Britain, the Albanian National Question
and the fall of the Ottoman Empire
1876–1914

Britain, the Albanian National Question and the fall of the Ottoman Empire 1876–1914

By
Daut Dauti

BLOOMSBURY ACADEMIC
LONDON • NEW YORK • OXFORD • NEW DELHI • SYDNEY

BLOOMSBURY ACADEMIC
Bloomsbury Publishing Plc
50 Bedford Square, London, WC1B 3DP, UK
1385 Broadway, New York, NY 10018, USA
29 Earlsfort Terrace, Dublin 2, Ireland

BLOOMSBURY, BLOOMSBURY ACADEMIC and the Diana logo
are trademarks of Bloomsbury Publishing Plc

First published in Great Britain 2023

Copyright © Daut Dauti 2023
This paperback edition published 2025

Daut Dauti have asserted his right under the Copyright,
Designs and Patents Act, 1988, to be identified as author of this work.

Cover image: The Malissori before the Council of Admirals protest against the annexation
of their country in Montenegro (© Niday Picture Library / Alamy)

Bloomsbury Publishing Plc does not have any control over, or responsibility for, any
third-party websites referred to or in this book. All internet addresses given in this
book were correct at the time of going to press. The author and publisher regret
any inconvenience caused if addresses have changed or sites have ceased
to exist, but can accept no responsibility for any such changes.

Every effort has been made to trace the copyright holders and obtain permission
to reproduce the copyright material. Please do get in touch with any enquiries
or any information relating to such material or the rights holder. We would be
pleased to rectify any omissions in subsequent editions of this
publication should they be drawn to our attention.

A catalogue record for this book is available from the British Library.

A catalog record for this book is available from the Library of Congress.

Library of Congress Cataloging-in-Publication Data

Names: Dauti, Daut, 1960- author.
Title: Britain, the Albanian national question and the fall of the Ottoman
Empire, 1876-1914 / by Daut Dauti.
Description: London ; New York : Bloomsbury Academic, 2023. | Includes bibliographical
references and index. | Summary: "An exploration of Britain and its foreign policy, the
Albania question and the fall of the Ottoman empire from 1876 to 1914"– Provided by publisher.
Identifiers: LCCN 2023026315 (print) | LCCN 2023026316 (ebook) | ISBN 9781350349537
(hardback) | ISBN 9781350349575 (paperback) | ISBN 9781350349544 (ebook) |
ISBN 9781350349551 (epub) Subjects: LCSH: Albania–Foreign relations–Great Britain. | Great
Britain–Foreign relations–Albania. | Albania–History–1840-1912. | Eastern question (Balkan)
| Great Britain–Foreign relations–1837-1901. | Great Britain–Foreign relations–1901-1936
Classification: LCC DR966.18 .D38 2023 (print) | LCC DR966.18 (ebook) |
DDC 327.496504109/034–dc23/eng/20230624
LC record available at https://lccn.loc.gov/2023026315
LC ebook record available at https://lccn.loc.gov/2023026316

ISBN:	HB:	978-1-3503-4953-7
	PB:	978-1-3503-4957-5
	ePDF:	978-1-3503-4954-4
	eBook:	978-1-3503-4955-1

Typeset by Integra Software Services Pvt. Ltd.

To find out more about our authors and books visit www.bloomsbury.com
and sign up for our newsletters.

To my granddaughter Annabelle and grandson Noah

Contents

Introduction   1

1   Albania – a travellers writers' discovery   7
2   The Congress of Berlin and the Albanian Question between policies of Disraeli and Gladstone 1876–81   27
3   Impact of the British Liberalism on Albanian Question   47
4   Albanian Nationalism and Macedonian Question   61
5   Against the Young Turks, 1908–10   77
6   From autonomy to independence   101
7   The Balkans for the Balkan people   121
8   Refuting Gladstonian liberalism   137

Conclusion   157

Appendix   161
Notes   162
Selected Bibliography   190
Index   205

Introduction

The Albanian national movement grew as a reaction to other Balkan national movements, the Macedonian crisis of the 1890s and the weakening of the Ottoman Empire. The British government showed only limited attention to the Albanian national question, with the exception of a few specific periods, because of their lack of major or direct interests in the Balkans. The very fact that the British had no interests at stake in the Balkans and were a democratic and economic superpower became the reason why Albanians wanted British support and protection.

The intention of the Albanian leaders to have Great Britain to their side grew to the point that they wanted a British king as head of their country. This was an effort to place Albania under the protection of a European Power. The leaders of the Albanian movement believed that a British king could secure a prosperous economic and political future for Albania. This also reflected Albania's perceived need to distance itself from the East, specifically from a declining Ottoman Empire. In this regard, the Albanians, like other Balkan nations, had adopted the 'Western style of modernity' and wanted to be included in the 'process of Europeanization'.[1]

The lack of interests was reflected in British public and academic circles, demonstrated by the fact that during the period of 1876–1914, and even today, Albania remains a largely unknown country. Those who intend to research and study this field will face a relative absence of books or secondary sources. The number of scholars and experts who dealt with the Albanian Question of the nineteenth and beginning of the twentieth century was small, and their work remains almost unknown today in Britain. One such scholar was Edith Durham (1863–1944), a Balkan specialist and a rare expert on Albania's national movement, politics and ethnographic composition. Because of lack of interest on this subject, Durham remained largely unknown in Britain. Recently there has been some renewed interest in Durham's life and her work. A book[2], a number of her letters and writings were published to offer help to those interested in this subject.[3]

In most history books, including contemporary secondary sources on the Balkans during this period, the Albanians are described as playing minor role in historical events. Therefore, Albanians, more than often, are characterized as being late starters as far as national awareness is concerned, and the last to form their nation state. In reality, a study on the role of the Albanians in the history of Ottoman Europe proves that this matter has been widely overlooked and underestimated. The Albanian role in the Ottoman Empire and numerous insurrections, specifically those of 1908–12, could prove that the Albanians have played a major role in the history of the Balkans. Several reasons could be given as to why the Albanians and their history received considerably less coverage compared to their Balkan neighbours. National historiography of the Balkan peoples (Serbs and Greeks in this case) has established a positive narrative of their nationhood. Belgrade had an institution of higher education since 1808 while Athens a university from 1837. Both countries produced their version of national historiography at the time when vast majority of Albanians could not read and write in their mother tongue. After the Second World War, specifically after 1961, when Albania broke all ties with the Soviet Union, the communist ideology of the Albanian state incorporated a 'peculiar strident of nationalism', as other Balkan countries had done it earlier. Although Albanian historians did produce serious historical publications, because of this 'peculiarity' they were seen with doubts and ignored by Western historians and readers.[4]

According to Noel Malcolm and some other historians, the older works of non-Albanian Balkan authors have imposed their views on English speaking scholars. These authors have minimized the role of the Albanians by introducing the Slavs and Greeks as principal actors in the general narrative of the Balkan history. Therefore, in this framework, the Albanians are presented as 'auxiliary actors'. An additional factor is that most scholars have no reading knowledge of either Albanian or the Ottoman-Turkish language. Another reason, emphasized by James Tallon, is that the Albanians, the majority of whom are Muslim, did not fit well into any of the 'schemes frequently laid out in the general monographs on Balkan History'. Therefore, notions such as 'Turkish Yoke', 'Turcocratia' or 'Turkish Long Night' do not necessarily apply to the Muslim population of the Balkans, meaning the Albanians tended to fall into the category of the 'oppressor' and not the 'oppressed', a term reserved exclusively for the Christian population.[5]

Until 1998, when Noel Malcolm's book *Kosovo, A Short History*[6] was published, the only available solid scholarly work on the history of Albania in English language was Stavro Skendi's book published in 1967.[7] After the fall of communism and the disintegration of the Yugoslav federation, Albania and Kosovo have attracted some attention among historians and scholars of other fields. As a result, several valuable works that study particular segments of Albanian history have emerged. George Gawrych's book, *The Crescent and the Eagle,* is one such work.[8] Gawrych has recognized the existence of the Albanian ethnic identity in the early nineteenth century, which went on to develop into nationalism during the period between the activities of the Albanian League of 1878 and the insurrections of 1908–12. By examining the efforts of Albanian nationalists, who aimed to gain nationality rights, and the efforts of conservatives to maintain local privileges under Ottoman rule, Gawrych has provided new and important perspectives on the development of Albanian nationalism. Majority of historians maintain that the development of Albanian nationalism took place from 1878 to 1913, a period of time similar to that outlined by Gawrych.

To a degree, this established pattern is acceptable. But, in addition it should be added that the birth of Albanian nationalism is to be sought in the early nineteenth century and went on to develop with higher intensity between 1878 and 1912. Furthermore, the efforts of Albanian intellectuals to develop the Albanian language, and the question of Macedonia, became the driving forces behind the development of Albanian nationalism in the late nineteenth and early twentieth centuries.

The Albanian Question has also attracted limited attention in other recent publications, which primarily address the Macedonian or Balkan Question of the first decade of the twentieth century. In this regard, several authors have studied the Macedonian Question, the Young Turk Movement and Revolution of 1908 from different points of view and have given a wide account of the events. However, all of them have overlooked the role of the Albanian nationalists in the Young Turk Movement and their conflict with Turkism. In few other works the role of the Albanians in the Young Turk Revolution is recognized, but the Albanian Question in Macedonia does not receive a proper attention. The Albanian Question and nationalism are missing, as this part of history presents the Macedonian Question mainly as a Muslim–Christian problem.

The literature published so far has rather superficially addressed the subject of the Albanian national and cultural revival, the British position on the Albanian Question and the Ottoman rule. These issues and their importance have not been studied in sufficient depth as this book intends to address. Thus, the intention of this book is to widen and deepen our understanding with new sources and with greater scrutiny by posing the main research question: whether British policy and the Albanian nationalist movement had a common interest during the period 1876–1914 and what was their stance towards the Ottoman Empire?

The fallout between the Albanian nationalist leaders and the Young Turks was evident through the issue of language, which served as a subject of confrontation between Albanian nationalists and the Turkish nationalism that emerged from the ranks of the Young Turks. This confrontation, which ended with armed conflict, also heralded the end of the Ottoman Empire and the birth of the Albanian state.

The lack of the British interest in the Albanian Question reflected into the process of the image making of Albania in Britain during the nineteenth century and how it had developed by the early twentieth century. There were two views which contributed to the image-building process, the foundations of which were laid by British travel writers and diplomats. The first view described the Balkans and Albania without consideration for religion. It was subsequently adopted by the Conservative party in Britain and its leader Benjamin Disraeli, and played important role in British political life and diplomacy. The second view, which was also established by travel writers and diplomats, regarded religion as an important element in building the image of Albania. Among the members of this group, William Gladstone played an important role in establishing the British Liberal view, which also became known as Gladstonian Liberalism. The first, non-religious Conservative view favoured the Albanian national cause while the second religious Liberal view ignored the Albanians, the majority of whom were Muslim, and gave priority to the Christians in the Balkans.

The religious and Liberal view led the public opinion and politicians to believe that under Islamic Ottoman rule the concept of state and religion were intertwined and to see the two elements as separate was viewed as 'completely alien to Mohamedan mind'.[9] The contradiction between religion and their national demands has spread further confusion among European, and particularly British, liberal politicians and public opinion, who were unable to see a distinction between Ottoman and Albanian identity. Overall, there was little knowledge about Albania in Britain and Europe. Ignoring the existence of an Albanian nationality and their political ambitions was simpler than reckoning with it.

The main political demand of the Albanian nationalist leaders was autonomy, and as such, it was important and could be demonstrated by analysing the British Conservative and Liberal approaches to the Albanian national cause. The question of Albanian autonomy was a subject which was linked with Ottoman and British policy. In this regard, a considerable attention should be given to the Congress of Berlin (1878) and the Albanian political and military struggle which was led by the Albanian League from 1878 to 1881.

Although the Albanians had proved capable of autonomous government with the activities of the League, their request for autonomy was denied. The Congress of Berlin had a great impact on Albanian nationalist leaders, who had marked the four *vilayets* (Ottoman administrative provinces) of Kosovo, Shkodra, Janina and Manastir as Albanian territories to be included in the future state of Albania. The importance of the Congress of Berlin can also be seen in its consequences which are felt to this day. The borders decided upon then still have the potential to create new conflicts or to rekindle old ones.

The Great Powers, including Britain, at the Congress of Berlin showed little regard for the principle of nationality when deciding the new borders. Since then, because of this disregard, many wars have been fought. The Balkan Wars of 1912 and 1913 and the First World War (1914–18) both came as a result of struggles for border changes. At the London Conference of Ambassadors (1912–13), the Paris Peace Conference (1919) and the resulting Treaty of Versailles, the Powers continued with the attitude expressed at the Congress of Berlin and showed no respect for the principle of nationality when deciding the borders of the Balkan countries. As a result, more than half of the territories inhabited by Albanians were included in Greece and in the new state which became known as the Kingdom of Serbs, Croats and Slovenes and later Yugoslavia. Yugoslavia, again, did not satisfy the principle of nationality breaking up violently at the end of the twentieth century and ending with the Kosovo War in 1999.

The British government, because of a lack of interest in the Balkans, had no separate policy regarding the Albanian Question and viewed this matter within the broader framework of the Eastern Question. The Albanian Question came under the consideration of the British government only during the international crises that took place in the Ottoman part of the Balkans. Such crises were addressed during the period of the Congress of Berlin, during the Macedonian crisis (1903–8), and the Conference of London that came as a result of the Balkan Wars.

The debate between the Liberals and Conservatives in the British Parliament, and the press about the Albanian Question went on during and after the Congress of Berlin. However, eventually, there was little difference between the two parties regarding the main objectives of British foreign policy. Even Gladstone had accepted that maintaining the Ottoman Empire meant protecting the route to India.[10] Both political parties had also declared that the Balkans, as a region, stands outside the British vital interest. However, since Disraeli and the Conservatives had recognized the existence of the Albanian nationality, there was hope for Albanian leaders to find support for their national cause in the future.

The chances for Albanian leaders to win British support became slim with the development of the Gladstonian Liberal policy. After the Macedonian crisis of 1903, British public opinion and Liberal organizations, such as the Balkan Committee, pressured the government for closer engagement in the Balkans.

The birth of the Albanian state came as a result of the Balkan Wars and the fall of the Ottoman Empire. However, in the British public opinion Gladstonian Liberal ideas were not manifested in favour of the Albanian national cause. It is for this reason that Edith Durham, Aubrey Herbert and a group of British intellectuals, who formed the Albanian Committee in 1912, became engaged in refuting such public opinion and policy which were not in favour of applying the principle of nationality in the Balkans, specifically in the case of Albania.

1

Albania – a travellers writers' discovery

What is the Balkans and where is Albania

No travel writer has described Albania and the Albanians better, nor indeed liked them more, than Lord Byron (1788–1824). In describing the Albanians, Byron has pointed out that to him and to the Albanians religion was not important:

> I like the Albanians much; they are not all Turks; some tribes are Christians. But their religion makes little difference in their manner or conduct.[1]

Yet, religion did matter to other people in Britain and was a factor which played a fundamental role in forming an image of Albania in British public opinion and politics. Trying to understand nineteenth-century Albania and how its image was built, one should ask the same question about the Balkans more broadly. In 1881 Prince Bismarck in the Balkans included Greece, Serbia, Bulgaria and Eastern Rumelia. According to a map that was published in 1903 in *The Times*, the Balkans comprised Albania, Montenegro, Bosnia, Serbia, Rumania, Bulgaria, Macedonia and Eastern Rumelia.[2] Today, Encyclopaedia Britannica defines the Balkans as a region comprising the countries of former Yugoslavia (Slovenia, Croatia, Bosnia and Herzegovina, Serbia, Montenegro, Kosovo and Macedonia), Albania, Bulgaria, Rumania, Moldova, and portions of Greece and Turkey.[3] There is no universal agreement on defining the region in cultural, historic and geographic terms and it is for this reason the entire territory of Greece is missing from the description of Encyclopaedia Britannica. Yet, there is a general agreement and acceptance that 'Balkan' is a Turkish word and name which means 'mountain' that entered into use with the arrival of the Ottomans in this part of Europe.[4]

The name Balkan in British literature was first used by John Morritt (1772–1843), a British traveller, politician and scholar. Travelling from Bucharest to Constantinople in 1794, Morritt crossed the mountains at Shipka Pass (Bulgaria) and wrote about a mountain called 'Bal. Kan.', which is the name for ancient Haemus.[5] The first description of the Balkans as a peninsula was made in 1827 by Robert Walsh (1772–1852), an Irish priest who served as a chaplain in several British embassies. He described the region as a territory between two seas: the Adriatic and Black Sea. He wrote about a range of mountains that starts in Croatia and ends in Bulgaria.[6]

However, the term Balkan did not find immediate use in Europe. Until the Congress of Berlin (1878) the official name used by the British and other European governments was 'European Turkey' or 'Turkey in Europe'. The official name used by the Ottomans was 'Rumeli', meaning 'the land of the Romans' and also the area of ancient Greece. The Ottomans also used the term 'Avrupa Osmanli' (Ottoman Europe). The Ottomans first used the name 'Balkan in Rumelia' to specify the exact geography. Before 1878, different European authors preferred ancient names describing the region as Hellenic, Dardanian, Roman, Byzantine and Thracian.[7]

During the nineteenth century, the name Balkan became a synonym for a different Europe or Near East and as such became an object of discussion in history and politics. In developing her theory on 'balkanism', Maria Todorova has refused to accept the tendency to treat the relationship of the Balkans with the West as a variant of orientalism, as it was argued by Milica Bakić-Hayden and Elli Skopetea. Edward Said's denial of the existence of a real Orient has further enforced Todorova's argument that the orientalist discourse is not an identical, but rather similar, phenomenon to 'balkanism'. The fact that the Balkans have produced an opposition or division between East and West in Europe is one such similarity. For Todorova this division is 'as old as written history', and the Balkans must thus be treated as having a specific history and concrete geography.[8]

This division between East and West started with the ancient Greeks, who divided the world between the civilized, with them belonging in this group, and the barbarians. Barbarians were the northerners while in the East, the Persians were semi-civilized people. The Roman Empire, during the rule of Diocletian (244–312 AD), introduced an administrative division between East and West which was later taken as a division between Catholicism and Orthodoxy or Christianity and Islam. Albania is an example of where all these divisions converged. This division of the Albanian land created conditions and circumstances for Albanians to play a role in Western European state affairs and in the political history of the Byzantine or Ottoman Empire. Therefore, Albanians through history crossed this political and cultural division and played an important role in East-West relations.[9]

In all cases, divisions were based on religious, cultural and political factors. Yet only after the fall of Constantinople into Ottoman hands in 1453 and later the growth of economic prosperity in the West, the East was seen either as an Orthodox or Islamic world, and, as such, poor and inferior.[10] The Ottomans, new rulers of the East, were also characterized as 'barbarians' or 'saevi' (wild or savage people) and the level of division and animosity between the East and the West grew further. Noel Malcolm has shown how the Western writers have described the critical level between the East and the West or Christianity and Islam which followed the fall of Constantinople.[11]

The division of Europe between East and West, as known today, is largely an invention of eighteenth-century Western European writers who produced a philosophy 'responsible for the conceptual reorientation of Europe along an East-West axis'.[12] From the eighteenth century, the Ottoman Empire entered into a decline while the rest of Europe prospered economically as a result of the Industrial Revolution and social changes introduced by the Enlightenment. Since then, the East, including the Balkans and Albania, lagged behind economically and culturally and was associated with backwardness, underdevelopment of social relations and an absence of democratic institutions. By the end of the nineteenth century, the Balkans became a label or cliché which presupposed the existence of geographical and non-geographical referent. In political debates, journalistic essays and in other conversations, the name Balkans was used to show the existence of a region which has a specific identity and certain common features which fitted the accepted clichés.[13]

These clichés seem to have had an effect on the Balkan languages themselves regarding the use of the name Balkan. Excluding the Albanian language, the name Balkan has a derogative meaning in all other Balkan languages and stands for uncultured, uncivilized, backward and disorderly people.[14]

Even today labels and clichés stand behind the hegemonic usage of 'balkanism'. For Slavoj Žižek, a well-known Slovenian philosopher, the Balkans are still viewed with prejudice by the West. The West's mistrust, contempt and animosity towards the Balkans and its people are viewed by Žižek as a racist projection:

> First, there is the old-fashioned, unabashed rejection of the Balkan Other (despotic, barbarian, Orthodox, Muslim, corrupt, Oriental) in favour of true values (Western, civilised, democratic, Christian).[15]

'Balkanism', as defined by Todorova, was shaped over the course of two centuries and took a specific form around the Balkan Wars and First World War. Yet 'balkanism' also evolved as a result of disappointment among those Western Europeans who hoped to fulfil their 'classical expectations' in the Balkans. These travellers, most of them British, were among the first to express their disappointment, particularly in the case of Greece. John Morritt (1772–1843) was surprised to discover that modern Greeks had lost the physical and cultural resemblance they possessed in antiquity.[16] Reverend Thomas Smart Hughes (1786–1847), a scholar, historian and travel writer, probably expected to find Greece inhabited exclusively by ancient Greeks, and was thus surprised to find a vast number of Albanians living deep into the territories of Greece, as far as Attica, and including Athens.[17]

The love of the British for Greece during the first decade of the nineteenth century created huge disappointment when Greece turned out to be different from the images they had composed in their minds.[18] In this sense, Albania was not a disappointment because the travellers had no prior expectations of the country and its people. Albania was generally unknown to most of them and, therefore, in most cases, appeared as a pleasant surprise.

Yet much more than classical expectations, the question of religion had a great impact on the British public and politicians and was also fed by some of the travellers' works. The process of independence of the Balkan countries, excluding the case of Albania, was seen not only as a liberation from Ottoman rule, but as a religious mission, too. On this Todorova, wrote:

> The Balkan's predominant Christian character, moreover, fed for a long time the crusading potential of Christianity against Islam. Despite many attempts to depict its (Orthodox) Christianity as simply a subspecies of oriental despotism and thus

as inherently non-European or non-Western, still the boundary between Islam and Christianity in general continued to be perceived as the principal one.[19]

Malcolm, Todorova, Žižek and many others have pointed out that although religion was not the only boundary between the West and the Balkans, it was the main base upon which the West has constructed perceptions and prejudices about the East, the Balkans in general and Albania specifically. Direct links, which usually came from state interests between Britain and the Balkans as a region, were also important. Such a link was missing between Britain and Albania during the nineteenth century, but this absence of direct interests did not stop the process of image building. As indicated above, the image of Albania in Britain was built through religious and non-religious views which were introduced by diplomats and travel writers.

An unclear view of unknown Albania

The effect of constructed images has proved to be powerful. Karl May (1842–1912), the famous creator of the literary characters Old Shatterhand and Winnetou, also became popular for his novels on the Near East. Although he never visited any countries in the Balkans, his novels were well researched, being based on travellers' books, historic and geographic works. During the late 1970s, a German linguist visited Kosovo and Albania, admitting that these places were not much different from the images he had created in his childhood, probably by reading Karl May's *Durch das Land der Skypetaren*.[20]

Flora Sandes, an English woman who served as a sergeant in the Serbian army during the First World War, is another example which illustrates the capacity of images to heighten expectations and stretching the limits of reality. When her unit retreated through Albania to Corfu, Sandes met Albanian villagers for the first time. Impoverished Albanians of destroyed villages from the Balkan Wars and First World War did not look the way she had imagined them. She probably expected to see them as they had been presented by Lord Byron, a 'very picturesque race of men wearing spotless native costumes, and slung about with fascinating looking daggers and curious weapons of all kinds'. The majority of the Albanians, as described by Sandes, were 'a perfect picture of squalor and filth' and a 'very degenerate looking race'.[21]

In Britain images and perceptions of the Balkan people were created through a long and gradual process. For Andrew Hammond this process of 'imagology' lasted a century and a half and was created to explain 'mutations that have marked British balkanism'.[22]

The spread of information which contributed to creating an image of Albania in the British public sphere should be divided into two phases. The first phase takes place throughout the nineteenth century. The second phase starts in the twentieth century and brought a wider awareness of Balkan affairs and Albania with a requirement for a closer British engagement.[23]

During the first phase, the dispersal of information took place mainly through publications by diplomats and travel writers, who used religious and non-religious criteria to describe Albania as a geographic notion and Albanians as a people, ethnic entity or nation. While the works of these travel writers could be considered independent in that they presented their own views, the independence of some publications should be questioned after 1830. This is especially true during and after the period of the Congress of Berlin (1878), when Britain, because of the emergence of Russia as an important power, adopted a policy of preserving the territorial integrity of the Ottoman Empire. As a result, some authors opted to follow this policy line in their works.

Until the beginning of the twentieth century Albania remained largely unknown to ordinary members of the British public. In this respect Albania was 'the Balkans within the Balkans' and went on to be less known during the Cold War when it became a 'curtain-within-a-curtain'.[24] This lack of interest among the public was reflected in government policy, which had no direct or major interests in the Balkans. Britain had owned the island of Vis between 1811 and 1814, which today belongs to Croatia, but at this time the eastern Adriatic coast was still called Illyria by the British.[25]

The British also owned Parga, a town which is now in Greece. Further north of Parga, just off the Albanian coast, the British also ruled the island of Corfu, from 1815 to 1864. These were the only three cases that the British, for a short period, had direct interests in the Balkans. Although this period was short, Parga and Corfu played an important role in building the religious view in Britain which reflected negatively on Albania's image. The British government's lack of interest in the Balkans was noticeable in media coverage of the region, which was never as serious as that of other European Powers.[26]

The desire to see classical Greece initially attracted British travellers to visit the region. The region had not yet acquired the name the Balkans but became known in Britain, especially in intellectual circles and among politicians, because of developments which led to the formation of the powerful state of Ali Pasha Tepelena (1740-1822), the Napoleonic Wars and the independence of Greece. It was because of these developments that the British government opened its first consular representation in Arta in 1769.[27] By 1803 the representation became permanent when John Philip Morrier was appointed 'General Council in the Morea and Albania' with the centre in Janina, which in reality was the court of Ali Pasha.[28] This is probably the earliest official recognition of the name Albania by the British government. However, in 1795 John Hawkins, a geologist and antiquary, was the very first Englishman to visit the region and to meet Ali Pasha. In 1803 William Hamilton was the first British government functionary to visit Ali Pasha in an official capacity. He wrote that Ali Pasha has established a secure environment for all his subjects who live a prosperous, safer and richer life than anywhere else in the Ottoman part of Europe.[29]

France, Italy and Austria-Hungary also established their consular offices in Janina and this opened the way for diplomats to become pioneers of travel writing on Albania. French historian and diplomat François Charles Pouqueville (1770-1838) was the initiator of this trend at the very beginning of the nineteenth century. British writer, topographer and diplomat William Martin Leake (1777-1860) was sent to 'European Turkey' in 1804 to help defend this territory against French attacks and a few years later was appointed as a British consular representative in Janina, Albania. Another diplomat who had significant influence on future travel writers was the Austro-Hungarian consul and scholar Johan Georg von Hahn, who travelled in Albania and gathered information on history, philology and folklore and published '*Albanesische Studien*' (Albanian Studies) in 1853.

To a great degree, it was Leake who initiated the process of building images of Albania in Britain and who influenced other British travel writers to continue the process. His work was published in four volumes and included travel studies which he undertook in Albania, Macedonia and Greece from 1804 to 1807.[30] The situation changed considerably in 1809 when Lord Byron and John Cameron Hobhause (1786–1869), later known as Lord Broughton, went to Albania. The aim of their travel to Albania was to meet Ali Pasha and see the country which was thus far largely unknown in Britain. In 1813 Hobhouse published his book describing the places that he and Byron had visited and the meetings they had with Ali Pasha. Although Hobhouse's visit was made four years after Leake's arrival in Albania, his book was the first major publication on this matter.[31] Leake's, Byron's and Hobhouse's publications established the non-religious view that contributed to the construction of the image of Albania. However, these publications did not build a clear image of Albanian and were only read by a certain number of intellectuals and did not reach a wide public.

Illyricum Albania

In 1790 Mozart's opera *Cos! Fan Tutte* opened in Vienna. The opera was set in Naples but had an Albanian motif. The story was about two Italian suitors, Ferrando and Guglielmo, who decided to test the temptation of their fiancees. Pretending that they were going to war, said farewell to their women. But, dressed gallantly as Albanian noblemen they came back home after few days. The maid, Greek in origin, is greatly impressed by the look of the 'Albanians' and announced them to their ladies with great excitement: 'What appearances! what costumes! what figures! what mustaches! I don't know if these creatures are Vlachs or Turks?'[32] Despite the effort, Ferrando and Guglielmo failed to pass as Albanians. In the eighteenth century the number of Europeans who could recognize an Albanian by the look was incredibly small.

Before the arrival of British travel writers, Albania existed as the name of a territory in the Balkans but without clear shape, form or figure. With the travellers' contribution, an image of Albania, in the form of a murky picture, or puzzle was created. It is not easy to say which one of the travellers contributed most to 'creating' Albania, but Lord Byron remains the best known in both Britain and Albania. He considered Albania as almost his own discovery and, in a letter, he sent to his friend Henry Drury, he touched on this matter by comparing the 'known' Greece with the 'unknown' Albania:

> Greece, ancient and modern, you know too well to require description. Albania, indeed, I have seen more of than any Englishman (except a Mr. Leake) for it is a country rarely visited, from the savage character of the natives, though abounding in more natural beauties than the classical regions of Greece, which however, are still eminently beautiful, particularly Delphi and Cope Colona in Attica. Yet these

are nothing to parts of Illyria and Epirus, where places without names, and rivers not laid down in maps.³³

Because of the great effect that Ali Pasha's personality had on travellers, territories ruled by him were initially taken as a base for describing the size of Albania in a geographic sense. For Lord Byron Albania was a country that once used to be Illyricum but was now ruled by Ali Pasha.³⁴ Most of the travellers mention Illyria or Illyricum to emphasize the size of Albania, but also to give historic weight to their descriptions of the country which was inhabited by Albanians, who were characterized as descendants of the Illyrians. As they were 'discovering' Albania, Illyria was probably thought to be an attractive name for the British public and, as it turned out later, very appealing to Albanian national ideologists. Over the gate of his castle, Ali Pasha had an inscription claiming descendance from Pyrrhus, King of Epirus.³⁵ Whatever the origin of Ali Pasha and the Albanians, the Albania of the nineteenth century was considerably different from how it was known as Illyria and other ancient regions by the Romans. As there was no clear geographical layout, no precise distribution of population and no clear exercise of power, Albania appeared as an imagined country, as were all other Balkan countries before becoming nation states.

Henry Holland (1788–1873) concluded that because of absence of knowledge of the population distribution, Albania could not be defined by any strict line or boundary. The country began in the north of the gulf of Arta, Greece, and continued northwards to end at the border of Montenegro, but he had no clear idea of how far to the east the border should be marked.³⁶ Because of the mixture of the population, none of the travellers were able to identify the eastern border, all pointing out that it should be somewhere in Macedonia. Holland suggested that language and other characteristics of the population should determine the outline in the east, and also used language to prove that the Albanians were direct descendants of the original population or remnants of the ancient Illyrians.³⁷

Another geographic layout, again under the rule of Ali Pasha, was offered by Thomas Jollife (1780–1872) author and travel writer. For Jolliffe Albania included the whole of Epirus, southern Illyricum, a considerable portion of Macedonia, the greater part of Thessaly, Acarnania, Phocis, Aetolia and the division of Boetia.³⁸ In 1848 poet and painter Edward Lear (1812–88) painted different parts of Albania and wrote an account of his journey which he called 'Travels to Illyricum Albania'. Lear's Albania is divided into two parts but he gave no layout. He went north to Shkodra (Scutari) and called it 'the capital of Illyricum', while Janina was the capital of the south.³⁹

The geographic layout outlined by most of the travel writers was close to the territories of the two *pashaliks* which had come into being by the end of the eighteenth century. By the beginning of nineteenth century the Sultan had decided to appoint Albanian *pashas* to administer their native territories, who ruled their *pashaliks* by employing local Albanians in the administration and military. Ali Pasha used this opportunity to get away from the Sultan's rule and enlarged his *Pashalik* of Janina. At this time, when the travel writers visited the Balkans, the two *pashaliks* had emerged as two centres of powers in the Balkan territories which were inhabited by Albanians. Ali Pasha ruled in the south, centred in Janina, and the Bushati family ruled in the north with Shkodra as a centre. Because the travellers mostly visited the south, we do not have many descriptions of the north, but from other historic sources we know that the Bushati's influence was established by Mehmet Pasha between 1757 and 1775. He extended his area of control to the north-east, widened his political jurisdiction and refused to pay taxes to the Porte.[40]

The Bushati's managed to mark the north-east (Kosovo and Macedonia) and central part as Albania, a territory which Ali Pasha could not reach from the south. By the beginning of the nineteenth century both *pashaliks* roughly covered the territory of what is today Albania, northern Greece, western Macedonia, Kosovo and the south east of Montenegro. In a later stage Albanian nationalists used this as a fact that these autonomous territories, created by their leaders, became sources for their political and cultural inspiration.[41] Both *pashaliks* were ruled independently by Albanian *pashas* and this created a sense of ethnic belonging for Albanians, which consequently led to a permanent conflict with the Porte.[42] This fact also created a need for Albanians to seek an autonomous relationship with the Porte and was most probably the reason that most anti-Ottoman travel writers viewed the Albanians with admiration. Just before the Congress of Berlin, the Porte divided this territory into four administrative units that became known as Albanian *vilayets*: Janina, Manastir, Kosovo and Shkodra. This did not mean that Albanians composed the majority of the population in all *vilayets*. The *Vilayet* of Kosovo included the *Sanjak* of Novi Pazar and almost the entire territory of what is today known as south Serbia and parts of Macedonia. This administrative division came as a result of the Porte's effort to prevent the development of Albanian nationalism and the creation of homogenous Albanian *vilayets*. Although this division was made almost half a century after most of the travel books were written, this new administrative form created only a demarcation of an Albania which was a rather 'vague geographic expression'.[43]

Back in the beginning of the nineteenth century travel writers applied the criteria of religion, language, national dress and manners to characterize Albanians. Scottish traveller and diplomat James Henry Skene (1812–66) used different principles to differentiate between the three groups of inhabitants in the Ottoman provinces in Europe. Greeks and 'Osmanlis' were the biggest groups differing in religion and origin. Albanians comprised the third group and differed from both of them regarding their origin but were divided between two religions: Islam and Christianity. Skene also underlined that Albanians did not attract the attention of Europe as much as the other two groups and this was why they remained unknown in Europe.[44]

Because Albanians of the south were Muslim and Orthodox Christian, Hobhouse took language and not religion as a criterion to distinguish them from the Greeks.[45] Byron, like his companion Hobhouse, divided Albanians religiously into Turks (Muslims) and Christians.[46]

The fact that religion made no difference to the Albanians seemed to have impressed Byron deeply. As Woodhouse noted, to Byron 'religion was cant', not because he was unfamiliar with religious doctrines but because he had studied them. In many reviews of *Childe Harold*, Byron was even accused of lack of patriotism and religious unorthodoxy.[47] However, it was Byron who made a more effective introduction of Albanians to Britain and greatly influenced future travel writers. Byron fell in love with the country and there he was inspired to write his epic poem *Childe Harold's Pilgrimage*. In order to present a familiar picture in Britain, Byron compared the Albanians with the Highlanders of Scotland, whom they supposedly resembled in dress, figure and manner of living. To Byron, even the mountains of Albania seemed Caledonian but with a milder climate, their habits seemed similar and the Albanian language sounded to him like Celtic.[48]

In London in 1813, Byron put on the Albanian costume, which he bought in Preveza, and stood in front of the portrait painter Thomas Phillips. The painting, which became very popular, was named '*Portrait of a Nobleman in the dress of an Albanian*' and was exhibited at the Royal Academy. The painting was also to prove that Byron identified himself with Albanians 'whom he recognizes as fellow Europeans',[49] and showed his attachment to Albania.

The painting has initiated considerable debate among intellectuals in Britain and elsewhere. In her recent studies, Katarina Gephardt has suggested that the portrait was commissioned by Byron only to promote his 'self-image as the author of *Childe Harrold's Pilgrimage*', and not to promote Albania. Gephardt has argued that before visiting Albania Byron, held a 'peripheral position in English society', being a 'landless aristocrat' of Scottish descent and, as such, a 'relative outsider' in the British establishment.[50] Byron was fascinated with Albania and probably thought that the British public would also be fascinated by this unknown and exotic country. Therefore, it could be argued that Byron wanted to promote both himself and Albania.

When Byron's first two cantos of the poem were published in London in March 1812, the expensive first printing sold out within three days. It caused a sensation among the public, which rather surprised Byron, who wrote in his memorandum book: 'I awoke one morning and found myself famous.'[51] With Byron's fame and the sensation about his work, it appeared that Albania had made a magnificent entry in Britain. But this was not the case, as his work made some impact in the literary world, the effect in the public and political spheres was not significant. Byron, with his first publications, introduced both Albania and Greece to the British public. Representations of Albania had also been made in 1806 with Pouqoville's translation, and later in 1813 by Hobhouse and in 1815 by Holland were unable to match the spread of image and enthusiasm for Greece. At this stage Albania's picture remained unknown and murky to the British public and it was Greece that won British sympathy and support.

As a matter of fact, there is no evidence to suggest that Byron asked the British public or the government to support the Albanians or the Greeks. Yet, it cannot be denied that Byron contributed to spreading some love for Greece and Albania. He introduced Albanians as a free people living in their state under their leader, Ali Pasha, whom he considered as a 'man of first abilities who governs the whole of Albania'.[52] For Byron and most travel writers, Ali Pasha, the 'Albanian tyrant of Ioannina [Janina] was a paragon of learning' compared to the Greeks. Furthermore, in Byron's view, Albanians were 'less degenerate than both the ruling Turks and the oppressed Greeks'.[53] To some British Philhellenes, Albania was an additional reason which contributed to their disappointment with the Greeks. They discovered that Greeks were 'ignorant' and most excellent Greek schools and libraries were in Janina, which was ruled by Albanians.[54]

However, the notion of liberating the Greeks from the Ottoman Empire was becoming increasingly accepted by British intellectuals. Many thought that Russia should take over Greece and some like Douglas Dakin 'thought that the Albanians would do so'.[55] Byron and a dozen or so British travellers, who had met Ali Pasha, noted that he portrayed himself and Albanians as friends of the British nation. They also noted that the Albanians, who were living independently, were not oppressed by the Porte and Ali Pasha was seeking to establish some kind of alliance with the British government.[56] Therefore, Albanians and Albania did not seem like they needed any help from the British, but, rather, it was the Greeks who were in greater need of British support.

As Byron's biographers noted, Byron's travel writing power was immense and no one has described better national differences, costumes, manners and governments.[57] Byron, like no one else before, presented the Greeks as living under the 'Turkish yoke' but he never made a public call to help them. The call to help the Greeks in Britain was spread by other Philhellenes and travel writers. By 1823 the Philhellenes had created a feeling among the British public, or at least among intellectuals, that something had to be done in support of the 'heroic Greeks' so they could be liberated from the 'centuries-old yoke of their Ottoman, un-Christian and cruel oppressors'.[58] As seen, Philhellenes gave importance to the religion by emphasizing that the 'cruel Ottoman oppressor' was 'un-Christian'.

On 8 March 1823 a group of Philhellenes formed the *London Greek Committee*, an organization which would support the Greek national cause and reject Albanian nationalism. Byron did not attend the meeting and played no part in this initiative, but members of the Committee sent him a letter to ask for his 'kind and cordial support' and 'allow his name to be added to the list'.[59] The Committee immediately started fund raising and awareness raising on behalf of the Greeks. Edward Blaquire, a Committee activist, set off in the spring of 1823 for Greece and stopped at Genoa, Italy, to ask Byron if he was interested in leading an armed expedition to Greece. Byron accepted the invitation and during the summer of 1823 made his second journey to Greece to join the war of independence.[60]

Even in Greece, Byron preferred to be among Albanians who were fighting the Ottomans for the Greek cause. In August 1823, on board the ship Hercules, Byron was waiting to join Albanian Suliot forces led by Marko Boçari (Marco Botzaris). Boçari had sent a letter to Byron to thank him for his moral and financial support and to let him know that he would receive him as a noble ally on his landing. That very night, 21 August 1823, Boçari was killed in the attack he led against the Ottoman army consisted mainly by Albanians.[61] A few months later, on 19 April 1924, Lord Byron died of fever in Missolonghi and became a hero in Greece and a legend in Albania. Ali Pasha had died two years earlier defending his castle in Janina in his last battle against the Ottomans. This was the end of Albania as some of the British travel writers knew it and as was praised by Byron. From that moment on, Albanians came under the Porte's direct rule and found themselves in a similar position to that of the Greeks before independence.

Gothic, Conservative and liberal views

Some travellers, many of them promoters of liberal ideas and social reforms at home, saw Ali Pasha as a cruel tyrant but Byron, Hobhouse and some others did not look at him that way. Charles Cockerell (1788-1863), who visited Albania in 1814 and met Ali Pasha, wrote that the tyrant and his governance should be admired because he had built roads, fortified borders and 'raised Albania into a power of some importance in Europe'.[62]

Ali Pasha was not only known for establishing law and order in his *pashalik*. During his rule and with his support the best Greek schools were established in Janina. There, Henry Holland found a ceiling with decorations which showed aspects of Copernican astronomy. Holland discussed European and American politics with Ali Pasha and wrote that Pasha had considerable knowledge of science.[63] Above all, Pasha asked important and clever questions, such as why so many Englishmen were coming to Janina.[64] 'The correct answer was to meet the great Pasha himself', wrote Woodhouse.[65]

Historical circumstances, as well as his own actions, had raised Ali Pasha to the position of negotiating on equal terms with Napoleon and other Western governments of his time. Before the Napoleonic wars the contact of Europeans with Albania was through travellers, and therefore on personal basis. Because of the Albania's geostrategic position, Ali Pasha established official contacts with the powers, including Britain. For this reason, British government established official presence and maintained friendly relations with Ali Pasha. Therefore, British officials, from the Foreign Secretary to military and diplomatic envoys corresponded with Pasha.[66] In 1807 the mutual cooperation reached a very high degree. In August that year, Sir Arthur Paget, who was sent to Constantinople to repair Ottoman-British relations, contacted William Leake, British representative at the Court of Ali Pasha, to instruct him how to proceed with Ali and Albania. Ali Pasha was told that if he continues with his desire and if he has a capability to maintain his independence, His Majesty's Government will recognize the fact and will support him offering military assistance (Naval Force) if needed in case of Russian or French attack. But the recognition of independence was to happen only if the Ottoman Empire collapses during the Napoleonic Wars. A year later (1808) the British support reached Ali Pasha: thirty cannons, ten smaller artillery pieces and gunpowder.[67] As Napoleon lost the war and the Ottoman Empire did not collapse, the British saw no reason to continue their high-level friendship with Ali Pasha. Nevertheless, the hope of the Ottoman collapse and the British support for independence remained in the minds of Albanians and Ali Pasha.

However, to diplomatic envoys and travellers, Pasha played the role of a believer in the democratic principles of the French Revolution, although his character and actions suggested otherwise.[68] Yet he certainly knew how to impress his British guests. Seeking to establish friendship or alliance with Britain, he received British diplomats, travellers and politicians with great honour. He once served dinner on golden plates in honour of the Earl of Guildford in his magnificent garden on the lake of Janina.[69]

Ali Pasha's friendly behaviour towards his guests and his interest in science and world politics were not the only reasons most British travellers continued Byron's and

Hobhouse's style of writing, their admiration for the tyrant and their love for Albania and Albanians. In 1851, Edward Lear used Byron's words to present Albania as 'savage, yet classic, picturesqueness, perfectly exquisite'. Even seven decades after Byron, in 1888, another travel writer H. A. Brown, described Albania as a country of 'diabolic mountains' where 'the wind howled like a wild beast'.[70]

Many travel writers applied Gothicism to their works, a literary form which was used as a genre by British novelists and travel writers in search of images, symbols and motifs to 'depict the perceived monstrosity of a variety of post-colonial regions'.[71] Gothicism was anti-religious and important to Byron's writing. He derived from it a template for his more mysterious, alienated characters, along with his preoccupation with ruins or architectural decay.[72] He found plenty of these elements in Albania. Byron and Hobhouse, like many after them, were delighted to meet Ali Pasha probably because his despotic character fitted well into this imagined Gothic environment. Apart from political tyranny, they also found plenty of situations to enjoy and beautiful places to admire. In Byron's descriptions, Albanians and their land also appear in romantic images, described as unknown, heroic, dangerous, enigmatic and beautiful. Albania, in his words, was 'a shore unknown which all admire, but many dread to view'. In *Childe Harold,* Byron pushed the existing boundaries of poetry and entered into new poetic territory, creating images which influenced the British perception of Albania and Albanians in literature.[73] However, these images, being glorified, often romanticized and containing Gothic elements, were not close to reality. Yet despite all these dramatic depictions of Albania, the point to be emphasized here is that Byron and other writers who used Gothicism did not create prejudice against Albania and Albanians on a religious basis.

Albania, Montenegro and some other Balkan countries were rare places left in Europe where Gothic travel writers found powerful stimulus for their imaginations. For Gothic writers, Albania and other Balkan countries were the Europe of the past. In Albania they saw a frozen picture of Europe. The Gothic style also appeared in travel writings about other Balkan countries like Rumania, Serbia, Bulgaria and Montenegro but describing them in negative way.[74]

Nationalist movements in the Balkans were not seen with sympathy by most travel writers. The territorial reduction and gradual fall of the Ottoman Empire were seen as a threat to the British Empire whose trade and influence were endangered, and the fall of the Ottoman Empire was seen as an example of how the British colonies could be lost.[75] This negative depiction was applied partly because the Gothic style required it be so, but mostly acted as a form of revenge against those nations who rose against the Ottoman Empire. From 1800 to 1878, within which period most of these books were published, Albanians did not have an active nationalist movement and were seen as protectors of the Ottoman Empire. Until 1878 they had risen against the empire many times, but not for the same purpose as their neighbours, and it is for this reason that Albanians were spared such negative depictions.

Benjamin Disraeli (1804–81) visited Albania in 1830 when he was twenty-six years of age. In Disraeli's life, like in Byron's, religion did not play an important role. However, Disraeli's Albania was specific and differed from the way it was portrayed by Byron and other travellers. Although he was an ardent admirer of Byron, and it was because of him that he visited Albania, his sympathies were in favour of the Porte and therefore against the Albanians who, after the death of Ali Pasha, had risen against the Ottoman Empire. When Disraeli was still in Corfu, his intentions were to join the Ottoman army against the Albanians and Greeks.[76] There was nothing strange in this decision, considering that he was a Conservative politician and in favour of preserving the Ottoman Empire. On his way to Albania, he spent some time in Malta, where he was further influenced by British army officers and merchants who wanted a peaceful Mediterranean coast. The army seemed to have been against the warlike Albanians and the merchants were against the Greek pirates who preyed upon British ships and merchandise.[77]

Disraeli spent few weeks in British ruled Corfu, waiting until the Albanian insurrection was over. After the insurrection, the Ottoman Grand Vizier and supreme army commander, Mehmet Reshid Pasha, had invited 300 or so Albanian leaders to Manastir to pardon and reward them for the insurrection and the role they played in the war against Greek independence. On 26 August 1830 he massacred them all during the banquet he had organized for them. Afterwards Mehmet Reshid Pasha moved north to subdue the northern Albanian *pashalik* of Mehmet Pasha Bushati.[78]

This massacre and the submission of southern and northern parts of Albania were committed with the aim of preventing any potential spread of the Albanian national resistance movement. The Porte believed that Albanian leaders were inspired by the Greek war of independence and other nationalist movements that were occurring in the Balkans. However, this could be considered as the first intervention of the Porte against an early Albanian nationalist movement.[79] The massacre had taken place only few weeks before Disraeli arrived in Albania. On his arrival the first thing he noticed was this massacre, on which he wrote that 'the practice of politics in the East may be defined by one word, dissimulation'.[80]

This situation made Disraeli question his belief in Ottoman politics and see Albania through the prism of reality, as opposed to simply through the imagined ideas that Byron had created. Disraeli called the country Albania, with Janina as the capital, although when he visited it had fallen under the direct rule of Constantinople. Surprisingly, Albanians still impressed him, even though they were subdued and their country was turned to ruins. In the town of Arta, the only two buildings he saw standing and undamaged were the main mosque and the house of the British Consulate. He was touched by the situation and wrote about his feelings:

> Here for the first time I reposed upon a divan, and for the first time heard the muezzin from the minaret, a ceremony which is highly affecting when performed, as it usually is, by a rich and powerful voice.[81]

The Albanians were heavily armed and to Disraeli looked dangerous and ready for the next rebellion. Their weapons, and the way they looked and acted, are incorporated into his historical romance *The Rise of Iskander*.[82] He praised Skanderbeg, the fifteenth-century Albanian national hero, with glorifying and Gothic words similar to those that Lord Byron had used in *Childe Harold*. Disraeli, like other Gothic writers, considered Ali Pasha a 'formidable ruler that had made Albania so independent'.[83] On his way to Janina he described ruined buildings and Pasha's rule:

> We found ourselves at a vast but dilapidated khan as big as a Gothic castle, situated on a high range, and built as a sort of half-way house for travelers by Ali Pasha when his long, gracious, and unmolested reign had permitted him to turn this unrivalled country, which combines all the excellences of Southern Europe and Western Asia, to some of the purposes for which it is fitted.[84]

Almost eight years after Ali Pasha's death, Disraeli, like Byron and other travel writers, admired the Pasha's efforts for 'specifying Albania and extending its boundaries'. Above all, Disraeli was impressed by Pasha because under Pasha's rule 'Janina had become the literary capital of the Greek nation'.[85] Nevertheless, Disraeli enjoyed his visit, saw ethnic differences between Albanians and Greeks and also recognized the will and the ability of the Albanians for self-rule.

However, Disraeli did not apply the Gothic style to all his writings on Albania. In this respect, he made way for the new era of travel writing, which would continue to be represented by David Urquhart, who was seeking to lay the foundation of a pro-oriental project in British foreign policy.[86] This pro-oriental policy would have also been a pro-Albanian policy.

Urquhart was known as the best example of 'thwarted philhellenism' that started after the independence of Greece.[87] He contributed enormously to the Greek cause by taking an active role in the war of independence, where he was wounded. After his disappointment with the Greeks, he reversed the whole stereotype of philhellenism, and in his book *The Spirit of the East* went on to champion the case of the Ottoman Empire and praise the Albanians. With his pro Ottoman and anti-Russian political views, Urquhart found a prominent place in Disraeli's political camp and served as an example of how to influence the press. For Urquhart, the Porte had built an amazing political system of checks and balances and he pointed out that this system had allowed, and even favoured, the local independence of different religions and nationalities. Here he saw the chance for nationalities, including Albanians, to prosper within the empire.[88] Yet this prosperity would only be possible if the Porte was reformed with the help of the British government, and since this remained unlikely, he described Albania as a place which was suffering under the weight of an Ottoman Empire in the process of decay and collapse. Within this framework he saw the Albanians, and the Porte as open enemies and permanently engaged in armed conflict.[89] Although he was a supporter of the Ottoman Empire, he did not exclude the possibility of Albania becoming autonomous. Urquhart looked at the Albanian Question from the position of a politician and diplomat, and from this angle analysed the situation and gave his sympathy to Albania. He was also the first travel writer to bring north Albania into view as an important political and military factor, evoking important historic moments of the past and proposing political strategies in case the conflict between Albanians and the Porte escalated further.[90]

Urquhart, like many British travel writers, noticed that the Albanians were interested in winning British support. 'The Albanians seem most anxious to display, on all occasions, their respect for England,' wrote Urquhart and added: 'our power and our motives are equally incomprehensible to them; and no wonder.' It is for this reason that the Albanians would not send British travel writers and other visitors away with a bad opinion of Albania.[91]

Urquhart should be considered the first British travel writer who voiced the need for Albanians to be supported by the British public and government. He suggested that the British government should establish trade and cultural relations with this part of the Ottoman Empire, and gave a detailed account of an ancient decision-making process he observed among Albanians, a matter which had been largely ignored by other travel writers. He did not hide his admiration for Albanians.[92] Without doubt, Urquhart was the first British travel writer of the nineteenth century to write with the purpose of influencing the British government and public opinion on the Eastern Question, and by extension the Albanian Question.

With this contribution, Urquhart gave rise to a new group of British travel writers who sought to influence the public and persuade the government to form policies in favour of the countries they supported in the Balkans. Urquhart's example was followed by other travel writers, but their influence went against his ideas and efforts. Urquhart was the last British travel writer who broke with the Gothic tradition of writing and who did not apply the religious criterion to his depiction of Albania. His efforts in influencing the British public and government were soon overshadowed by William Gladstone's activities. In this respect, Urquhart should also be seen as the last British travel writer to have applied the non-religious view and the last to have tried to create a supportive climate for Albania in Britain. In other words, with Urquhart, the nineteenth-century battle to win over the British public in favour of Albania, was over. The end of this phase paved the way for Gladstonian Liberalism, which was much more influenced by religious interpretations of the Albanian Question.

Godless Albania

From November 1858 to February 1859, Gladstone had served as High Commissioner Extraordinary of Corfu and played an important role in giving the island to Greece.[93] A visit by the British delegation to Albania in November 1858 heralded significant changes in British politics and public opinion. The delegation arrived in Albania from Corfu to visit the town of Filates and according to John Morley (1838–1923) a journalist, writer and later a Liberal politician, the Albanian population there had organized a magnificent reception for their British guests. The entire population had come out to welcome them and the host, Jaffier Pasha, impressed most of the guests.[94] Morley was accompanying the most important guest, William Gladstone, who was not impressed by the host and who did not enjoy the visit at all. During a long dinner, Pasha's son told Gladstone that he should become a *pasha* in Albania. Gladstone was not impressed by this 'offer' either. To Gladstone, Albania, particularly the mosque and muezzin, did not create the same impression as they had for Disraeli. On this matter and the whole visit, which lasted only one day and one night, Gladstone wrote in his diary:

> Visited the mosque, heard the muezzin, & went through the town (Philiates). Turkish dinner in rude abundance. The whole impression is most saddening: it is all indolence, decay, stagnation: the image of God seems as if it were nowhere.[95]

This was the only time that Gladstone visited 'Godless' Albania or any other part of the Ottoman Empire, but the visit led him to 'fix a prejudicial image of the Ottoman realm in his mind'. This was also an important moment for Gladstone to develop his doctrine of British Liberalism.[96] Gladstone was already known for his idea that Europe, particularly the Concert of Europe, should be a community of Christian nations.[97] However, it was in Albania that Gladstone's preconceptions of Ottoman rule and Muslims were reinforced.

Albania had another great effect on Gladstone's life. As a result of the visit, Gladstone studied Hahn's '*Albanesische Studien*' a work that seems to have directed him towards another study. Hahn's study focused on the fact that the modern Albanians of Epirus descended from the ancient Pelasgians and Gladstone seem to have accepted this fact. In August 1862 he selected the book for 'systematic summer reading'.[98] Gladstone referred to Hahn's studies on many occasions throughout his book[99] and was noted to have said that he 'learned a great deal from *Albanesische Studien*' and highly valued Hahn's work.[100] During 1862, Gladstone was also seen displaying Hahn's book predominantly as he travelled. In Penmaenmawr (modern-day Wales) he 'quizzed the Bishop of Gloucester's wife about Albania'.[101] But, Gladstone was not interested in the origins of the Albanians, their geographic distribution, language, ethnic or national issues. His interest was in the religious side of Hahn's work, or more precisely, the question of: how Pelasgian spirituality had contributed to Hellenic faith and Greek art?[102]

Gladstone had developed religious liberalism, the idea that there should be equality and opportunity for all believers of the Church of England and those of other religious persuasions. In 1863 Gladstone was recorded as having strong ties with slave ownership or the slave economy.[103] However, for him, politics and religion went hand in hand and he maintained that his faith is for all humankind. As Fawcett noted, Gladstone 'remained unshaken in that characteristically liberal mix of Enlightenment and Christian universalism'.[104] In international politics and regarding the Balkans, Gladstone maintained that Christians should be first liberated and then assisted with the Enlightenment. Therefore, by the 1860s, it became obvious that Gladstone was applying religious interpretation to his views on the Ottoman Empire, Balkans and Albania. Furthermore, in applying this view, he did not see Albania as a distinct part of the Ottoman Empire as most other travel writers and diplomats had. Albania which had been described without religious prejudices by Byron, Disraeli and others seemed not to exist for Gladstone.

However, Gladstone was not the first British personality or travel writer to see Albania through the prism of religion. This view was expressed decades earlier, almost in parallel with the non-religious view, and was linked with the town of Parga. In 1817 Ali Pasha bought Parga from the British government and this act did not go unnoticed by the public. Reverend Thomas Smart Hughes wrote on this occasion that every Englishman must 'feel the blush of shame tingle in his cheeks', and felt that delivering Parga to Ali Pasha was a 'cruel and impolitic' act. Furthermore, Hughes was 'distressed by the thought of a Christian power' giving up this important town 'to an infidel tyrant'.[105] The point which he underlined here is that the rejection of Parga being transferred to a 'Muslim power' was made on religious grounds and Reverend Hughes had established a pattern of viewing Albania from a religious point of view. In April that year, a similar view was expressed by Thomas Maitland, who served as High Commissioner of the Ionian Islands, which were put under British control by the Treaty of Paris in 1815. On this matter, Maitland wrote to the Colonial Minister, Earl Bathurst, and expressed the same view as Hughes.[106]

Parga was also discussed at great length in the British Parliament. It was Lord John Russell who brought up the religious aspect, accusing the British government of failing to preserve the Christian religion of the people of Parga.[107]

The religious remarks of Reverend Hughes, Maitland and Russell did not create any immediate effect on the British government or public. Yet four decades later, the religious idea was to gain more weight under the patronage of Gladstone, who was to become important in the British political and intellectual scenes. The religiously informed idea, which contained a considerable anti-Albanian sentiment, was continued by two travel writers Georgina Muir Mackenzie (1833–74) and Adeline Paulina Irby (1831–1911) who introduced southern Slavs to Britain. Between 1861 and 1863 they travelled to Bosnia, Albania and Montenegro but spent most of their time in Serbia. Their passion for advocating for liberating the Christian Slavs from the 'Turkish yoke' is seen throughout their book which was published in 1867 under the title: *Travels in the Slavonic Provinces of Turkey in Europe*. The authors were so taken with Serbia, so they wrote that Kosovo, Montenegro, Bosnia and Herzegovina should be part of Serbia. They showed little consideration for non-Slavs and non-Christians and descended into 'denigratory Balkanism' when they spoke about the Muslims who were portrayed as 'savages, cruel and lawless'. Albanian Catholics were even more disliked by Mackenzie and Irby, who appeared to them to be worse than their Muslim brethren and were accused of 'making Judas bargains with the Turks'.[108]

Mackenzie and Irby went on to describe Albanians as being considerably less successful in everything when compared with Montenegrins and Serbs. They did not hesitate to describe Albanian women as 'ugly and dirty'. Their work built an unwanted picture of Albania in Britain, and this denigration was made with the intention of 'undermining the idea of Albanian independence'.[109] Their book was so appealing to the British public that in 1877, when the second edition came out, it was proof read by Florence Nightingale and prefaced by William Gladstone. By now, Gladstone had served as prime minister from 1868 to 1874. The book served Gladstone in his repetition of the need to liberate the Christians and to call for overthrowing 'the fabric of Turkish rule over a Serbian people'.[110]

The popularity of Gladstone grew considerably during 1876, when he accused the Porte of atrocities against the Bulgarians and criticized Disraeli's Conservative government for 'concealing the wholesale massacres' of the Christian population in the Balkans. Simultaneously he praised the Serbs for their bravery against the Porte.[111]

Gladstone was not alone in spreading his liberal view on Muslim Ottoman rule in the Balkans. By the 1870s this view became increasingly anti-Islamic and was mainly spread by those who supported the Greeks during the war of independence. The 'Bulgarian atrocities' of 1876 further heated the public debate in Britain concerning the role of the Ottomans in the Balkans.[112] The circle of intellectuals supporting Gladstone's religious view widened and came to include Liberal politicians such as Lord John Russell, William Harcourt, the Duke of Argyll, John Bright and intellectuals such as Charles Darwin, Herbert Spencer, Thomas Carlyle and many others.[113] In 1876 Thomas Carlyle wrote to *The Times* newspaper calling on the British and European governments for the 'immediate and summery expulsion of the Turks from Europe'. He proposed that some 'Mongol inhabitants', as he called the Turks or probably all Muslims, should be allowed to stay if they were peaceful but he insisted that the 'governing Turk should be ordered to disappear from Europe and never to return'.[114]

Another significant support to Gladstone came from Arthur Evans (1851–1941), archaeologist and journalist who became famous for unearthing the palace of Knossos in Crete. He also unearthed artefacts elsewhere in the Mediterranean, including north Albania where he discovered Illyrian coins from the second century BCE. With his publications as a correspondent for the *Manchester Guardian*, Evans inspired Gladstone and the Liberals and was considered a partisan of protecting the Christians in the Balkans. Evans also took the role of the leading 'Atrocitarian' in Britain. This was appreciated by Gladstone who used Evans' writings as a reference for his political speeches and as first-hand evidence to tell the public and voters how the Christians were persecuted.[115]

Evans used Serbian terminology when explaining the names of places in Albania and in his reports, he proposed Kosovo be given to Serbia after the Ottoman withdrawal. However, Albanian nationalists showed some respect for him, as some parts of his work became useful during the process of their national renaissance. Evans brought back into use *Dardania*, the old Illyrian and Roman name for Kosovo and north Macedonia. He was also appreciated because of his support for the theory that the Albanians were descendants of the Illyrians, and because he was considered to have published fair articles regarding the Albanian League.[116] During his visit to Albania in 1878 he changed his mind. He was impressed with the Albanian League and viewed the Albanians with admiration.[117]

Evans' writings on Albania were published during and after 1878 when it was too late to influence the British government, the public or the decision-making process of the Powers in the Congress of Berlin. Before he became interested in the Albanian Question, he was very active in Croatia and Bosnia in supporting the Christian Slavs against Austria-Hungary. In Dubrovnik he was once arrested and accused of being Gladstone's spy. Because of his anti-Austro-Hungarian activity he helped Gladstone to maintain anti-Austro-Hungarian feelings in Britain.[118]

Gladstone's passionate political and intellectual activities inspired Oscar Wilde to write 'Sonnet on the Massacres of Bulgarian Christians'. It is known that Wilde wrote the sonnet after he read Gladstone's essay 'Bulgarian Horrors and the Question of the East'.[119] At the same time Gladstone managed to convince Alfred Tennyson, another well-known British poet, of taking up the role of the 'Montenegrin's Byron'. Neither of these poets had ever set foot in the Balkans, nor had Gladstone save his one-day trip to Albania. However, Tennyson wrote a poem which was published accompanied by an 'account of Montenegro penned by William Gladstone'.[120] In the popular poem *Montenegro*, Tennyson praised Montenegrin warriors for beating 'Turkish Islam'.[121] In his accompaniment, Gladstone wrote that Montenegrins were intellectually comparable to other European nations because they carried the printing press into the mountains and used it to print laws, but mostly because they fought for 'freedom and Christianity'.[122]

By praising the Montenegrins and asking the British public to support Montenegro in 1877, and earlier making the same call about other Christian nations such as the Greeks, Serbs and Bulgarians, Gladstone had completed his circle around Albania. From the fact that Gladstone never mentioned Albania or Albanians, it could be suggested that he either ignored their existence or regarded them as simply being Ottoman Muslims. The Russo-Turkish War had started a year earlier in 1876, and all Balkan countries that were praised by Gladstone were advancing towards the territory of four *vilayets* that the Albanians regarded as their own land.

By now Gladstone had established his Liberalism and won the support of the British public, but the Conservative government held a different view and applied a different policy towards the Balkans. At this time Disraeli, who showed little or no consideration for religion and some sympathy for Albanians, was in power. The political clash between Disraeli's Conservatives and Gladstone's Liberals was fierce and the Albanian Question would often come into their midst.

Disraeli, by showing sympathy for Albania, took on the views of Lord Byron. Disraeli's views did not create a long-lasting impact on British public opinion and politics but he remained known as a sympathizer of the Albanian national cause. As late as 1939 *The Manchester Guardian* noted that in British news Albania 'generally recalls a few names: Scanderbeg, Ali Pasha, the Lion of Janina, and – Benjamin Disraeli'.[123]

2

The Congress of Berlin and the Albanian Question between policies of Disraeli and Gladstone 1876–81

San Stefano: A threat that mobilized the Albanian elite

Montenegro entered the Turko-Russian War (1877–8) on the side of Russia. At the beginning of January 1878, the most north-western coastal town of the Ottoman Empire, Antivari, fell into the hands of Montenegrins. The town was taken during an armistice agreed upon by the Porte on one side and the Russians and their allies on the other.[1] The Montenegrin army refused to acknowledge the ceasefire and expelled the population of the town, whose inhabitants were Albanian Muslims and Catholics.[2] The territories the Montenegrins occupied were almost entirely inhabited by Albanians, who were forced to leave their homes and properties behind and never to return.

The refugee problem soon became an international issue, causing great embarrassment to the Porte and some of the Great Powers. In Constantinople, the Austro-Hungarian ambassador, Count Ferenc Zichy, told the British ambassador, Henry Layard, that his government was deeply embarrassed by the entrance of some 30,000 Albanian refugees who had fled into Austro-Hungarian territory following the fall of Antivari (Bar in Serbo-Croatian or Tivar in Albanian) and other places. The Austro-Hungarians were not prepared for such a situation and simply could not cope. They were unable to convince the Montenegrins to take the refugees back and the numbers continued to grow. Meanwhile, the Montenegrins and Serbs were moving everywhere they could without any regard for armistice conditions.[3]

On the northern border of the Ottoman Empire, the Serbian army was advancing with similar speed and causing the same strategic dilemma as the Montenegrins. By June 1878, the Serbs had expelled the Albanians from their conquered territories. At the end of February Rifat Pasha, the *vali* (governor) of Prishtina, asked the British vice consul Harry Cooper if he could ask his government, or even British charitable institutions, for help in tackling the Albanian refugee crisis, whose number, he said, was over 100,000. Cooper believed that the number of refugees was exaggerated, but there was little doubt they had become an unbearable burden for the Ottoman government. Their presence had worsened an already tense situation, with some of the refugees and *bashi-bazouks* (irregular or paramilitary soldiers of the Ottoman army) instigating revenge attacks on the Christian population and the *vali* was unable to prevent it.[4] In the *vilayets* of Kosovo and Manastir the number of refugees was over 140,000. A British investigator Cullen, who was appointed by the Powers to investigate the situation of the Muslims in 'European Turkey', reported a difficult situation. Other British diplomats, including Edmund Calvert, sent reports with horrendous news about Muslims being forced to leave their homes in places that were lost by the Porte.[5] However, this hardly made any news in British or European press, which rather supported Liberal ideas and continued to report mainly on the situation of the Christians.

On 3 March 1878 the Russians forced the Porte to sign the Treaty of San Stefano. This effectively constituted a Russian diktat and an autonomous Bulgaria was formed as a result. The borders of Bulgaria penetrated deep into Albanian lands. Serbia and Montenegro, being in the camp of the victors, gained considerable swathes of Kosovo and Albania. To the Albanians, the Porte had shown little or no regard for their four *vilayets*, and the Treaty of San Stefano saw the Albanian leadership react swiftly. From Constantinople, Layard forwarded to London several letters that were addressed to him by Albanian delegates from the affected territories and from other parts of northern Albania, protesting against the annexation of their lands to Montenegro. The Christian and Muslim Albanians of Kosovo objected to the political decisions taken at San Stefano and were not prepared to see their territory ceded to Montenegro, Bulgaria or Serbia.[6] Inhabitants of Dibra dispatched a petition against being included in Bulgaria.[7]

The British General Consul in Albania, Kirby Green, sent an advisory letter to his superior, the Marques of Salisbury (1830–1903), concerning the Treaty of San Stefano. Montenegro, a small and landlocked country, had tripled in size under the terms of the Treaty. He suggested that the borders envisaged at San Stefano would engender a major problem among the Albanians and maintained that this ominous possibility should not be lightly accepted by European elites. Explaining the meaning of the situation on the ground and its consequences, he wrote:

> The Porte has handed over, by a stroke of pen, to Montenegro some of the most influential and hardy of the Roman Catholic mountain tribes. [...] The barrier which might and ought to have been raised against Slav encroachment is thus broken through.[8]

As a result of the Treaty of San Stefano, Albanians gave up their hope of any further support from Constantinople. They believed that the Ottoman army, consisted mainly of Syrian and other Middle Eastern conscripts, was not putting up a serious defence along the northern border of the empire where their land touched both Serbian and Montenegrin territory. Albanian leaders were readying themselves to convince the population to resist any attempt to enforce the Treaty of San Stefano on the ground. A number of spontaneous meetings were held throughout northern and eastern Albania where demands for taking action were heard. Albanians, in the north-west, around the border with Montenegro, formed a league whose members swore 'to resist until death all attempts coming from abroad or from the Supreme Government [the Porte] to change the present state of their territory'.[9] The league took steps to establish contacts with the Albanians of the north as far as Prishtina, east as far as Dibra and Ohri, and south to Janina, which led them to hold a far bigger meeting with greater political significance. Meanwhile, the British government and most of the Powers were getting ready to reject San Stefano and organize another peace conference.

Until 1878 there was no political organization claiming to represent the whole of Albania or demanding a political solution to their plight. Before 1878 Albanian leaders were engaged in local or regional political projects. This cluster of Albanian groups and their activities were narrow and local in character and, as such, did not cover the entire scope of the Albanian issue. After the Treaty of San Stefano this matter became more acute. The Albanian elite, who resided mainly in Constantinople and feared the threat of further territorial losses, believed it necessary to organize at the highest level in order to represent the entire national cause. When it became clear that the Powers of Europe would not accept the Treaty of San Stefano and were gathering to revise it in Berlin, Albanian leaders decided to hold a general assembly to discuss the matter of their future.

The Albanian League and the Congress of Berlin

On 10 June 1878, around 300 delegates from all parts of the four *vilayets* assembled in the town of Prizren in Kosovo. The meeting lasted two weeks and the proceedings were conducted in utmost secrecy.[10] The Porte did not try to stop the gathering, nor did it interfere in any of its activities during the assembly. After electing Ilaz Pasha Dibra as president, the assembly formed a military organization and called it Lidhja (League), which later was to be known as the Albanian League or the League of Prizren (Lidhja e Prizrenit), named after the town in which it was formed. The assembly passed both the *Kararname* (Resolution) of the League and the *Talimat* (Instructions) for the organization of a government administration and the creation of an army. A decree of eight points was also passed which dealt with army organization and its deployment.[11]

For more than a week the assembly, dominated by conservative landlords and a sultanist movement, which favoured a moderate approach towards the Porte, did not tackle the issues related to reforms, schools or autonomy. They did not even discuss the issue of uniting the four *vilayets* into one, which was the aim of the radicals led by Abdyl Frashëri (1839-92).[12] As a matter of fact the League was, to a great degree, an initiative led by activists from a group of Albanian elites and intellectuals in Constantinople represented in Prizren by Frashëri. Therefore, the League also represented the differences that existed between Albanian intellectuals who lived abroad and powerful landlords and traditional clan leaders at home. However, both wings, radicals and moderates, agreed from the beginning to defend the integrity of Albanian lands but to remain under the Ottoman umbrella.

When the League ended its two weeks of sessions, the leaders of all sides agreed to put a request to the Porte for uniting the four *vilayets* into one politically autonomous administrative and territorial unit. British newspapers, such as *The Spectator*, wrote that Albanians were determined 'to be governed by Albanian Committees, elected by universal suffrage'.[13]

Many observers, including Kirby Green, proclaimed that the Porte was behind the Albanian League. Others, mainly Slavs, believed that it was Britain who had set up the League. A great number of politicians, intellectuals and newspapers in Russia went even further by saying that the League did not really exist. According to them, not only was the League a figment of imagination put forward by the Sublime Porte in order to stop the implementation of the Treaty of Berlin, but there was in fact no Albanian nation save a few tribes.[14]

Several weeks before the Albanian League was formed, the Powers has been preparing for a peace conference. In London, following his appointment as Foreign Secretary, Marquees of Salisbury (1830–1903) produced a policy statement concerning his vision for British foreign policy. The document, known as the Salisbury Circular of 1 April 1878, became famous in the world of European diplomacy. The Cabinet accepted this new policy with great enthusiasm and it was telegraphed all over Europe, with the aim of demonstrating that Disraeli's Conservative government had adopted a new approach and was in energetic hands.[15]

The Circular principally called for a review of the Treaty of San Stefano. A big and strong Slav Bulgaria, under the control of Russia, was a prospect that the British could not accept and extension of Bulgaria into Greek and Albanian lands was considered a territorial severance of the Porte.[16] It was also made clear that London would preserve the presence of the Ottoman Empire in Europe, which left no place to discuss the Albanian Question as a separate issue.

In Constantinople, Layard had suggested that the Sultan appoint a 'credible Turk like Sadik Pasha', as head of the Ottoman delegation, to which the Sultan agreed. To Layard's surprise, a few days before the start of the Congress, the Sultan changed his mind. He told Layard that he had appointed Karatheodory Pasha and Mehmet Ali Pasha as plenipotentiaries who were to be joined by Sadullah Bey, the Ottoman ambassador in Berlin.[17] Karatheodory was a Greek Christian born in Berlin and, being the son of the Sultan's personal doctor, had made a successful career in Ottoman politics. At the Congress he was the principal representative of the Ottoman Empire and also held the position of Minister for Foreign Affairs. As he struggled to preserve Ottoman interests, he was 'constantly and rudely snubbed by Bismarck' who told him on many occasions that he was there 'only to accept what the Powers dictated'.[18] Mehmet Ali Pasha was born in Magdeburg, Germany, and was originally called Ludwig Karl Detroit. As a young man he went to Constantinople, joined the Ottoman army, became a Muslim and climbed to the military grade of Marshall.[19] During the Congress, it was also noted that Bismarck addressed him dismissively as *der Magdeburger*. The Albanians called him Ali Pashë Maxhari (Ali Pasha – the Hungarian). He was well known among the Albanians and was deeply unpopular because he had led a mission a few years earlier to disarm them.[20]

In Europe the Powers hurried to secure their positions before the beginning of the Congress. All made secret contact with each other and some signed agreements, with Britain signing a total of three secret agreements between March and June. None of these agreements touched on the Albanian Question. However, Albania was mentioned in another secret agreement, the Budapest Convention, which was reached between Austria–Hungary and Russia, and signed on 15 January. The third article of the second convention, which was signed a year earlier, on 18 March 1877, dealt with the future of the Balkans in the event of the collapse of the Ottoman Empire. If this was to happen, Russia was not to interfere directly in the Balkans, no large Slavic state was to be created and Albania, as well as Bulgaria, might become independent.[21]

In Berlin the Albanian Question was not discussed as a separate or independent issue as there was no power to bring it to the agenda. Among the Albanians there was some hope that Italy might raise the question, since during 1876 Francesco Crispi, President of the Italian Parliament and himself of Albanian origin, had expressed to the Powers the Italian interest in Albania.[22] Crispi visited Bismarck, who considered the Italian conquest of Albania a possibility. He told Crispi that Germany would not break with Vienna for the sake of Italy, but if Austria-Hungary were to take Bosnia and Herzegovina then Rome would be free to take Albania.[23] However, in March 1877 there was a change of government in Rome and the new Italian government decided to take a neutral position on this matter.

In the Protocols it was noted that on 1 July Karatheodory Pasha argued against the cession of Antivari to Montenegro. Furthermore, he said that Antivari was an Albanian town which had been taken by Montenegro during an armistice period and could only be kept by Montenegro by force and against the will of the Albanian population.[24]

The British delegation supported the Porte when the French and Italian delegates, William Waddington and Count Corti, proposed a ratification of the frontiers of Greece. Karatheodory Pasha did not agree with the proposal. He stated that the Porte was determined to keep the territories with the population, alluding to Albanians, who were worried about the idea of Greek expansion. Salisbury, and particularly Disraeli, who was familiar with that part of Epirus and Thessaly, supported Karatheodory Pasha and proposed that the issue of boundaries be left to the goodwill of the Porte. Apart from the Ottoman delegates, everyone agreed to recommend the session of territory as proposed by Waddington and Corti.[25]

During the main session of the Congress, the Albanian Question came up only in fragments. Sush was the case of the French delegate, Saint-Valier, who proposed to the Congress to continue securing the rights of Albanian Catholics of Mirdita that they enjoyed on the basis of *ab antico*. The proposal was rejected by the Porte and the British. Salisbury emphasized that this may cause difficulties as this matter asked to sanction privileges which were not clear and by which, the Congress would give international recognition to the Albanian local customary law. Although the French and the Austro-Hungarians insisted that the issue was linked with the traditional autonomy and rights of the Christian population, the proposal did not pass. Instead, a compromise was made: the Ottomans agreed not to make any new changes regarding the status of Mirdita and this was included as a statement in the text of the Treaty.[26]

Austria-Hungary was behind the Mirdita issue. They had managed to mark Albania, or at least the northern part which was inhabited by Albanian Catholics, as their zone of interest. Furthermore, Austria-Hungary succeeded in winning the right to build a road and railway extension from Herzegovina, through Montenegro, to Albania.[27] Austria-Hungary did not succeed in becoming militarily established near Shkodra, as it had hoped, but compared with her rival, Italy, Vienna had by far emerged as a winner from the Congress. Austria-Hungary became territorially linked with Albania on the frontiers of Kosovo, through the *Sanjak* of Novi Pazar. Article XXV of the Treaty allowed an Austro-Hungarian military presence in Sanjak but the place was to remain part of the *Vilayet* of Kosovo and as such under the Sultan's sovereign rights.[28] However, from Sanjak Austro-Hungarians were only a few miles from the railway station of Mitrovica in Kosovo. They were coming close to Salonika, the place they planned to occupy in the case of the collapse of the Ottoman Empire.

A nationality ignored

The Liberals managed to impose religion as an essential element in the rise of nationality in the Balkans. Crucially, many politicians, historians and the public in Britain and Europe viewed the Eastern Question through the prism of Christians living under the 'barbarous and infidel state' of the Ottomans.[29] The rise of new states was considered as a struggle of new Christian nations against the Ottoman Empire, which was viewed as Muslim in essence.

Albanians did not fit easily into this framework. The majority of the population were Muslim, and although Albanians were integrated into the Ottoman system, they were nevertheless looking for an exit strategy, as they felt the collapse of the empire was drawing near. The Albanians were the first nation with a Muslim majority to have risen against the Porte and demand autonomy.

The existence of a distinct Albanian identity was noticed by British travellers in the Balkans long before the Congress of Berlin. Most travel writers observed that the Albanians constituted a separate ethnicity from those that surrounded them or indeed even a nation, being distinct in origin, language, tradition, religion, behaviour and dress. It is necessary to recall Hobhouse's notes on this matter:

> It is certain that the Christians who can fairly be called Albanians are scarcely, if at all, to be distinguished from the Mahometans [Muslims]. They carry arms, and many of them are enrolled in the service of Ali [Pasha], and differ in no respect from his other soldiers. There is a spirit of independence and a love of their country in the whole people which, in a great measure, does away the vast distinction observable in other parts of Turkey between the followers of the two religions; for when the natives of other provinces, upon being asked who they are, will say, "We are Turks," or "We are Christians," a man of this country answers, "I am an Albanian".[30]

It is also useful to recall, once again, Lord Byron's impressions of Albanians. Concerning their religion, nationality, behaviour and the position that the Albanians held in the eyes of their neighbouring nations, Byron wrote:

> No nation are so detested and dreaded by their neighbours as the Albanese; the Greeks hardly regard them as Christians, or the Turks as Moslems, and in fact they are a mixture of both, and sometimes neither.[31]

Ali Pasha's rule had contributed to furthering these characteristics. His role was becoming important even after his death although his intention was not to create a nation state. However, the legacy he left behind was used by the Albanian elite to build their nationalist platform. After his death, northern Albania, together with Kosovo, gradually became the cradle of nationalist activities and uprisings against the Porte.[32]

The beginning of what became known as the 'Albanian National Renaissance' or 'Rilindja' (Revival) took place in the early 1830s and did not differ considerably from other national movements in the Balkans.[33] However, the Albanians did not manage to create a single and united representative body before 1878 with the formation of the Albanian League. The League, established as a result of nationalist ideas circulating in the Albanian elite, became the first political organization to be accepted by the population at large. As a result of the border conflicts with Greece and Montenegro, the League, directed from Prizren, became active in Janina and Shkodra. The League proved capable of threatening northern Greece and Montenegro militarily. In the north the League had permanently mobilized 30,000 armed men while in the south it was prepared to put 40,000 men under arms within a short time. Regarding the situation in the south, the League made it known that if the Powers and the Porte gave any territory in Epirus to Greece, the Albanians would proclaim independence and demand a protectorate guaranteed by a European Power. The British Consul in Corfu informed London that this menacing attitude within the Albanian League came out of their sense of being a 'separate national identity, coupled with religious fanaticism and secret encouragement from abroad, particularly from Italy'.[34]

The Congress of Berlin did not open the door for the Albanian League, although the League made efforts to prove it was capable of representing the entire nation. However, Bismarck had previously declared that he did not recognize the existence of a distinct Albanian nation. Furthermore, Austria-Hungary cared only for the Albanian Catholics while other Powers, except Britain, remained silent on this matter. In the memorandum submitted to Disraeli, the League asked the British government to present the Albanian case at the Congress of Berlin. The memorandum, which became the political programme of the League, explained their historical background and went on to explain and affirm both Albanian nationality and its frontiers:

> All we want is to be Albanian. Albania cannot be united with Greece. Profound differences in nationality, language, customs and culture would make such a union untenable [...] Albania will never stand the Slavic domination. Albanian will never be Turkish [...] From the banks of the Boyana [the river bordering Montenegro] to the gates of Janina there is one compact and homogenous core of population, with common characteristics and a common national identity.[35]

Explaining why Britain should undertake such a role, the memorandum elaborated:

> Only Great Britain can take up our requests and make them heard at the Congress. In doing so, it will not lack the support of the other Powers who have recognised our political existence and destiny from the moment the principle of nationality became the primary basis of European public law. Independent of

the issue of justice, Great Britain has great interest in creating an impregnable cordon to check the Slavic invasion advancing and flooding towards the Adriatic, and this cordon must and can only be created by the peoples who are most imperilled by the inexorable threat of their neighbours [...] Great Britain, that ancient seat and mistress of liberty for all peoples, foremost among all the Powers has recognised the right of other nations to their independence.[36]

The British government and its delegation to the Congress, headed by Disraeli, did recognize the existence of the Albanian nationality but took no steps to sponsor their request. Whenever members of Disraeli's government and the Conservative Party considered the Albanian issue, they came under strong criticism from the Liberal opposition. The harshest criticism was directed at Salisbury, who as Foreign Secretary received a delegation from the Albanian League. The two delegates, Abdyl Frashëri and Mehmet Vrioni, arrived in London after meeting high officials in Rome and Paris.[37] Salisbury saw them on 12 May 1879. Both delegates were former Deputies to the Ottoman Parliament from the region of Janina.

Among other issues, these two delegates discussed the issues of language, education and religion which posed problems for the Albanian national cause in the south. At that time the Albanians lacked a unified alphabet and had adopted Greek as their language of education because the use of the Albanian language was prohibited by the Porte. Albanians in the south spoke Greek and were educated in Janina in the Greek. The Albanian delegates told Salisbury that the language issue should not confuse him, arguing that it would be an error to classify these Albanians as either Greeks or exclusively as Christian. They also stated that a large number of Christian Albanians lived in the north and the south of Albania but had no desire to be included in Greece or Montenegro. Of a population of 600,000 in South Albania, about 60,000 spoke Greek, but these were only men and the figure excluded both women and children.[38]

With regard to other points, raised during the meeting, Salisbury wrote:

> They desire to lay their wishes and their claims with all humility before the European Powers in the hope that justice would be done to them; but they did not conceal their resolution to persevere in resistance to alien domination which for many centuries their fathers had maintained. Whatever the results of the pending discussion might be, the King of Greece would only become master of any portion of Albania if he was able to subdue it by the force of arms.[39]

Salisbury did not express to the delegates any opinion concerning their national cause remaining cautious and declaring no official position on the matter. He advised them to continue to provide the other Powers in Constantinople with information of this kind. He informed Layard in Constantinople that he had told the two Albanian delegates that 'it was the wish of the Powers to do impartial justice to all races which inhabit the Balkan Peninsula'.[40]

In the House of Commons, the Liberal MP Charles Dilke argued that the members of this delegation could not be considered representatives of the Albanian nation, as they had introduced themselves. He said they were Ottoman paid functionaries and the Porte did not prevent their visit to Europe.[41] During the meeting the Albanian delegation handed a memorandum to Salisbury,[42] and from London went to Berlin in the hope of meeting Bismarck. Prince Bismarck, however, refused to see them. Back in the House of Commons, Dilke suggested that Salisbury should have acted the same way as Bismarck.

When Janina and the border with Greece were discussed during 1879, Conservatives often asked the House to consider Albanians a nationality. A year later, the Liberal MP Joseph Cowen asked Prime Minister Gladstone 'whether, in seeking to extend Montenegrin territory in the north and the Greek territory in the south, regard will be had to the [Albanian] nationality in the centre?'

Gladstone, although not known as a friend of the Albanians, recognized their nationality. With diplomatic and politically correct language, he replied:

> We are bound to have the same fair regard to all the facts of the case, and to the element of nationality and to the peculiar circumstances of Albania, as we should do in reference to any other portion of territory.[43]

Many Conservative MPs thought Gladstone's approach towards Albania was unfair, believing that he had disregarded Albanian nationality. When the British government pressurized Albanians and the Porte to give Ulqin and its surroundings to Montenegro, Henry Drummond Wolf, a Conservative MP, accused Gladstone of 'plundering Turkey' and 'coercing the Albanian nation'.[44]

However, a group of well-known Liberal politicians and diplomats of the Gladstone circle, consisting of Dilke, Granville, Goschen and Fitzmaurice, recognized the need to accommodate the Albanians within an autonomous or independent state or even in Personal Union with Greece. Throughout 1880 and 1881 they sought a solution for the Albanians and convincing the British government to apply one of these three options.

From Constantinople, Fitzmaurice suggested that Kosovo and some parts of Macedonia, being predominantly Muslim and Albanian, should be put under a new *Projet de Loi* (Project of Law) and treated separately by the International Commission which had a duty of overseeing reforms in the Ottoman Empire. He proposed other measures to be taken regarding reforms in Albania[45] which were supported by ambassador Goschen. He reminded the Foreign Office of the unsolved Albanian issue, which was causing problems because their nationhood was ignored but should be considered. He urged Earl Granville:

> I venture to submit to Your Lordship, as I have done before, that the Albanian excitement cannot be passed over as a mere manoeuvre conducted by Turks in order to mislead Europe, and evade its will. Nor can it be denied that the Albanian movement is perfectly natural. An ancient and distinct race as any by whom they are surrounded, they have seen the nationality of these neighbouring races taken under the protection of various European Powers, and their aspirations gratified for a more independent existence [...] They see the Eastern Question being solved on the principle of nationality, meanwhile they see that themselves do not

receive similar treatment. Their nationality is ignored and territory inhabited by Albanians is handed over in the north to the Montenegrins, to satisfy Montenegro, the protégé of Russia, and in the south to Greece, the protégé of England and France. Exchanges of territory are proposed, other difficulties arise, but still it is in expense of Albanians, and Albanians are to be handed over to Slavs and Greeks without reference to the principle of nationality.[46]

Goschen proposed the creation of a strong Albania before the Ottoman Empire collapsed, otherwise, as he emphasized, Albania would disappear along with the empire. If Albania was to be created as a state, a balance of power in the Balkans would prevail, otherwise no European Power alone would be able to subdue the Albanians. It would not be wise to break up Albanians and divide their lands because, he said, Albanians are a difficult race to manage. Dividing them into north and south would also be unwise. Therefore, Goschen had an alternative proposal regarding the future of Albania and advised Earl Granville to consider the possibility of 'attaching Albania by a dynastic link to Greece'.[47]

Charles Dilke had a similar plan for combining Albanian autonomy with Personal Union with Greece, 'finding that the Albanians were willing to accept the King of the Hellenes'.[48] The Greek *Charge d'Affaires* in London, Gennadius, told Dilke that a proposal for a Personal Union between Albania and Greece was made to the king of Greece. The Greek diplomat, wishing to deny Albanians were a nationality, saw this as a predictable move because the southern Albanians, according to him, were 'to all intents and purposes Greeks but the initiative ought to proceed from the Albanians'.[49]

As Gennadius knew, there had been contacts in the past between the Albanian leaders and Greek government officials. In 1877, Albanian leaders had secretly negotiated with Greece on a joint war against the Porte. However, Abdyl Frashëri had rejected the hypothetical union with Greece and told the Greek delegate, Skouloudis, that Albanians were determined to 'save the Albanian nationality'.[50]

Goschen thought that the proposed union would be a solution for Europe but he was aware of the difficulties in convincing the Albanians, who were strong in Constantinople and trusted all over the Empire. However, Goschen was convinced that the Albanians 'would and must have an autonomy in some shape'.[51]

On 4 September 1880, the question of Albanian nationality came up again in the House of Commons. Cowen criticized the way the British government was handling the crisis and did not agree with the government helping the Montenegrins to 'take Albanian land without their will or approval'. As he characterized Albanians as the oldest people in the Balkans and fighters for independence, a loud voice was heard in the House: 'They are not a nationality'. To this Cowen replied:

Not a nationality, his hon. Friend said. That was Prince Bismarck's remark at Berlin. He said he did not know of the existence of the Albanian nation. Such a statement was not at all surprising. Prince Bismarck did not know of the nationality of Denmark or of Holland either. And another Prince, quite as potent then as Prince Bismarck is now, contended at the Congress of Vienna that he did not know of the nationality of Italy.[52]

A small group of MPs, among them Cowen, criticized the Liberal government for having sympathy towards the Slav nationalities but showing no regard to their rival peoples in the Balkans. Cowen maintained that the Treaty of Berlin was being 'carried out irrespective of nationalities and creeds' while her Majesty's Government and other Powers of Europe, by extending the Greek and Montenegrin territories, were 'encroaching upon the nationality of Albania'.[53] This group argued that the government was applying the principle of nationality only partially, a policy which was seen as selective because the government was playing the role of Christian emancipators and liberators in the region. Cowen stated that the attitude of the British government towards Albania was the same as that shown towards Ireland but the ignorance the British and other European Powers showed towards Albania was greater than that towards Ireland, he emphasized.[54]

Benjamin Disraeli and William Gladstone had been leaders of their parties since 1868 and together dominated British politics. They came from contrasting social and ethnic backgrounds and differed in many aspects, particularly in foreign affairs and over the Eastern Question and Albania within it. For Disraeli, the Ottoman Empire was a bulwark against a Russian invasion of the British dominions in Asia and potential capture of the route to India. This made Disraeli seek to protect the territories of the Ottoman Empire in Europe against the Russian threat.[55]

According to Disraeli's strategy on the Eastern Question, Russia was an enemy and had to be prevented from advancing into Europe or occupying Constantinople at any cost, even that of war. Disraeli even reminded the Queen of this position in a letter he sent from Berlin before the Congress began in 1878. The Congress was to deal with such 'topics as the port of Antivari', which he thought would be insignificant, just as he regarded the borders of Montenegro and Serbia as having the same low importance.[56]

Gladstone expressed readiness to include Russia in joint European actions and avoiding direct confrontation with St. Petersburg. For him, the emancipation of Christian states in the Balkans would be easier with Russian help and would tie into the aims of his liberalism. He supported the national programmes of the Balkan nations. He was devoted to the Hellenic cause and praised the Montenegrins, Bulgarians and other Balkan nations for their war against the Ottoman Empire.[57] As we saw earlier, he did not include the Albanians in this list.

In their second terms as prime ministers, both Disraeli and Gladstone dealt with the Albanian Question. Disraeli addressed it during and after the Congress of Berlin and Gladstone did so in implementing The Treaty of Berlin. The Albanians were the only Balkan people for whom Disraeli showed sympathy during the Congress and throughout the rest of his second term in office. Although the Albanian League pleaded with him to take their case to the Congress, he did not answer their call, but later did bring up the need for the Great Powers to support the Albanians. In his opinion, Albanians were 'the main guarantors of the preservation of the Ottoman Empire in Europe'.[58]

Disraeli had gained considerable knowledge and experience of Albania before coming to power. His visit had a significant impact on him because he came to know the Albanians and became familiar with the Albanian-Greek problem. He had considered Janina the capital of Albania.[59] During and after the Congress of Berlin, his government refused to acknowledge Greek territorial pretensions over Albania. He was firm that Janina and other southern Albanian towns should not be ceded to Greece as some diplomatic voices, headed by the French, requested at Berlin and after.

Unlike Disraeli, Gladstone did not show much interest in Albania before he came to power, though he recognized the authority of the Albanian League. In his election campaign of 1880, he spoke at the Music Hall in Edinburgh about the Porte's inability to hold territories in Europe. 'Albania is possessed by a League' he told his supporters.[60] However in his second term as prime minister (1880–5) Gladstone seemed to have more interest in this matter. Disraeli saw the Albanians and their territories as an important element for the Ottoman Empire in Europe. Therefore, he favoured a cautious relationship with the Albanians in order to maintain stability in that part of the empire. Yet, the British government under Disraeli, and even less under Gladstone, had no strategy or doctrine for an official position towards the Albanians and their national programme. Albanian interests were examined only when the interests of other nations in the Balkans were considered.[61]

Great disagreements between Conservatives and Liberals over the Eastern Question, and consequently the Albanian Question, came to the surface in 1877, when Disraeli appointed Henry Layard as ambassador to Constantinople.[62] Gladstone and his Liberals expressed fierce disagreement at Layard's posting to Constantinople, 'fearing that he will bring another Crimean War'.[63]

The Liberals continuously accused Layard of being a Turcophile. However, during his service in Constantinople Layard, who disliked Gladstone in return, managed to establish a good relationship with Sultan Abdul Hamid II and exercised some influence over him. He became familiar with the Albanian Question and on several occasions raised the importance of this question for Britain and other European Powers. Some of the Liberals, including Dilke, Lord Goschen and Lord Fitzmaurice, were convinced that Disraeli was showing too much interest in the Albanian Question while in opposition, but changed their mind when they came to power. They realized that the Albanian Question required proper attention and engaged themselves seriously in solving this problem.

Difficulties in implementing the Treaty of Berlin

When the Porte took steps to implement the Treaty, the relationship with the League worsened quickly. The Porte sent Mehmet Ali Pasha to northern Albania to persuade the Albanians to accept the Treaty. As mentioned earlier, he was well known among the Albanians and was deeply unpopular.[64] The Sultan thought that Mehmet Ali Pasha was the best man for the job since he was an Ottoman plenipotentiary at Berlin, knew the region and had friends in Kosovo. On 19 August 1878 the Pasha told Layard that he was leaving for Albania, where he was being sent as a Commissioner to execute the Treaty in relation to the territorial cessions to Montenegro and Serbia 'and reconcile the Albanians to them'. Pasha also told Layard that the Porte will need British support in implementing the Treaty at the Albanian side of the border with Montenegro and Serbia.[65]

Mehmet Ali Pasha arrived in Prizren on 25 August 1878. The next day, in a meeting with the leaders of the League, the Pasha told them to submit to the will of the Powers and obey the Treaty. The reception he received was very hostile. When he tried to read the Sultan's *firman* (imperial decree) about the Treaty, he was shouted down.[66] Then he gave the League twenty-four hours to think about his proposal and come up with a positive reply. No one attended the next meeting the Pasha had called. News spread that the Pasha, after the delivery of Gucia and Plava to Montenegro, would go on to disband the League in Prizren and its branch in Shkodra. That day his telegrapher was killed, as he was suspected of secret communications with the Porte.[67]

Mehmet Ali Pasha left Prizren and continued towards Plava and Gucia, but stopped in Gjakova to spend the night of 1 September 1878 as a guest of Abdullah Pasha Dreni, the governor of Gjakova and a member of the League. The next morning, they found themselves surrounded by a large crowd of Albanians, believed to have been led by Ali Pasha Gucia, who commanded the armed Albanians along the border of Montenegro and refused to surrender Plava and Gucia. They called on Abdullah Pasha to hand over Mehmet Ali Pasha. He refused, telling the besiegers that it was against traditional Albanian law to hand over friends and guests. Shooting began and lasted four days. Finally, Mehmet Ali Pasha, Abdullah Pasha Dreni, their guards and a unit of Ottoman soldiers were all killed.[68]

This event terrified the Porte. The Powers realized that implementing the Treaty would not be as easy as they had thought in Berlin. Cooperation between the League and the Porte ended and the will of the Albanians to resist any cession of territory grew. The episode also brought the Albanian Question to the attention of European governments and public opinion.[69] The Albanian League, through Abdyl Frashëri, used this situation to put forward demands previously adopted by the southern branch of the League in Janina.[70]

The incident in Gjakova halted all proceedings of the Commission about the border of Montenegro. The British Consul in Shkodra, Kirby Green, advised the Foreign Office to postpone any activity of this nature. The delimitation, he said, would be used by the League to further confront the Ottoman authorities and to assume defence of the whole country of Albania. The assassination of Mehmet Ali Pasha created more difficulties than were ever anticipated in deciding on the handover of Plava and Gucia. However, Green advised London that 80,000 Ottoman soldiers would be required to repel armed units of the Albanian League on the border with Montenegro. He suggested that these imperial forces should come from Anatolia or other parts of the empire and should consist of soldiers who had no sympathy for Albania.[71]

Ali Pasha Gucia, in command of 30,000 armed Albanians, was waiting for a signal to enter Montenegro. Albanian soldiers and other personnel were deserting the Ottomans *en masse* to join the Albanian force. The League had passed death sentences on some of its members who had refused to break with the Ottoman authorities.[72] Under these circumstances the delimitation of the frontier by the European Commission had to be stopped. The Porte was not willing to proceed with Treaty arrangements until an alternative solution for the Albanians was found. As had been suggested by Green, the Porte was having difficulties sending fresh and sufficient numbers of troops to Albania.[73]

Keeping Plava and Gucia became a danger for the Porte. Giving these places to Montenegro was not a solution either. The armed forces of the League were imposing a conflict between the Albanians and Montenegro. On the other side, the League brought the Porte into difficulties with the Powers and Albanians.[74] It became obvious that the rectification of borders could not happen in the near future.

After the Congress of Berlin, the border problem and the activities of the League became daily concerns of the Powers. The League was established quickly in the south, led by the most powerful and wealthiest Albanian families. By the beginning of 1879, Albanian notables assembled in Preveza, coming from Epirus and the rest of Albania to monitor changes in the border. They declared openly that they were determined to resist by force any annexation of part of Epirus by Greece and were prepared to put 40,000 men under arms. It was obvious that they had 'plenty of money, men, arms and ammunition to carry a long war'.[75]

This situation worried Greece. The Powers, including the British, could only observe and think of alternatives. The national ambitions of the League worried the Porte, although the Sultan was pleased at this delay in the cession of territory since negotiations between Ottomans and Greeks were not moving forward. The Albanian League became more than a threat. In the north, the situation with the Montenegrin border was no better. The League caused serious problems and 'succeeded in defeating the attempt of Europe' to detach areas in the south and north.[76] Practically, the Berlin Treaty, in many ways, was dead.

The Foreign Minister of France William Waddington, who was also a French plenipotentiary at the Congress of Berlin, looked for a way out of this difficult situation. He favoured actions benefitting the Greek Government and wanted to reach an understanding with the British on the Greek question. He told the British ambassador in Paris, Lord Lyons, that France had received offers from the Russian and the German governments to send warships to the Mediterranean to execute the part of the Treaty concerning Greece.[77] However, he refused both offers because he preferred this matter be dealt with by France and Britain. Waddington insisted that Thessaly and Epirus should be considered as a source of strength for Greece but Disraeli's government refused these proposed annexations because it would have weakened the Porte and angered the Albanians. Yet the British were in favour of a moderate extension of the Greek border, though not including Janina and the surrounding region, as Waddington had advocated.

The Ottoman government, as an answer to this situation, issued a memorandum in which they refused the French proposal of separating Epirus from Albania. The Porte regarded that the 'Tosques' (Albanians of the south) would be severely damaged because they would be denied the natural link with the port of Preveza in the Adriatic. The Porte insisted that Epirus was inhabited by 'Tosques' from the Valley of Callamas to the north with Vlora as the centre.[78]

Almost one year after the Congress, negotiations over the Greek borders were going nowhere. The Liberals, while in opposition, never ceased to remind Disraeli that ministers of England had always promoted the extension of Greece as a strategy for a 'solution of the Eastern Question in accordance with the real interests of England'.[79]

Disraeli did not ignore the issue of the Greek border. For him, the Greeks were a danger but the Albanians, who were neglected, were a greater danger. Disraeli had mainly disregarded Waddington's plans but on some occasions let him know that it was the Albanians and the Porte he was worried about, rather than the Greeks. Disraeli had other plans and was trying to win the support of Bismarck. Concerned about the poor fulfilment of the Treaty, on 13 July 1879 he wrote to Bismarck:

> The Janina question is not one of Turkish *amour propre*, at which we should all laugh. It involves an Albanian war, which would probably be long and devastating, and precipitate results which it is the interest of Germany and England to postpone.[80]

The call from Gladstone for Disraeli to implement the Treaty of Berlin was strong. He criticized the government for allowing France to champion the case of the 'Hellenic races'. Charles Dilke also pushed both Government and Parliament to accept a French memorandum sent to Disraeli regarding mediation. He told the Parliament that Disraeli's government appeared as an obstacle to European mediation. In other words, Disraeli was obstructing the initiative of France and Italy, and not pressuring the Porte to execute the Treaty.[81]

The Porte searched for alternative solutions and Italy was asked to mediate. At the beginning of 1879, Count Corti came up with a proposal for territorial exchange. As Plava and Gucia were inhabited by Muslim Albanians, Corti thought it would be easy to give Montenegro Kuçi Kraina, Hoti and Gruda, which were inhabited by Catholic Albanians. Although Montenegro indicated readiness to accept this proposal, Albanian Catholics refused inclusion in Montenegro. Salisbury told Layard to officially support the arrangement in Constantinople but not to push it if Austria-Hungary expressed strong objections to it.[82] The proposal further united the Albanian Catholics with the Albanian Muslims and Albanian armed units along the border became a real threat.

The Great Powers shifted position and decided to give Montenegro the coastal town of Ulqin and its surroundings, which were also predominantly Albanian but Muslim in religion. During the spring of the same year, the Ottoman army began to withdraw from other positions to allow the Montenegrin occupation as ordered by the Treaty. But many of these positions, instead of being held by Montenegrins, were in fact occupied by the forces of the League. Clashes between the Montenegrins and the Albanian League were frequent yet neither side was winning, thus creating a problem for the Powers and the Porte.

The change in British foreign policy and the Conference of Berlin

The British election of May 1880 brought the Liberals to power with Gladstone as prime minister. Earl Granville became Foreign Secretary with Charles Dilke as his deputy. Another immediate change was the ambassador to Constantinople. Ambassador Layard, whom the Liberals disliked so intensely, was replaced by Joachim Goschen.

Lord Edmond Fitzmaurice was appointed Commissioner at Constantinople with the duty to oversee the reorganization and reforms of the European provinces of the Ottoman Empire as foreseen by the Treaty of Berlin.

British foreign policy and its position towards the Eastern Question changed. The Porte, especially the Albanians who were aware of Gladstone's liberalism, were most concerned. Yet surprisingly the Liberals became more active than the Conservatives had been previously in trying to find a solution to the Albanian Question. Gladstone, through Goschen as a special representative, was showing the Porte that his government was determined to insist, in concert with the other Powers, that the time had come to fulfil the obligations of the Treaty of Berlin. Therefore, Goschen's main duty was to convince the Sultan that the British would not tolerate further delays regarding the border demarcation of Montenegro and Greece.[83]

The new government gave fresh impetus to the Treaty negotiations. As a result of this new British foreign policy, the Powers became more active and pressure on the Porte and on Albanians was intensified. Gladstone was now in a position to pressurize the Powers to speed up preparations for another peace conference and bring about an end to the border problems in the Balkans. In July 1880 the Great Powers gathered once again to solve the problem of the Greek and Montenegrin borders. Almost the entire part of Thessaly and a great part of Epirus were assigned to Greece though the Montenegrin border was not discussed in great detail. The Powers considered the matter closed because Montenegro was to get Hoti and Gruda, or the town of Ulqin with its surrounding district. As before, the Albanian Question was not treated as a separate issue. The British wanted to deal with the Albanian matter as they still, even under Gladstone, considered the Albanians important for the existence of the Ottoman Empire. However, they were not supported by the other Powers, with Russia and France strongly rejecting any talks about Albania and Austria-Hungary and Germany taking neutral positions.[84]

The Albanian League, again, did not accept the decisions of the Conference. In September it became known that Ulqin would be given to Montenegro and that the British, leading a naval blockade, would assist in the cession and complete the rectification of the border. The idea of a naval blockade on Smyrna, although it did not happen, frightened the Sultan who saw it as a potential humiliation. The Powers had viewed this insistence unfavourably and Gladstone was left alone to deal with the Porte. Bismarck said that 'Dulcigno [Ulqin] was madness and Gladstone was a crazy professor'.[85] Even the Queen seemed to have agreed with Bismarck and continued to remind Gladstone that Disraeli's policy towards the Ottoman Empire should not be abandoned, nor would she give her consent to a war with the Porte, whom she regarded as an old ally. Yet Gladstone believed that it would not be good 'if Turkey befools Europe at Dulcigno [Ulqin]'. Bismarck also regarded this act as Gladstone's policy of 'promoting Russian interest in the East and neglecting the English'.[86]

As a result of Gladstone's threat, the Porte sent more troops to Albania to convince the Albanians to hand over Ulqin to the Montenegrins. After some clashes between the forces of the League and the Ottomans, on 27 November 1880 the border question was over. Finally, on 24 May 1881 the Conference of Ambassadors in Constantinople drew the demarcation line with Greece, giving the greatest part of Thessaly to Greece as well as part of Epirus, along with the entire region of Arta, which surrendered on 6 July 1881. Janina was not included. Greece got considerably less territory than it and its friends had asked for.[87] For the League, this was a loss the Albanians could live with.

Throughout 1880 the League was running the territory of modern-day Kosovo, north Albania and northwest Macedonia as a *de facto* government. In February Abdyl Frashëri told the Central Committee of the League in Prizren that the Porte would do nothing about Albania and would give part of their territory to Montenegro and Greece. 'Let us be Albanians and make one Albania,' said Frashëri in a meeting of the League.[88] A well-known British artist and illustrator, Richard Caton Woodville, registered the same spirit of independence in Shkodra. Woodville and his companions were allowed to attend a secret meeting of the Albanian League because they were British. Woodville characterized the meeting of the Albanian leaders of the League as resembling any European senate of that time. In an anti-Ottoman atmosphere, he drew a sketch and registered a speech of one of the leaders:

> What want we with matters in the land of Arbenii [Albania]? Are we babes, that we cannot go alone? What does the Sultanate for us? Does it protect our lives? No. Does it roof our houses? No. Does it feed our starving? No. Shall we be silent and eat dirt? […] I will tell you. What is the will of our masters? That we give it up to the Slavs of Kara Dagh [Montenegro]? For what? Because the Sultanet wills it? Because the Cuvend [Assembly] of Berlin wills it? Because the Ruski [Russia] wills it? […] Let us speak – but with steel and lead, with yataghan [sword] and pouska [gun].[89]

The activities of the League were noted throughout that year by the European press, which had started to show considerable attention to the Albanian Question. An article published in the *Manchester Guardian* criticized the British government for not addressing the Albanian Question.[90] The League's success, which was evident by August 1880, had caused excitement among some Albanian leaders which led them to think of independence. This fact was also noted by newspapers in Britain that reported, with some exaggeration, that the League had declared independence and established full control over most parts of Albania and Macedonia.[91]

However, after the loss of Ulqin, a military clash between the League and the Porte was inevitable. Fearing that the League would move towards independence, in March 1881 the Porte sent 20,000 troops to Skopje. Dervish Pasha moved 10,000 troops and heavy artillery to Kosovo and confronted 5,000 armed men of the League in Shtime. The Ottomans won the battle but fighting continued elsewhere. In May the Ottoman army occupied all of Kosovo and the hunt began for the leaders of the Albanian League. More than 4,000 people were arrested and hundreds were exiled.[92]

This was the end of the Albanian League. Although it had prevented the annexation of much of the territory to Greece, Montenegro and Serbia, in general the League must be seen as a failure since it did not succeed in fulfilling its objective to unite the Albanians under one single *vilayet* or other autonomous administrative unit.[93] With this, Gladstone believed that Albania was pacified and the future of the Ottoman Empire, and indeed peace in Europe, was secured.

However, the aftermath of the Congress of Berlin also revealed that Conservatives and Liberals had accepted the need to maintain an Ottoman presence in the Balkans. In this both parties aimed to protect broader British interests.[94] Although Gladstone publicly appeared to believe that the Albanian Question had been solved with his actions, he was still convinced that the Balkans was a troubled place. Therefore, Gladstone aimed to normalize relations with the Porte, which had deteriorated over the Albanian Question. Thus, Gladstone announced a solution for the Balkans. If this solution was to be realized, the nationalisms of the Balkans had to be restrained while Austria-Hungary and Russia were not to be allowed to intervene in Balkan affairs. In order to protect British interests, the Liberals aimed to introduce 'tranquillity in the Balkans'.[95]

In connection with this, many Liberal politicians regarded the Balkan states (Serbia, Montenegro, Greece and Bulgaria) as 'reasonable instruments for safeguarding Britain's principal interests in the eastern Mediterranean'.[96] In return, the Liberals would supply the governments of these countries with advice, loans and arms, but would not offer any help in the form of military intervention.[97] Above all, Albania was not included in their plans because it was regarded as part of the Ottoman Empire.

The impact in decision-making process

Various reports sent during this period by the ambassadors Layard, Goschen and Lord Fitzmaurice from Constantinople did have some impact in London. They understood the peculiar situation of the Albanians and asked their superiors in London to find a proper solution for the Albanian Question. On some occasions they exercised considerable influence. It is likely that it was Fitzmaurice and Goschen who convinced Gladstone that part of Epirus, with Janina as a centre, was not given to Greece. To a certain degree, this was the position held by Disraeli who already understood the situation but, even taking into account this prior knowledge, Layard's reports helped him in particular situations when dealing with the Powers. By 1881 Goschen's and Fitzmaurice's initiative, which called for creating an autonomous or independent Albanian state, faded away. The reason for abandoning such an initiative was not known for a long time. Decades later Edith Durham revealed the reason. Durham befriended Lord Fitzmaurice who continued his personal interest in Albania. In a lecture that Durham gave in February 1941 at the Royal Institution of Great Britain, she told the audience that the Albanians were treated with prejudice because of their religion.[98]

Lord Fitzmaurice was a Liberal but on the subject of Albania he did not share the views of Gladstone and most members of his party. Instead, he made it known that it was religious biases which prevented the Albanian Question, from receiving the sympathy of the British public. He saw that, as a consequence, the British public did not pressurize the government to adopt policies in favour of the Albanians.

The situation was different with the British diplomatic and consular representatives on the ground, in Albanian territory. Kirby Green in Shkodra and St. John in Prizren, having a lower status, had less impact in London. They both showed no sympathy for Albanians and their cause. In their reports they often created confusion by calling the Albanians Arnauts, Muslims or even Turks.

Kirby Green was under the influence of the Austro-Hungarian consul, Lipich, who was of Slav origin and favoured the Montenegrins and Serbs. Albanians were aware of this fact and held him in no high regard. It was obvious that Green did not like the Albanians and their warlike attitude. His duty was to convince the Albanians to give up their ideas of autonomy or independence, discourage them from fighting the Porte and the Montenegrins and obey decisions and orders from the Great Powers. When the Albanian League was formed, he considered it an exclusively Muslim and fanatical organization and did not change his mind even after Albanian Catholics joined it in large numbers. When a British journalist asked him about the political centre and the chief characteristics of the League, he said that the Albanian League is an 'organization of the most fanatical Mussulmen of the country'.[99]

Kirby Green maintained that the League was an Ottoman creation and had difficulties to change his mind even when the Albanians opposed the Porte militarily. The British diplomats in Constantinople were not always happy with the work of Green in Albania and Montenegro. Green convinced London to accept his plan for the annexation of Ulqin (Dulcigno Arrangement) and was supported by his Austro-Hungarian colleague, Lipich. Yet, Green did not see the Albanians organized as a nation and never agreed that their actions were the result of nationalism.[100]

Goschen was strongly determined to discredit some of Green's reports and the eventual influence he may have had on this matter in the Foreign Office and the wider British Government. Therefore, Goschen swiftly advised the Foreign Secretary to dismiss Green's reports. Goschen also wrote several reports to explain the nature of the Albanian nationalism which manifested similar demands on same manner as those of other Balkan nations.[101]

At the end of July 1880, Fitzmaurice complained to London about St. John, who was sending contradictory reports from Prizren, completely disregarding the Albanians in Kosovo. In his reports St. John suggested that Kosovo was a Serb region and inhabited predominantly by Serbs. He called Kosovo 'Stara Srbia' (Old Serbia), a term used for Kosovo which found place among Serbian nationalists of the nineteenth century.[102] Contents of his reports were contrary to all other reports available to British diplomats and those published in the European press. In reality his reports were not much different from those of Yastrebov, the Russian Consul in Prizren, under whose influence St. John had fallen.

3

Impact of the British Liberalism on Albanian Question

Prelude to the Macedonian Crisis

In the summer of 1883, the mountaineers in northern Albania organized an insurrection against the Porte. They approached the British consul in Shkodra and asked if 'there was any hope of support from the British Government'. The reply from London said:

> There is only one British interest in North Albania, and that is that the perfect harmony should exist between the Sultan and his subjects – a state of things which could not be if the mountaineers fancied they could put pressure on the Turkish Government through foreign aid.[1]

Two years later, there was another event which attracted British attention. This time, the Albanian Question in Macedonia came to the British government's attention in a strange way. At the beginning of 1885 a certain G. W. Leybourne, who presented himself as president of the Albanian Committee, started sending letters to European leaders in order to inform them that Albanians were preparing to liberate Macedonia. In a proclamation issued on 5 June 1885, Leybourne called on Bulgarian and Macedonian personalities and organizations to join the 'Children of Skanderbeg', as he called the Albanians, to rise together against the 'Turkish Infidel' and create the Republic of Macedonia.[2] Austro-Hungarian diplomats called this organization, which was based at Corfu, the English-Albanian Committee and worried that future actions of the Committee may disturb the region and endanger their interests in the Balkans.[3]

The Porte and the British government were particularly worried, as it was believed the troubles that would take place in Macedonia would be organized by the Albanians and led by a British subject. The Ottoman ambassador in London, Musurush Pasha, contacted British Foreign Secretary, Lord Salisbury, to find out who Leybourne was and who was sending letters and issuing proclamations from London.[4] After a long investigation, on 6 October 1885, Lord Salisbury advised Musurush Pasha not to worry about Leybourne and his activities because the supposed committee had ceased to exist. However, both British and Austro-Hungarian diplomats noticed that

Leybourne had worked closely with two Albanians, Prenk Gjoka and Emin Bey, both on the pay roll of the Greek government. They tried to organize an insurrection and claimed to have British support. Gjoka had even met the British consul in Shkodra, whom he told that 'the revolution in favour of the English, and also the Greeks, is ready'.[5] At the beginning of 1883 the pair escaped to Greece as they were wanted by the Porte as ordinary criminals. Together with Leybourne they tried to revive the Albanian League but their efforts ended without success and they fled the ottoman territory. In the end, Salisbury told the Porte that in the future such a person and others like him would be 'prevented from misleading the Albanians'.[6]

Although Leybourn was merely an adventurer, he managed to alarm the Porte and the British government. This case showed that the Albanians and Macedonia would soon become a problem for which the British government did not have a plan and did not want its citizens to be involved in. The Leybourne case, although a false alarm, was a strange prelude to the Macedonian crisis.

However, it was the Bulgarians who initiated the complicated problem of Macedonia. Towards the end of the nineteenth century, the idea of creating an independent Bulgarian state, and particularly a Bulgarian Church (Exarchate), independent from the Greek Patriarchate, became a reality and brought the Macedonian Question into the view of the European Powers.[7] The internal ethnic problems of Macedonia became an acute question that the Powers had to address.

The British government continued to support the territorial integrity of the Ottoman Empire in Europe and viewed the Balkans as a region outside its vital area of interest. Within such a context, there was no need to create a separate policy for the Albanian Question. On the topic of the Balkans, the British government believed that 'behind the Macedonian Question lies the Turkish question'.[8] This meant that the Ottoman Empire depended very much on the stability of Macedonia. The only worry of the British continued to be Russia which was to be stopped from reaching the Balkans or the Bosporus, a move that would destabilize the Ottoman Empire.

However, at the beginning of the twentieth century British foreign policy towards the region started to change slowly. This departure from pro-Ottoman policy took place for many reasons the most important of which was growing pressure from the British public which became more knowledgeable about the region and demanded more protection for the Christians.[9] This pressure was channelled through the activities of the Balkan Committee and the press. British financiers also played their role by reminding the government about the Porte's inability to repay its loans. One more reason, probably the most worrying, was German influence over the economy and politics of the Porte. Collectively these led the British government to be more cautious about the creation of more autonomous or independent states and to seek a closer relationship with Russia. Yet the British believed that Russia should not be given a 'free hand to pursue her interests unimpeded' in the Balkans and Constantinople.[10]

Although the creation of new autonomous or independent states was not favoured by the British government, some Albanian leaders had approached Gladstone to ask for support. When Gladstone formed his new government in 1886 he appointed the Earl of Rosebery as Foreign Secretary, who declared that there would be a policy of continuity in foreign affairs. To many observers in Britain, and probably to some

Albanians, this announcement may have been understood to mean that the Liberal government would continue to apply some aspects of the Conservative approach in foreign policy. As a matter of fact, what Rosebury meant was that the continuity, as a guiding principle, was to be Liberal as established by Gladstone.[11] An Albanian intellectual, Faik Konitza (1876-1942), who published the newspaper *Albania* in Brussels and London between 1899 and 1909, hoped to get support from the British government. He considered the Greeks the main obstacle to forming an Albanian state.[12] He also felt that the British Liberal government was treating the Greeks more favourably than the Albanians. In 1897, on behalf of the League for Albanian Independence, Konitza wrote to 'the Great Old Man', as he called Gladstone, with the intention of explaining the Albanian position and, possibly, 'correcting' British policy. Gladstone sent a short reply:

> I do not make any distinction between Albanians, Greeks and other people with regard to their national rights to liberty, justice and humanity. It seems to me inappropriate for you to begin your plea for the Albanians by laying severe charges against the Greeks, who are at this moment engaged in an honourable task. In the present state of my knowledge of the question I regret being unable to say more.[13]

Gladstone's negative reply confirmed his Liberal policy, which was not in favour of the Albanian national cause. As a result, Konitza wrote to Ibrahim Temo (1865-1945) to inform him that the British government has 'refused to take Albania under protection'.[14] Temo, one of the founders of the Young Turks, and Konitza were supporters of Austro-Hungarian policy and took Gladstone's reply as a sign that the Albanian leaders should seek closer links with Vienna. However, the early twentieth century would bring changes in British public opinion which would result in a reorientation of British foreign policy.

The Balkan Committee's liberal approach

With the start of the twentieth century the public in Britain showed more interest in closer engagement with the Balkans. The rise and expansion of mass media, along with the development of communications and transport, increased interest in international affairs and brought Britain into closer contact with the world. With the spread of information, which reached a wider spectrum of the British public and increased their awareness, knowledge of the Balkans 'ceased being a matter of the few'.[15]

Despite this increase in available information, media coverage of the Balkans was irregular and covered only those themes which were deemed extraordinary. The events that caught the public's imagination and the attention of the press were usually violent ones. Two such situations, the murder of the royal family in Belgrade and the Ilinden Uprising in Macedonia, occurred in the early summer of 1903 and triggered two different responses in Britain. The brutal murder of King Alexander and Queen Draga in Serbia was presented with great interest. The story had all the elements needed to attract a wide readership and this shocking, violent act fortified

British preconceptions of the 'bloody-mindedness' of Serbs and violence in the Balkans.[16]

The press also showed similar attention to a second event, the Ilinden Uprising of 2 August 1903, which brought to the surface the multiple national questions of Macedonia, including the Albanian Question. The uprising took place while Ottoman troops were engaged in suppressing an Albanian uprising in the *vilayet* of Kosovo. The Ilinden Uprising was supported by local Albanians who supplied Macedonian bands with arms and ammunition. The insurgents occupied the town of Kruševo and formed a Provisional Assembly which had sixty delegates: twenty Macedonian, twenty Albanian and twenty Vlahs. Two Albanians, Gjorgji Çaçi and Nikolla Balo, were appointed among the six members of the Provisional Government. The Albanian press abroad and nationalist leaders called upon the Albanian population to further support the uprising in Macedonia.[17] At the same time, the press in Britain and Europe spread news that insurgents and the mob had used this situation to attack non-Christians and destroy their properties in Kruševo and the region of Manastir.[18]

In British public life, pressure to involve the government in the Balkans had started during the nineteenth century and intensified with the beginning of the twentieth century. This was due to the initiative of the Liberals, who continued to believe that problems in the Balkans would disappear only when the Ottoman Empire ceased to exist in this part of Europe. The Liberals supported, and in many cases initiated, propaganda against Ottoman misrule in Macedonia because they were convinced that peace in the Balkans would be possible only after a settlement was accepted by all Balkan people.[19] They continued to see the Balkans as a question of civilization. Ottoman rule, and in some cases also Austro-Hungarian rule, was considered by Liberals to be preventing the progress of the Balkan peoples. Yet the solution offered by the Liberals did not necessarily mean that the Balkan people should be granted the right of self-determination, but rather considered various forms of autonomy. British Liberal politicians were already familiar with this matter as they were engaged in the ongoing debates about 'Home Rule' as a solution to the Irish question. The Liberals were willing to forgo autonomy for the Balkan people but only if the Porte was to undertake satisfactory reforms.[20]

With this approach, the Liberals maintained that the British had reached a higher stage of civilization as a result of the development of democratic institutions and the economy which, in return, guaranteed them liberty and prosperity. Thus, they believed that they had the right and obligation to rule over 'less civilized' populations in the British Empire and at home. If British rule could not reach the 'less civilized' people outside their empire, then help would be offered to them. The historian R. W. Seton-Watson has described this help as conveying 'the image of the traditional moralising Briton who wished to radiate civilisation among those less fortunate'.[21]

In this context the Liberals felt obliged to get involved in changing the situation in the Balkans. To explain this commitment, the author George Bernard Shaw remarked that a Liberal is a man who has three duties: a duty to Ireland, Finland and Macedonia.[22] The Liberals believed that these three nations, each incorporated into three different multi-national empires, should be granted autonomy but only as constituent nations within each empire.[23]

A number of well-known British personalities, who were predominantly Liberal, were convinced that the press and the government were showing indifference towards the Balkans in general and the fate of Macedonia in particular. The problems of Macedonia made them come together in early July 1903 and form the Balkan Committee. Among the founding members were high-profile scholars, politicians, clerics and journalists, such as Noel Buxton, Robert William Seaton-Watson, Arthur Evans, William Miller, Arnold Toynbee, Harold Nicholson, Aubrey Herbert, Edith Durham, Henry Brailsford and many others.[24] By 1906 the list included sixty-four MPs, fifty-five of whom were Liberals, six from the Labour Party and three from Conservative ranks. The membership also included the Archbishop of Canterbury and several bishops. The Committee also attracted radical critics of British foreign policy such as journalist Henry Nevinson.[25] The member's list grew long with both highly educated personalities and members of the ordinary public and also included Lord Herbert Gladstone, the youngest son of William Gladstone.

The activities of the Committee were directed towards awakening public interest in the Balkan people and reminding the British government of the responsibilities it had assumed in the Treaty of Berlin, which included protection of the Christian population under the rule of the Porte. The publication titled 'Macedonia 1903' became the Committee's manifesto. according to which, the British government had not only the right, but the duty, to take any steps in her power to 'put an end to the appalling state of things'. The Committee acknowledged that Britain had no direct interest in the region like Austria-Hungary and Russia and therefore it was suggested that the British government should restrain itself from taking independent actions. Consequently, the Committee argued that Britain 'should endeavour to induce the other Powers to agree to a scheme', which would help the Balkan people and should ask the Powers to unite in demanding the withdrawal of Ottoman troops from Macedonia. The appointment of a European Governor, with complete control of the civil and military administration and the establishment of a gendarmerie commanded by European officers, were other necessary measures to follow.[26]

The Committee also published the 'Autonomy Proposal', a twelve-article document which was sent to the Sultan and relevant European governments to demand autonomy for Albania, Macedonia, Kosovo and Adrianople and outline details of a settlement for the region. It should be noted that considerable attention was shown to the Albanian Question in articles I and II.[27] It is hard to understand the reason or the criteria that led to this division of autonomous provinces. The 'Autonomy Proposal' was ambiguous and satisfied neither the Albanian nor the other nationalist movements in the Balkans. This ambiguity stemmed from the fact that the division of the suggested autonomous provinces was not based on ethnic nor religious principles. Albania would consist of only two *vilayets* (Shkodra and Janina) and not four *vilayets* as foreseen by the Albanian national programme. Kosovo, as proposed, was to become a separate autonomous province while the *vilayet* of Manastir would become part of Macedonia. The fact that Kosovo was to become a separate autonomous unit and called 'Old Serbia' must have caused worries among Albanian leaders and the Serbian government, as both claimed the place for themselves. Nevertheless, from the Albanian perspective the proposal contained some positive elements namely that this was the first proposal for the autonomy of Albania to be presented to the Porte and the European Powers by a British organization, a fact which was to become important later.

Led by chairman Noel Buxton, who became a Liberal MP in 1905, the Balkan Committee started furnishing the press and government with articles and letters containing information about the difficulties in Macedonia and suggestions on how to deal with these problems. Between 29 September and 16 November 1903, the Balkan Committee organized around 150 public meetings all over Britain. In every occasion Noel Buxton and other leading members informed the public and state officials that the Committee's plan for Macedonia was to remove the Sultan's direct rule and establish a government which would be responsible to the Powers.[28] As soon as the Committee was formed Edith Durham, Lady Thompson, Henry Brailsford and the brothers Noel and Charles Buxton went to Macedonia in an aid and fact-finding mission. As the delegation discovered, the Macedonian uprising was not simply directed against Ottoman rule and local Muslims but was also a dangerous conflict between the idea of Greater Bulgaria and the Greek 'Megali Idea'. Macedonia had also become a place for religious clashes between the Greek and Bulgarian Orthodox churches, a conflict also known as patriarchists *vs* exarchists.[29]

After the visit to Macedonia, Brailsford, Durham and Noel Buxton published their works and became known as travel and expert writers. This group, often called New Europe,[30] was joined by Aubrey Herbert and James David Burchier of *The Times*, the longest-serving British correspondent in the Balkans. However, none of these writers had any particular knowledge on Albania. Some members of the Committee or expert writers, including Brailsford, were among the last British philhellenes to be disappointed with Greece. In 1897 Brailsford had joined a regiment of British volunteers, inspired by Byron, to fight in the Greco-Turkish war but he left feeling no sympathy for the Greek cause. He soon found another cause to support, north of Greece, in Macedonia.[31] His knowledge about the region and its people was shown in his book, which became a reference on Macedonia.[32] Other publications continued with Noel Buxton's *Europe and the Turks* and with Edith Durham who covered Macedonia and the wider area of the Balkans.

With these books and other numerous academic publications and articles the Balkan Committee marked a new and important period in forming the image of the Balkans in Britain. The Balkans was presented as a region that should matter to the British public and government. The Committee brought together experts and members of the public interested in this region where previously diplomats had been the main source of information and debates were mainly initiated by politicians. For obvious reasons, the Foreign Office was not keen on the appearance of self-appointed expert writers and the Committee and officials, diplomats and politicians publicly questioned their abilities and credentials while privately ridiculing them.[33] Yet officials were also worried that these expert writers possessed the knowledge and the ability to exercise influence over the British public. To explain the power of these experts, historian A. J. P. Taylor later wrote that those interested in Balkan affairs would have done well to refer to Durham on Albania, Brailsford on Macedonia, R. W. Seton-Watson on Hungary or Serbia.

Taylor maintained that one who reads these authors 'would be better informed than if he had stuck to official channels'.[34]

The Committee's initiative for involvement in the Balkans was not a new idea. As noted earlier, the idea emerged during the early nineteenth century and resulted in the formation of the Greek Committee which went on to build a positive picture of Bulgaria and Serbia. The Balkan Committee represented a modernized version of the nineteenth-century tradition of engagement with the Balkans 'which was personified by Lord Byron and William Gladstone' who were in favour of the Balkan nationalist movement.[35] Noel Buxton emphasized Gladstone's role and the duty of Europe to support the Balkan Christians:

> As Mr. Gladstone said, the Christian who retained his faith at the price of slavery, when by recanting he could obtain every favour, is entitled to the name of martyr, and to him also Europe owes the gratitude that is due to the rampart which saved it.[36]

In the Balkan Committee Noel Buxton represented the principle thoughts of the Liberals and saw the relationship between East and West as a 'conflict of two fundamental principles of life'. He continued to explain this relationship as 'the Mahomedan principle, namely, of a belief in conquering power, and the Christian principle which looks to the forces of the spirit and the mind'. Therefore, he suggested that this 'reality' is a 'matter of foreign affaires' and called for the British government to act in favour of the Christians.[37]

But, the Committee, with the presence of Aubrey Herbert and a few others, also represented the political views of the Conservatives under Disraeli, who had shown sympathy for the Ottomans and for the Albanian nationalist movement. Herbert, who became a Member of Parliament in 1911, became an advocate of Albanian independence. As such, Herbert was a unique example of a Conservative politician who made efforts to bring the British political scene in favour of closer engagement with the Balkans.

Although the Balkans were not a direct British interest, the British government saw the future of the Balkans as a possible strategic objective. Brailsford maintained that 'the Slav peasant has no passwords to the foreigner's heart'.[38] In other words, the Slavs could not attract the attention of the British as the classical heritage of the Greeks had done. However, the Balkans became a place that managed to attract attention in Britain and elsewhere in Western Europe.

Edith Durham was convinced that the Balkans were not a serious concern for British politicians nor for the press. She compared the liberal, radical and conservative press coverage and concluded that the Balkans were simply being used to influence politics at home and most of their concern was about the future of the British Empire. On this matter, Durham wrote that not one of the British newspapers 'cares twopenny jam about the good of the Balkan peoples'. She added that the press used the Balkan situation merely 'as a lever for tipping home governments in or out, and thereby building or blowing up the British Empire'.[39]

However, Durham was the first expert to identify the Albanian Question as the main problem in the Balkans and to show that this question was neglected by the Balkan Committee and the British government. She believed that ignoring the Albanian Question was a big mistake and felt the fact that the Albanian Question 'was always left out of consideration was a constant source of difficulty'.[40]

The Powers' failure in Macedonia and triumph of Gladstonian Liberalism

The Balkan Committee played its role in influencing the British government to organize an international intervention in Macedonia and in the pro-Macedonian agitation which spread quickly in Europe. This pressure resulted in speeding up the reforms foreseen by the Mürzsteg Agreement, signed on 2 October 1903 by Austria-Hungary and Russia. The agreement aimed to oversee the implementation of reforms designed to restore law and order in Macedonia, which was to be done through a reorganization of the gendarmerie. These reforms were similar to several of the points adopted by the Balkan Committee, but it was clear that they did not focus on establishing the autonomy of Macedonia understood as the *vilayets* of Salonika, Manastir and a part of Kosovo.[41] The reforms therefore emphasized the maintenance of Ottoman territorial integrity, despite their interference in Ottoman affairs.

In January 1904, the Italian government selected General de Giorgis to supervise the reorganization of the Macedonian gendarmerie as part of the implementation of the reform programme. Colonel Fairholme was appointed as British Staff Officer and was assigned to the region of Drama. Among the Powers there were discussions of including some of the Albanian districts such as Korça in the reforms, but these were excluded from the operation of the scheme.[42] In reality, many other such districts were included but the Powers chose to ignore the presence of those Albanians who inhabited a considerable part of the *vilayets* of Manastir and Kosovo. Such was the region of Skopje, which was given to the Austro-Hungarians and Manastir to the Italians. In the districts of Ohri (Ohrida), Resna, Prespa, Kruševo, Demir Hisar and Kërçova (Kičevo), Albanian revolutionary bands made an appearance in reaction to Macedonian, Bulgarian, Greek and Serbian bands. Reports from the British consul showed that the Muslim populations (mainly Albanian) of Skopje, Ishtip and Kumanovo were alarmed about more than seventy murders committed against them within a short time and considered organizing themselves like the other Macedonian revolutionary bands. The few European police officers who were there to reform the gendarmerie found themselves powerless. Colonel Fairholme reported that the Greeks, Bulgarians and Serbs were 'allowed to cut each other's throats with impunity and the Albanians were showing signs of moving'.[43]

In years to come, the Bulgarian exarchist campaign against the Greek patriarchists continued. Bulgarian, Serbian and Greek bands who entered Macedonia exercised terrorism against Muslims and, more often against each other.[44] From 1903 to 1908 in Macedonia, which was thought to consist of 1.5 million inhabitants, over 10,000 people were murdered. In most violent ways, the bands were competing to establish superiority and win European sympathy and support. The call of the Balkan Committee for international intervention was ignored. The British, as well as other Powers, refused any military engagement on the ground. When massacres took place and properties were destroyed, European officers could only observe, take photographs and prepare reports.[45]

In January 1905, the British Foreign Secretary Lansdowne wrote that Macedonia had become the most difficult and embarrassing problem for Britain and the Powers. As a result of the Balkan Committee's influence 'Lansdowne lived in terror' and made 'efforts to stiffen the reform proposals of the Mürzteg Powers and to secure more influence for British officials on the reform commissions'.[46]

Lansdowne acknowledged that gendarmes alone were not an answer to this problem and pointed out the need to adopt an Organic Statute in Macedonia like the one adopted in Crete as foreseen by Article XXIII of the Treaty of Berlin. This was also one of the demands made by the Balkan Committee. In a memorandum Lansdowne proposed new measures to be taken on the Macedonian problem[47] which came close to the Balkan Committee's request, but it never materialized. In December 1905 Lansdowne was replaced by Edward Grey, who resisted the Balkan Committee's pressure. The new Foreign Secretary believed that the Balkan Committee and other organizations that pressured for British involvement in the Balkans did not have the support of the public.

Albanian leaders had not been happy with the reform programme from the start. They were characterized as Christians, as the majority of them were in southern Macedonia, but they wanted to be known only as Albanians. After the Ilinden Uprising was supressed by the Porte, Albanian nationalist leaders abroad gathered in their colony in Bucharest and sent a memorandum to the Powers. They demanded recognition as a nationality, the opening of Albanian schools, the establishment of an Albanian Orthodox Church and the appointment of a representative in the Commission of Reforms in Manastir.[48] Their demands were ignored.

The Porte also complained about the reforms and about European officers serving in the gendarmerie. The Ottoman government addressed a complaint to the Powers about Italian intrigues in the Albanian part of Macedonia. Morica, one of the Italian gendarmerie officers, who was an Albanian from southern Italy, was creating a network with Albanian nationalist leaders and the population of the region of Ohri, where he was stationed. Morica's aim was to organize Albanians for reopening schools in their language and prepare them to work towards independence under Italian influence. The Porte was worried because Morica had become very popular among Albanians.[49]

The Porte was also aware that Italy and Austria-Hungary had reached an understanding in 1897 on a common policy towards Albania and that both governments subsidized Albanian nationalist leaders. Since 1895 around 200,000 Albanians in southern Italy, under the leadership of Jeronim de Rada, had pressurized their government in Rome to take actions to protect Albania. This movement worried the Austro-Hungarian government, who believed that the activities of Italo-Albanians would result in an Italian protectorate in Albania. Both governments in Vienna and Rome were convinced that the other was working for supremacy in Adriatic.[50] Other rivalries and misunderstandings between Russia and Austria-Hungary culminated in the Sultan's approval to construct a railway from Novi Pazar to Mitrovica. Russia and other Powers feared that Austria-Hungary was preparing for access to Salonika and to occupy Macedonia. This situation strained relations between Austria-Hungary and Russia and, as a result, the Mürzsteg Agreement was abandoned in February 1908.

Similar rivalries also existed among the Balkan Committee members, with each seeking to support their preferred Balkan country. Thus, the Balkan Committee was not as homogenous as it had intended to be and efforts to keep up the appearance of unity were short lived. As noted above, the committee was dominated by Liberal politicians and religious leaders who continued the Gladstonian tradition of supporting Bulgaria, Greece or Serbia, being anti-Ottoman and disregarding the Muslim population. Whenever tensions were raised or conflicts took place in the region, the committee members were ready to fight a 'proxy Balkan war' in the British press and lecture halls.[51]

Nevertheless, these expert writers managed to occupy the public sphere and to decide which events should attract public attention. They established a trend which regarded the Ottoman Empire as a regime of tyranny, unmanageable and unable to reform and the vast majority of them held pro-Christian and anti-Ottoman (Muslim) views.[52] Their work was built on these two pillars, which also formed the basis on which they initiated and led discussions on the Balkan problem. Edith Durham, although being anti-Ottoman, challenged this discourse:

> When a Moslem kills a Moslem it does not count; when a Christian kills a Moslem it is a righteous act; when a Christian kills a Christian it is an error of judgment better not talked about; it is only when a Moslem kills a Christian that we arrive at a full-blown 'atrocity'.[53]

In general, the Balkan Committee succeeded in presenting Balkan affairs in the British public sphere but failed in fulfilling its main aim: to create autonomous provinces by applying reforms and bringing positive changes to protect the people of Macedonia. The committee never attempted to overcome the prejudices against Islam which were created by Gladstone's Liberal policy and this could be considered the main reason for its failure. Most of the members failed to recognize problems that the population in Macedonia faced. Instead they saw the situation only through the prism of religion – Christians suffering under the rule of the Ottomans and, by extension, Muslims. A significant number of the Muslim (the majority of whom were Albanian), Vlah and Jewish populations, were simply ignored. The situation was also complicated by the administrative division that the Porte had imposed in Macedonia. As a matter of fact, the Porte did not use nor recognized the term Macedonia but used the name Rumelia which consisted of the *vilayets* of Salonika, Manastir and Kosovo. Albanians numerically dominated the western part of the *vilayet* of Manastir and most of the *vilayet* of Kosovo, while their presence in *vilayet* of Salonika was low. The Porte continued with this division, which was made in such a way that the Muslim element was majority in all *vilayets* but it partitioned the Albanians in order to create obstacles to the 'formation of homogenous and united Albania'.[54]

Herbert and Durham believed that the Committee was largely overlooking the Albanian national question. The number of members of the Committee who opposed the idea of an independent Albania was significant and initially led by Robert William Seton-Watson. However, there were some members, such as Brailsford and Nevinson, who were not entirely supporters of Albanian nationalism but still maintained that the Albanians deserved their state. Brailsford believed that Albanians, particularly those of the south, were a 'relatively civilized population' and as such 'would bring progress and prosperity' to the Balkans if they were to establish their independent state. Brailsford maintained that the size and borders of Albania were 'essentially a question of civilisation rather than ethnography'.[55]

Brailsford, for a peculiar reason, played down the role and effect of Islam on Albanians whom he described as 'nearly all heretics'.[56] Like many other Committee members, he regarded Islam as an Asiatic religion and as such an 'alien culture' unbefitting of the European Albanians, who themselves had no similarities with the Muslim Turks. On this issue, he added:

> And yet they [Albanians] remain a race apart from the Turks and profoundly hostile to them. There is no community of blood between them and even in their mosques the barrier between East and West divides them. For the Albanian is essentially a European – a European of the Middle Ages. Alone of all races in Turkey, he [Albanian] has a hereditary aristocracy and a feudal system, Islam, among Eastern peoples, is everywhere a leveller.[57]

Brailsford, like all other Liberals, did not see Islam and Christianity as holding the same level of importance and considered religion, and not ethnicity, as a prime factor for Balkan nations. However, he believed the Albanians to have 'the makings of a united people' and therefore suggested that autonomy was the best solution for them. Autonomy would also solve the religious problem because 'under a Christian Prince vast number of Albanians would return to Christianity'.[58] Despite the emphasized religious differences and the fact that he was pro-Bulgarian, Brailsford suggested that the British government should use its influence to support autonomy for Albania. This would increase British predominance in the balance of power in the Balkan region, and Albanians would serve as a 'vanguard against the dangerous invasion of Pan Slavism in the East'.[59] However, the British government disregarded this advice and never endorsed such a policy.

Yet religion was not the only reason that the Balkan Committee did not take the Albanian Question seriously. The lack of general knowledge and understanding of Albania among members of the Committee remained an important factor, even in the twentieth century. After the First World War had started in 1914, James Bryce, who was regarded as one of the best experts of the Committee, told Noel Buxton:

> I have said nothing about Albania because I do not understand it, nor what precisely are the respective claims of Italy and Greece, but Albania ought to be left independent of any Slav control.[60]

The invasion of Macedonia by Balkan armies during the Balkan Wars and First World War ended the hope of the Balkan Committee to secure a safe and autonomous

Macedonia. In August 1913, the Balkan Committee asked the Foreign Office to respect the wishes of the local population in determining the government under which they wanted to be included in a Macedonia occupied by Serbian, Bulgarian and Greek armies. According to the Committee, the 'boundaries should not be drawn at will to suit the plans of cabinets in Athens, Belgrade and Sophia'.[61] Yet again the Committee ignored the presence and the will of the Albanian population in occupied Macedonia. When the Powers forced Bulgaria to withdraw from an area it had occupied in the western part of Macedonia, and when the Ottoman army reasserted its authority over the territory, the Committee believed that Albania would benefit from this move and asked Edward Grey to propose to the Powers a collective demand for the immediate withdrawal of the Ottomans.[62]

The failure of the Balkan Committee to secure autonomy and safety for the Macedonian people meant, in many ways, the triumph of Gladstone's approach. The Ottomans were forced out of the Balkans and the Christian nations won their liberty, but this was rather a different finale to what the Balkan Committee had planned, worked and hoped for in the beginning. Bulgaria and Greece were considerably enlarged, but it was Serbia who got the biggest part of Macedonia. Furthermore, Serbia's gains were unreservedly supported by the British government and many of the pro-Serb members of the Committee led by R. W. Seton-Watson. From 1903 to 1906, the British government had severed all relations with Serbia, whose image during that period was portrayed particularly badly through negative stereotyping in the press and literature publications. Serbia's case could serve as a good example of how the image-building process developed and the role played by travel and expert writers in this process.

The Austro-Hungarian annexation of Bosnia and the Bulgarian Declaration of Independence that took place immediately after the Young Turk Revolution of 1908, and particularly the start of First World War brought Britain and Serbia closer to each other. The British government viewed the Austro-Hungarian annexation of Bosnia and Herzegovina with fear. In London, it looked as the Austro-Hungarian Empire was about to extend further into the Balkans, through Macedonia, to reach the Aegean Sea. The Balkan Wars and First World War forced the British government to seek allies in the Balkans. Serbia, becoming anti-Austro-Hungarian in 1903 and now being at war with this empire, was in the best position among other Balkan nations to become the ally of Britain.[63] Now, the outlook towards Serbia and pejorative attitudes towards the Serbs shifted again, but this time in a positive sense. In Serbia's 'primitive peasant culture' now virtues were being discovered and Serbia became a place of 'poets' and 'heroes'. Pro-Serbian Gladstonians and others who had 'long recognised the aspiration to include all Serbs in a Greater Serbia' were back in fashion.[64]

During the Balkan Wars, the romanticization of Serb history was taken on board by many British writers, including Arnold Toynbee and L. F. Waring. Even Brailsford changed his mind and considered Kosovo as the 'heart of Serbia'.[65] Although traditional narratives tell of how Britain entered the First World War to defend Belgium, in the reality of this pro-Serbian climate the war started by defending Serbia against the Austro-Hungarian Empire. The British government practically became Serbia's agent in publicity and protector in the war.[66]

A mural which was displayed in a very prominent place at the top of the Foreign Office stair case explained this situation. Britannia Pacificatrix (Britannia the Peacemaker), painted by Sigmund Goetze, artistically and figuratively explained the position the British government held during the Balkan Wars and particularly the First World War. Under her arms, Britannia protects Belgium and Serbia while little Montenegro is cuddled by Serbia.[67] Goetze was inspired by a speech which was delivered on 4 May 1912 by the Archbishop of Canterbury at the Royal Academy. In November that year, a month after the Balkan War had started, Goetze approached the Foreign Office with a scheme, which illustrated the British foreign policy of that time, which was approved by the Foreign Secretary Edward Grey and the Prime Minister Herbert Asquith.[68]

This was not good news for Serbia's neighbours, especially for Albania whose independence had by then been acknowledged but its borders were not yet fixed. The 'cuddled' Kingdom of Montenegro 'disappeared' after the war, together with Macedonia and Kosovo when it was integrated into the new country of the Kingdom of the Serbs, Croats and Slovenes created in 1919. Macedonia was left with national problems, unsolved to this day. The large and aggressive Serbian extension became unacceptable even for R. W. Seton-Watson. He considered this extension as triumph of the pan Serbian idea and, as such, a triumph of Eastern over Western culture which was a 'fatal blow' to the future of the Balkans.[69] However, the positive image building process of Serbia that he enormously helped to construct, could not be reversed.

4

Albanian Nationalism and Macedonian Question

The British foreign policy and the role of the Albanian national movement in the Young Turk Revolution

The British Ambassador in Constantinople, Gerald Lowther, described the general situation in the Ottoman Empire for the year 1907 and informed Edward Grey about the rise of Albanian nationalism and its peculiar relationship with the secret organization – The Young Turks:

> Alongside, and yet independent of the Young Turkish movement, with which it appeared to be sometimes in collaboration and sometimes in direct opposition, there was noticeable throughout the year another Nationalist movement of which it seems probable that more will be heard in near future. This is the Albanian movement which, though known to exist as far back as the Congress of Berlin, had made little apparent progress up to the end of 1907.[1]

By the beginning of the twentieth century, British foreign policy made a slow departure from its traditional pro-Ottoman policy but could not go as far as taking independent or separate measures, as some members of the British Parliament and the public requested. Further changes were foreseen in the Agreement of Reval between Britain and Russia in June 1908. The meeting of King Edward VII and Tsar Nicholas II in Reval came after Russia and Austria-Hungary fell out over the implementation of the Mürzsteg Agreement. In Reval, the Russian and British governments reached an understanding about the pacification of Macedonia and the imposition of further reforms. They agreed to settle their differences and appoint a governor with the agreement of the European Powers. The Reval Agreement, which was opposed by Austria-Hungary, also heralded an alliance between Russia and Great Britain against the rising power of Germany.[2]

The low interest of the British government in Albania can be illustrated by the fact that, by the end of the nineteenth century, all diplomatic and consular representations were withdrawn from the country. In 1903 William Miller, a historian and member of the Balkan Committee, noted that 'at the present moment, when Albanian Question is before the public, we have no British Consul [...] Thus for the whole of Albania we have one at Scutari [Shkodra]'.[3] Even the representative in Shkodra, Nikollë Gjon Suma, was an Acting Vice Consul and native Albanian.[4] The British Foreign Office did not pay much attention to Macedonia either, although it had the means and opportunities to do so.[5]

Miller, a supporter of Gladstone's Liberal policy, wanted to exert pressure on the British government using the people who knew the region. His aim was to show that Macedonia should belong to Macedonians in the same way it had been shown and accepted that Bulgaria belonged to Bulgarians or Serbia to the Serbs. Miller, like most of the members of the Balkan Committee, was worried that the Macedonians were under pressure to assimilate by the Bulgarians, Greeks, Albanians and Serbs who competed for national superiority in Macedonia.[6] Yet they also admitted that winning the British government over to their way of thinking was a difficult task.

The governments of Bulgaria, Greece and Serbia continued to send their armed bands to Macedonia to work in their favour. The presence of the Serbian bands in Macedonia was even confirmed by Serbian diplomats in Skopje and it was known in Belgrade that a certain Milorad Gocevac had recruited men to join the armed bands sent to Macedonia.[7] All armed bands fought each other and frequently massacred the innocent population. The Ottomans rarely intervened but when they did, they used a heavy hand.

Durham, while in Macedonia, noted an increase in anti-British feelings among Slavic population, which came as a result of Russo-Japanese war of 1904–5. The Christian Slavs were greatly influenced by the Pan-Slav propaganda directed from Russia, and since the British government was not intervening in Macedonia and instead allied with Japan, Britain was seen as being anti-Russian and, therefore, anti-Christian. The Bulgarian Bishop believed that 'England had always been the foe of the Balkan Slavs and had attacked their only friend [Russia]'.[8]

Such situations made Macedonia a complicated matter for the British and the other Powers. Macedonian-speaking Christians regarded themselves as Macedonian but some saw themselves as Bulgarian. Some were members of the Bulgarian Church and some belonged to the Greek Church. The majority of the Albanians in Macedonia were Muslim while the rest, Christian Orthodox Albanians, identified themselves religiously with the Greek Church.

In 1904 Aubrey Herbert, while working at the British embassy in Constantinople and after visiting Macedonia, wrote:

> Even supposing one could cut Macedonia off from Turkey, one does not see what one could very well do with it. There are no reliable statistics, and it is ridiculous to talk of it administering itself with the Greeks, Jews, Bulgarians etc., most of whom are as ready or worse to cut each other's throats as the Turks themselves would be. The question is more political than religious really, though of course religion has been dragged in too.[9]

The situation was further complicated by the neighbouring nations who had territorial pretensions and refused to acknowledge the existence of the Macedonians as a separate ethnicity or Macedonia as a territorial unit. As McCarthy noted, 'if it were not confusing, it would have not been Macedonia'.[10]

As a result of these difficulties, but more due to lack of interest, the British government made the decision not to intervene. Prime Minister Balfour was blamed by the British press and pressure groups, such as Balkan Committee, for having admitted the horrors but for having condemned them in words only. Parts of the British press believed that Balfour's decision not to intervene went against the wish of a great many voters. An article published in *The Spectator* explained the Ottoman reaction against the bands and the population in Macedonia by comparing it with the actions of the British in their dominions in Asia:

> They [Ottomans] have burnt many villages, as we [British] are sometimes compelled to do in [the] Himalayas, there being no other way of teaching a wild people that they must live quietly.[11]

After the Ilinden Uprising no big revolt broke out in Macedonia and so the Powers were not forced to adopt a new policy. Therefore, nothing came out of the autonomy plan for Macedonia, a result which was in fact desired by the neighbours of Macedonia who wanted to carve up the area for themselves. Co-operation between Macedonians and Albanians might have been a solution for Macedonia and was an option that Britain and the Powers should have supported. Both Macedonians and Albanians, who probably together constituted the majority of the population in most areas, had worked closely together from the Ilinden Uprising until 1908 and after. On several occasions they asked Britain and the other Powers to acknowledge this co-operation.[12] Albanian-Macedonian cooperation was enlarged to include the will of the Vlahs and the Jews to create an autonomous Macedonia. This cooperation found support among some intellectuals in Britain who formed the London Macedonia Committee in 1913 which published its views in a newspaper called *Autonomy*.[13] However, there was no recognition of their will by Britain or other Powers because the reform programme was designed to protect the Christians and not to promote inter-religious or inter-ethnic plans in Macedonia.

On the initiative of Austria-Hungary, the reform programme had excluded most of the *vilayet* of Kosovo and most other parts of Albania. This made some of the Albanian leaders see Austria-Hungary as a protector of the Slavs, particularly the Serbs with whom Vienna had established a close relationship. For this reason, the Albanian leadership preferred British dominance over the reform programme and aimed to gain British sympathy or a protectorate over their cause.[14] In this respect Ismail Bey Qemali wrote to Edward Grey in April 1908. He called on the British government to take on the Albanian Question and organize a diplomatic conference in which the territorial integrity of Albania would be confirmed and recognized.[15] However, nothing came out of Albanian efforts to win British support.

In Britain some interest was expressed regarding the railway and economic and political situation of the *vilayet* of Kosovo. Noel Buxton urged the British government, business community and the public to help the development of the Balkan railways. He acknowledged the importance that the Austrian railway had in being extended to the south to reach Greece. Buxton was particularly interested in helping Serbia to build railways and considered the scheme as both strategic and economic.[16] However, the British government did not intend to get involved in any projects in the Balkans. 'Our attitude towards the various railway projects in the Balkans should be neutrality', declared Grey, and added that British government would certainly not support rival projects.[17]

Changes would indeed be made by the British government but not to the benefit of the populations of Albania or Macedonia, and not in the way that Durham and Buxton had called for. When Macedonia was discussed in the British Parliament in 1908, Edward Grey was criticized for doing far less than Lansdowne had done in 1903. Grey insisted that he was pursuing the policy of Lansdowne and had successfully acted on this matter in concert with the Powers. 'The utmost was obtained from it that could be obtained', concluded Grey. He also confirmed that the British government continued to leave the initiative to Austria-Hungary and Russia with regard to reforms in Macedonia.[18] Many members of the House were not happy with the 'Concert' and called for 'separate actions' in the form of intervention to be taken by the British government alone. Grey characterized Macedonia as an 'exceedingly complicated problem' and for this reason he ruled out separate actions.[19]

However, Grey did not tell the House that the British government was preparing an agreement with Russia. In 1907 Britain and Russia concluded the Anglo-Russian Entente to settle their disputes in Afghanistan, Persia and Tibet. As a consequence, this situation dictated another agreement between Britain and Russia which was finalized in June 1908, when King Edward VII and Tsar Nicholas II met in Reval and agreed to intervene in Constantinople with regard to administrative reforms. They aimed to fulfil the promise which was made by the Powers at the Congress of Berlin to the Christians of Macedonia.[20] In reality the agreement was designed to give a new lease to reforms in Macedonia, while the Powers were to guarantee the integrity of the *vilayets* of Manastir, Salonika and Kosovo and the reduction of Ottoman forces in Macedonia. A few days later, the Young Turk Revolution changed the whole situation.[21]

While the European Powers did not succeed in offering a solution for Macedonia and its inhabitants, who often were not sure to which ethnic group they belonged, nationalism, which itself came from Western Europe, developed its course.[22] The aggressive nationalism made the situation more difficult for all parties involved. The Macedonian problem was becoming more and more complicated and increasingly difficult for the Powers to solve. This had an effect particularly on the Albanians and produced two results: it contributed to the radicalization of Albanian nationalism and sped up the Young Turk Revolution.

Creating and implementing a nationalist plan

During the nineteenth century Albanian intellectuals were divided into two groups: intellectuals who lived abroad and those who lived within the territory of the Ottoman Empire. Those intellectuals who lived abroad contributed greatly to the development of the Albanian national ideology. They acted abroad because the Porte prohibited the use of the Albanian language in administration, schools and print, and because they believed that the battle for the Albanian national cause was to be fought and won in the hearts and minds of Western European governments.[23] Most of these ideological writers of the nineteenth and early twentieth centuries called for Albanian independence but because the Porte had banned the circulation of their writings in Albanian territories, their influence at home was extremely limited.

The second group of ideologists, such as the Frashëri brothers, Vaso Pasha (1825-92) and others, who lived within the territories of the Ottoman Empire and mainly in Constantinople, became more influential. Since they lived under very different circumstances from their fellow intellectuals at home, they developed a different approach to the future of Albania which planned the creation of the Albanian state in two stages: through initial autonomy leading to independence. To those Albanians in the territories of the Ottoman Empire this plan seemed more reasonable and therefore the views and plans of this group became widely accepted.

In 1874 in Constantinople Sami Frashëri, known among non-Albanians as Şemseddin Sami, through his play *Besa Yahud Ahde* ('Besa': Fulfilment of the pledge), showed the public that Albanians and Albania were integral parts of the Ottoman polity. Yet as Gawrych has noted, Frashëri had also a hidden agenda. He wanted to inspire ethnic pride among Albanians and encourage the development of Albanian consciousness during the era of Tanzimat and at a time when nationalist sentiments of other peoples in the Balkans were on the rise. His play also showed that Albanians maintained two distinct loyalties: devotion to the empire and an ethnic attachment to Albania.[24]

A similar view was given five years later by Vaso Pasha, who worked closely with Sami Frashëri. Together they formed the *Central Committee for the Defence of the Rights of the Albanian People* in Constantinople in 1877. Vaso Pasha started his diplomatic career as a secretary in the British Consulate in Shkodra and later entered the Ottoman diplomatic service, being sent to the Ottoman Embassy at the Court of St. James in London. From 1882 until his death 1892 he served as Governor of Lebanon, a position he was given because it was dictated by an international treaty that it should be given to a Catholic of Ottoman nationality. In his treaties, published in London in 1879[25], his view on Albania was shown to be very similar to that which Frashëri expressed in his play. Despite giving a historical account portraying Albanians as the most ancient people in the Balkans, he still saw the need for Albania to remain under Ottoman suzerainty and loyal to the empire.[26]

The situation of the Albanians in Macedonia led Sami Frashëri and other Albanian intellectuals to change their minds, as they saw no possibility for the Albanians to maintain loyalty to the empire if this meant losing Albanian territories. Frashëri believed that it was necessary to develop the idea of an Albanian national identity. Thus in 1899 he developed the concept of *Albanianism*, a term since used to describe Albanian nationalism in Albanian and Turkish historiography, as well as by some Western scholars. In March 1899, Frashëri secretly completed a book written in Albanian and titled *Shqipëria - Ç'ka qënë, çështë e çdo të bëhetë?* (Albania - What it was, what it is and will become of it?). The book was published in Albanian and in several languages and became a manifesto of Albanian nationalism. It became a revolutionary book because it contributed in changing the way Albanians regarded themselves and the Ottoman Empire.

Frashëri created the myth of national identity by claiming that Albanians, being the descendants of Pelasgians, were the oldest people in Europe and gave as evidence the writings of earlier European historians and travel writers.[27] The aim of Frashëri was to create a myth of origin and priority, by using core elements of nationalist discourse. Therefore, declaring the Albanians as owners of the territories they inhabited by proving their ancient origin. He listed the ancient people of the Balkans (Illyrians, Dardanians, Epirots, Macedonians and Thracians) as being Pelasgians in origin and therefore, Albanian.[28]

Frashëri also dealt with the Albania of his time by emphasizing the importance of ethnic homogeneity and cultural purity. Despite the religious and cultural differences between south and north or *Tosk* and *Geg*, he put forward the need for the unity of all Albanians. He explained that there were no similarities between Albanian Muslims and Turks, nor between Orthodox Albanians and Greeks. In his earlier work *Kamus-i Turki* (Turkish Dictionary) he included a new terminology describing the national character of the Albanians.[29]

If the Albanians did not detach themselves from the collapsing Empire, they would perish with it, warned Frashëri. Even if the empire somehow managed to survive, in a different form and with its territories curbed, it would mean death for Albania as the land would be divided between the Greeks and the Slavs. Frashëri also warned Albanians that Macedonia was soon to become an international problem and that they should make their voice heard in demanding their rights, as other peoples of the region had done. He went on to assure the Albanians that they were capable of governing and defending themselves yet emphasized this did not mean that Albanians should rise against the Porte, only warning that if the empire 'should be snuffed out, it must not take Albania with it to the grave'. He believed that Albanians had to unite and present their case to the Porte and the European Powers and that the Sultan, willingly or un-winningly, would listen to and approve the demands. Meanwhile Europe would help, as it had helped other nations, to compel the Porte.[30]

Frashëri, being aware of events in Macedonia and elsewhere, predicted the fall of the Ottoman Empire and worked to develop the national identity of other ethnic groups, including the Turks. With the Macedonian problem coming to a head, Frashëri's belief in the empire rapidly faded away in 1902, when the Sultan ordered the closure of the few Albanian schools while schools of other ethnicities in Macedonia were flourishing. When he died in 1904 many Albanians viewed him as the father of the Albanian nationalism while the supporters of Turkism regarded him as a Turkish nationalist.[31]

Nationalist, local and conservative leaders

During Frashëri's life and after his death, Albanian leaders were roughly divided into three groups that followed three different paths. The first group were the nationalists who adopted Frashëri's ideas and Macedonia became their main worry. The second group of local leaders consisted of those who pursued regional or their own personal interests. Frashëri believed that they harmed the national idea and for this reason he disliked them. The third group, the most powerful one until 1908, were the conservatives who supported the Sultan's regime and were against reforms in Albanian or any change in the empire. Macedonia was also their concern but they viewed it as an Ottoman rather than solely Albanian problem. This division became apparent by end of the nineteenth century when the Porte engaged around 150,000 troops to stabilize Macedonia and Albania. In 1898 the commander of the Ottoman Army in the *vilayet* of Kosovo, Marshall Ethem Pasha, backed by the Ottoman government, presented to the Sultan 'The Project on Albania'.[32] The 'Project' was also supported by Albanian conservative Pashas and some notables who were not concerned with Albanian national aspirations and saw no national future if excluded from the empire. Among them was Esat (Essad) Pasha Toptani (1863–1920) who backed Ethem Pasha's 'Project' unreservedly. Another conservative notable and landowner, Syreja Bey Vlora, sent the Sultan a plan, suggesting even more drastic measures against the Albanians in the south and north. The aim of the project was to alarm the Sultan about difficulties in the Vilayet of Kosovo and Manastir and to propose new measures for pacifying Albania. The complete disarmament of the Albanians and centralizing power in the hands of the Sultan in Constantinople were the two main points. These measures were foreseen to prevent a formation of an autonomous Albania and its exclusion from the empire.[33]

Ismail Bey Qemali (1847–1919) was the best example of a liberal Ottoman politician and diplomat who had made a successful career and grew into an Albanian nationalist leader of that time.[34] Ismail Bey became popular among the Albanians and others in the ruling elite in Constantinople, but until around 1900 he was unknown among the masses in Albania.[35] In 1892 he handed a memorandum to the Sultan expressing his views on reforming the empire. Regarding foreign politics, a field in which he excelled, he proposed to seek a special understanding with the British government to be finalized in a bilateral treaty. The Porte was to acknowledge Britain's special interest in the Mediterranean and assure the route to India. An 'Entente' with Britain, according to Ismail Bey, would stop Russia from advancing towards Constantinople and the Balkans.[36] He believed that the Balkan issue, and Macedonia within it, was a big concern for the Porte. With Russia out of the way, the Porte would be able to stabilize Macedonia by establishing 'an entente between the Balkan states' of Rumania, Greece, Bulgaria, Serbia and Montenegro by creating a defensive alliance and economic accord. Then, ambiguously, he suggested that in the process, a kind of union or a federation between the Balkan countries and the Ottoman Empire could be created. He probably thought that such a union or federation would have absorbed the problem of Macedonia. With a strong Empire, with Britain on its side and Russia out of the way, the Porte could serve as the centre.[37]

With this suggestion Ismail Bey probably aimed to solve the Macedonian and Albanian problems, although Albania was not mentioned at all in his memorandum. However, as he wrote, the Sultan never reflected on these 'projects and suggestions or to give practical solutions to them'. He added that a European power should have induced the Sultan to carry out such an important enterprise.[38] He did not mention which Power that should be, but he always favoured the involvement of Britain in the Balkans and possibly on the side of Albania. For this reason, Ismail Bey was already labelled by Ottoman officials as being pro-British and the Sultan's disregard left him deeply unhappy.

Regarding the relationship with the British government, the Sultan explained his position in his memoirs. Writing about the 'ambitions of England' of 1899, he accused the British government of breaking the Ottoman authority in Egypt and meddling further in territories such as Yemen. He blamed the British press for being biased and regarded Gladstone's Liberal policy as a crusade against the Ottomans. 'Gladstone', he added, 'was walking on the steps of Pope Pius II'.[39] With this attitude towards the British the Sultan showed no intention of considering the ideas raised in Ismail Bey's proposal. In his memoirs, as in many talks he had with European diplomats, the Sultan avoided addressing the Albanian Question.

There was another event which made Ismail Bey distance himself further from the Sultan. Albanian businessmen and political leaders showed great interest in the project of Albanian railways which was announced in 1892. They thought that the railway, which was to connect the Albanian coastal towns of Vlora and Shkodra with the Albanian part of Macedonia, where the line already existed, would enable the movement of people and goods. This would unite Albania politically and developed it economically. A British company was competing for concessions but the proposals were dropped by the Sultan.[40] Ismail Bey was involved in trying to win concessions for the portion from Manastir to his birthplace Vlora, where he also had business interests and felt that he was deliberately deceived by the Powers and the Porte because of political and personal reasons. The political reason, he believed, was that the Powers and the Porte did not want to develop Albania. The second reason, the personal one, was that the Sultan, who was the 'owner of considerable property at Salonika as well as the port itself, was not in favour of a line that was likely to compete with Salonika'.[41]

By the end of 1899 Ismail Bey was convinced that the prospect of reforming the empire and securing autonomy for Albania was practically non-existent. Therefore, he was left with one choice: to promote the case of autonomy or independence of Albania. Over the next two years he contacted important Albanian personalities in Constantinople and revealed his plan to them. As a matter of fact, his plan was more of a strategy of how to implement Frashëri's programme, which he planned to by visiting European governments and asking for their support for an autonomous or independent Albania. The plan also included winning the support of the Albanian diasporas in Europe and reorganizing them.[42] At the end of March 1900, the Sultan, being suspicious of Ismail Bey's involvement in conspiracies, decided to send him as far away as possible from Constantinople. He called Ismail Bey and told him that he was appointed governor of Tripoli in Libya with a doubled salary.[43]

On 1 May 1900, against the Sultan's will but in agreement with the British Embassy, Ismail Bey boarded a Khedive ship, flying under the British flag and left the Bosporus for Europe in order to escape his new appointment[44]. The Sultan asked his diplomatic representations to block Ismail Bey's contacts with European governments and sent envoys (from the ranks of Albanian conservatives) to Albania to discredit him. Within a few months Ottoman diplomatic missions sent reports to Constantinople informing the government and the Sultan that Ismail Bey was scoring positive results in his mission on Albania in Europe.⁴⁵

Meanwhile, Albania became almost ungovernable due to the troubles which were created by local Albanian leaders. Their actions were derived from personal, local or regional interests, but had the potential to force Ottoman troops to relocate from troubled Macedonia deep into Albanian territories, a situation that neither the Porte nor the Powers wanted. Albanian rebellions of this nature appeared frequently in the south and the north. The most dangerous local leader who disturbed the region was Isa Boletini (1864–1916) who gave signs of rebelling against the Porte. Boletini was a controversial character, whose actions in the beginning were difficult to categorize as either brigandage, local or nationalist in character. However, he would go on to become one of the main leaders of the Albanian armed struggle for independence, organizing his followers to reject the Porte's decision which allowed the opening of the Russian Consulate in Mitrovica.⁴⁶

As a result of the ongoing problems in Macedonia, security issues continued to rise in Albania which further emphasized the need to address the Albanian Question. The Sultan still refused to acknowledge this reality. After he crushed all resurrections and closed the few existing Albanian schools, he decided to put Albanians, who remained loyal to him, in several high positions of power in Constantinople. This gave conservative Albanians the opportunity to gain more power. The Sultan thought that Ferid Pasha (1851–1914) was one such conservative and appointed him as Grand Vizier in January 1903. He hoped that in his new position of power Pasha would be able to stop the Albanian opposition to the reforms in Macedonia and improve their relations with the Porte.⁴⁷ Ferid Pasha gave his word (Besa) to the Sultan that he would make sure the Albanians remained loyal to the empire. However, Ferid Pasha cared for Albania more than the Sultan had wished or hoped. During his mandate, the Grand Vizier, favoured two other Albanians in his government, Tefik Pasha (Minister of Foreign Affairs) and Turhan Pasha (Minister of Religious Estates) with whom he seemed to have shared a common cause on the future of Albania. At the same time Ferid Pasha suppressed Albanian conservatives, or at least stopped or delayed their promotions. Such a conservative was Hayredin Bey, Introducer of Ambassadors, whose promotion was stopped by the Grand Vizier. According to a British diplomatic report, Hayredin Bey denounced the Grand Vizier as a 'leader of the Albanian nationalist movement'.⁴⁸ There were tensions between Albanian nationalists and conservatives in the Ottoman government and probably also in the Palace.

Tensions between Albanian conservatives and nationalists in Macedonia and Kosovo had also risen and became more public two years earlier when in 1901 the Sultan had appointed General Shemsi Pasha, another conservative Albanian from the region of Peja, as a commander of the army in Kosovo. His duty was to act as the Sultan's trouble-shooter and guard the entry from the northern border with Serbia and Austria-Hungry into Kosovo. He was a darling of the Palace in Constantinople and so Albanian nationalists, as well as army officers from the Young Turk ranks, hated him. While he was able to restore some peace, he could not rule the part of Kosovo which remained under the control of local leaders.⁴⁹

Where Shemsi Pasha could not succeed with arms, the Sultan helped with money and rewards and had given military posts to emerging leaders like Riza Bey and Bajram Curri. The Sultan also had a plan for Isa Boletini who proved able to mobilize the masses. In 1902 Boletini, under the pretext of stopping the Russian and Austro-Hungarian invasion, organized 5,000 armed men and threatened the *Sanjak* of Novi Pazar. He also proved decisive in stopping the opening of the Russian Consulate in Mitrovica. Seeing the danger, the Sultan managed, through Shemsi Pasha, to persuade Boletini to leave Kosovo for the Imperial Palace in Constantinople where the post of commanding officer in the Albanian Guard was given to him.[50]

However, these measures did not prove sufficient to bring lasting peace and order. Boletini left behind a fear of invasion among Albanians and the idea of rejecting the Russian Consulate. Other nationalist leaders, who regarded Russia as their main enemy, took the decision to kill the Russian Consul, Grigorije Stepanovič Šcerbin.[51] In March 1903, thousands of armed Albanians entered Mitrovica to attack the Russian Consulate, clashing with the Ottoman army. On 18 March one of the Ottoman soldiers, an Albanian conscript, shot the consul who died ten days later.[52]

This was a big blow for the Porte which had tried to bring peace and offer security in the region. It also contributed to further worsening the relations between Albanians and Serbs in Kosovo, who saw the Russian Consul as their protector. A few months later, on 8 August 1903, another Albanian Ottoman soldier killed Aleksandar Arkadievich Rostkovski, the Russian Consul in Macedonia based in Manastir. Although not intended as a political murder, the event had highly political consequences.[53] Russia used this case to portray the Albanians as troublemakers and anti-Christian. However, the Porte and Albanian nationalists were worried about the chaotic situation which engulfed most of Macedonia and Albania. Many Ottoman army officers, as well as Albanian nationalists, were convinced that the present regime was not able to deal with such problems and therefore began to seek a new form of organization which would change the regime in Constantinople. Such an organization was the Young Turk movement which attracted the support of Albanian nationalists and some of the local leaders, while conservatives continued to support the regime of the Sultan.

The birth of the Young Turks

In early April 1896 British diplomatic reports from Constantinople spoke about signs of dissatisfaction that parts of Ottoman society expressed against the autocratic regime of the Sultan. There were different organizations working in favour of spreading agitation for a liberal government but one important organization was formed three years after the British diplomatic reports were sent to London.[54]

Young Army cadets were attracted by Western political thought and secretly debated the possibility of applying them in their country. In May 1889 a group of four students of the Military Medical College in Constantinople, among them Ibrahim Temo (1865–1945), an Albanian from Macedonia, gathered to form a clandestine organization aiming to depose the Sultan. The organization was named *Ittihat Osmanli Cemiyeti* (Ottoman Union Society).[55] Within a short time the group was rapidly enlarged with members from other schools, bureaucratic institutions and the military. Members were organized in secret cells and identified with personal numbers. Ibrahim Temo took the number 1/1, meaning that he was the first founding member or 'Young Turk number one' and was to play a leading role in the future of the organization.[56]

The organization, later named the Young Turks by the European Press, aimed to reinstate the constitution, centralize governmental power and unify the empire under strong Ottoman nationalism. This was contrary to what the majority of Albanians wanted.[57] However, many Albanian personalities with nationalistic backgrounds and many army officers saw the Young Turk organization as a way of advancing their national cause and joined the movement without much hesitation.

Ibrahim Temo, avoiding arrest, escaped to Rumania and there he worked with Nikolla Naço (1843–1913) to include among the Young Turk Movement their fellow Albanians already active in secret nationalist organizations. Local Young Turk committees sprung in many towns in Macedonia and Kosovo among the population and in army garrisons and by 1908 were dominated by Albanians.[58]

Nationalist Albanians also played an important role among the Young Turk societies in exile. Ismail Bey was among the most prominent members in the Congress which was held in Paris in 1902, organized by Prince Sabahudin,[59] to unite the various Young Turk factions. Ismail Bey proposed making a plea to the Powers for intervention but many Young Turks disagreed with Ismail Bey and told him that foreign powers were the greatest enemy of the Ottomans and seeking help from them was a disgrace. They argued that he was opening a way for the European imperialist designs to move and occupy territories of the empire.[60]

By putting forward such proposals, Ismail Bey wanted to secure the future of Albania with the help of the Powers. He never abandoned the Albanian cause and never fully supported the Young Turks. Xhemil Vlora worked in central Albania under his instructions while he helped other Albanian nationalists in Paris, headed by Jup Kastrati, to establish an Albanian nationalist organization. Albanian publications in Europe, which were supported by Ismail Bey, openly promoted autonomy or independence for Albania. The Albanian national cause was such an issue among the Young Turks in exile that the Porte used these facts to declare that Dahmad Mahmud Pasha and his sons were supporting the Albanian nationalist movement. This prompted Dahmad Pasha to deny these claims and affirmed his disapproval with the ideas of autonomy or independence for Albania.[61]

At that time, it became obvious that Ismail Bey was not in a position to lead Albanians abroad, as both the Young Turks and Albanian nationalists considered him to be pro-British and pro-Greek. He was also seen as favouring a diplomatic solution leading to the independence of Albania which was a slow process and, as such, rejected by many who favoured a guerrilla war against the Porte. The Greek members from Macedonia and other parts of the Ottoman Empire were also against Ismail Bey, as they did not like his ideas of foreign intervention and an autonomous or independent Albania.[62] Dervish Hima, another nationalist leader and also a delegate in the Congress, was a bigger player and was mistakenly regarded by the Porte to be a subordinate of Ismail Bey.[63]

Regarding foreign assistance, Prince Sabahudin and Ismail Bey decided to involve the British government in the plans to dethrone the Sultan. Ismail Bey acted by using his diplomatic experience and the ties he had established during his career with British diplomats and the Foreign Office. For their part, the British could have had reasons to endorse an attempted coup d'état. The Foreign Office was losing the influence it once exercised over the Porte and Germany was winning it. The Sultan had given the Baghdad railway concessions to the Germans and the British did their utmost to block this scheme during 1902 and 1903.[64] However, Ismail Bey's attempt to secure British backing and bring radical change in the Ottoman system of government proved unsuccessful because the British refused to get involved.[65]

The failure of executing a coup d'état caused the authority of Sabahudin and Ismail Bey to fade among their supporters. It was for this reason that Ismail Bey decided to distance himself from the Young Turks and showed more consideration for the case of the future of Albania.

The Congress of Paris in 1902 also showed that the Young Turks and Albanian nationalists in exile were more an intellectual than a political organization. They had not established strong connections with the organizations and the people within the territories of the empire. The Revolution was brewing in Macedonia and exiled Young Turks, among them Albanian nationalists, were out of touch with the situation on the ground. However, Albanian nationalists and army officers, who had joined the Young Turks in Macedonia and Kosovo, were better placed to change the situation.

The Revolution: An Albanian tale of three cities

The development of the Young Turk Revolution is, to a considerable extent, an Albanian tale involving three cities: Salonika, Manastir and Ferizaj. The Revolution was born, developed and erupted in these three places, which were culturally and strategically important for the Ottoman Empire in Europe.

At the beginning of the twentieth century the multi-ethnic, multi-religious, prosperous and tolerant city of Salonika became a centre of plotting against the rule of the Sultan. The transfer of the central CUP to Salonika in 1906 and its unification with the Paris branch a year later made the port city into a starting point of the Revolution. The support of the population for the CUP was strong and often was seen as a joint Jewish–Muslim movement. The Muslim middle class and part of the aristocracy, together with Jewish intellectuals and businessmen, gave the movement a high standard of political power.[66]

The Albanian population of Salonika was significantly lower in comparison with the Jewish majority and those who were known as Muslims or Turks, but their influence in the army was important. Dissatisfaction was growing among the officers of the Third Army, stationed in Salonika. To them, the empire, which had lost vast territories following the Congress of Berlin, was now about to lose Macedonia. Enver Bey (1881–1922), an Albanian officer, was among many officers who were worried about the empire whose fate was intertwined with that of Albania. Enver Bey played an important role in the movement and ultimately became the most famous Young Turk of all.⁶⁷ Another active army officer of Albanian origin was Salonika-born Mustafa Kemal (1881–1938).⁶⁸ However, Mustafa Kemal did not show much regard for the Albanian cause, but rather went on to become *Atatürk*, the father of Turkish Nation.

The activities of the Young Turks in Salonika were intensive, but the Revolution could not break out in this city. In 1903 a group of Young Turks told Richard Graves, the British Consul in Salonika, that they would be leading a revolt against the Sultan and asked for British support. The consul told them that if they had no support from the army and the police, they should forget about such a revolt. Graves did not even mention this meeting in his official reports but wrote about it in his memoires.⁶⁹ However, the consul was right. Salonika could feed the Young Turk movement but could not start a Revolution.

Manastir was another multi-ethnic and multi-religious city, situated further north in Macedonia, which offered better conditions for the Revolution. In Manastir the army, the police and, to a degree, the administration were three important institutions in which the Albanians had considerable influence and some control. The Albanian guerrilla bands and the local Albanian population were two valuable elements that the Revolution needed. In 1905 the Sultan reduced the number of Albanian soldiers in Macedonia by sending them to Yemen. Even after this move the rest of the army in Macedonia still consisted of a high number of Albanian soldiers which were known to be disobedient if they did not fight under Albanian command. They also refused to fight in Albanian areas. For this reason, Hairi Pasha, commander of the Third Army, did not want Albanian battalions in Macedonia and complained that Albanian soldiers were too anti-Christian to be suitable for intervention in Macedonia. He asked the Porte to move the remaining Albanian soldiers elsewhere but his request was denied.⁷⁰

While the discipline and morale of the Ottoman army were low, the activities of the Young Turk officers increased. Among them was Nijazi Bey (1873–1913) of Resna, an Albanian from Macedonia, who became as prominent as Enver Bey and together became two main heroes of the Revolution. Two other important personalities, Muzahir Bey, the brother of Nijazi Bey, and Nedim Bey were also active in spreading Young Turk ideas among the population in the area of Manastir. Ejup Sabri, another Albanian, was a commander of the *Redif* battalion and had enormous influence over the Albanian population of Ohri, which was his native town. At the same time the Albanian nationalist movement, mainly directed against Greece and Serbia, was growing rapidly in the *vilayet* of Manastir.⁷¹ The Ottoman authorities were aware of this movement but on many occasions tolerated it because Albanian nationalism, in the circumstances of Macedonia, was in favour of the Porte.

The next step that Nijazi Bey and his followers took was to win over the Albanian nationalist guerrilla bands which were formed in response to the difficult situation in Macedonia. Although initially they were formed for the defence of their national rights and as counter force to the other bands operating in Macedonia that attacked Albanians, they later fought against the Ottoman regime. The Committee for the Liberation of Albania was formed in Manastir in 1906 by Halil Bey, Georgi Qiriasi, Fehim Bey Zavalani and Bajo Topulli. All were from different parts of south Albania and developed a network which spread from south to north. The Committee was especially successful in Kosovo where they recruited some influential people.⁷²

The increased activities of the Albanian nationalist movement were noticed by British diplomats in a yearly report for 1907. Regarding the cooperation between the Albanian national movement and the Young Turks, the British Embassy in Constantinople reported that the Albanian nationalist movement was very active and on the rise.[73] By the beginning of 1908 Nijazi Bey, with the help of Galip Bey, the commander of Skopje garrison, managed to get the support of most Albanian leaders and members of their nationalist movement. Before June 1908 it was believed that in Kosovo two-thirds of the officers in the army and the gendarmerie had become members of the Young Turk movement.[74] This meant that almost the entire Albanian nationalist movement in Macedonia and Kosovo, as well as the majority of Albanian army officers, joined the Young Turks.

As the British and Russian monarchs discussed the question of Macedonia at their meeting in Reval on 9 June 1908, tensions were increasing among Albanians in the *vilayets* of Kosovo and Manastir. Nationalist Albanians felt that their national question was ignored and other foreign powers were about to move in.[75] Here, the Young Turks and the Albanians had a strong common interest as both wanted to save the territory of the empire. The Reval Agreement gave the signal for the Revolution. On 3 July 1908 Nijazi Bey, accompanied by some Ottoman officials and a few soldiers, most of them Albanian, proceeded to the mountains. There he joined other companies and formed a 'Young Turk' band which numbered 100 to 200 members.[76]

In their reports the British diplomats and the Foreign Office did not give much weight to this event which, within a few days, sparked great changes. One of the reports from early July said that an Ottoman army officer told British diplomats that the Revolutionary movement would break out in the course of a day or two and wanted to know the British attitude towards the Young Turks. The British vice-council, Heathcote, refused to discuss the issue.[77] By 18 July the Foreign Office started considering whether the movement would stop or spread. It was only around the end of July that they realized the progress made by Young Turks was resembling a Revolution.[78]

While British diplomats failed to recognize the signs of the Revolution in time, the Porte was alarmed immediately and ordered Shemsi Pasha to proceed from Kosovo to Macedonia and deal with the insurgents. Shemsi Pasha, with a contingent of 3000 Albanian soldiers, arrived in Manastir on 6 July. Upon their arrival, the Albanian soldiers declared openly that they would not fire on the Young Turks. Pasha found himself in a very difficult position and asked the Sultan to activate those conservative Albanians to whom he had given privileges for long time. He thought it was about time they should put their weight against Young Turk officers.[79] Shemsi Pasha was killed the same day while Albanian bodyguards offered little or no protection and the assassin escaped.[80] This prompted suspicions of an Albanian plot executed against Shemsi Pasha by those nationalists who had hated him so much and who had now become Young Turks.

A week later, in Manastir, an attempt was made by an Albanian on the life of Sadik Pasha, the Sultan's *aides-de-camp*, who was believed to have come to Macedonia on a spying mission. Three days earlier a 'regimental mufti' was also killed by Albanians in Salonika.[81] On 17 July, major-general Osman Hidayet was severely wounded while reading a telegram from the Sultan to the officers in the barracks in Manastir. Niazi Bey issued a proclamation: 'The object of the rising is to revive the 1876 Constitution.' The

Porte realized that this was a very dangerous movement as it had engulfed the army. The British Consul in Manastir wrote that majority of the officers of the Third Army were in 'favour of the Young Turks movement, and fully resolved to do their utmost for the realization of its objects'.[82]

The movement in the *vilayet* of Manastir reached wide proportions but it was still a military rebellion and could not be a revolution without the participation of the people. This happened further north of Manastir, in Ferizaj, Kosovo. Salonika and Manastir were old cities, ethnically and religiously mixed, while Ferizaj was a small and relatively new town, almost entirely inhabited by Albanians and grew fast after 1874 when the railway line began to pass through it and a station was built. The railway came from Salonika, via Manastir and Skopje and continued to end in Mitrovica where Austria-Hungary aspired to build links from Bosnia in order to reach the port of Salonika.

In spring 1908 Austria-Hungary initiated the old plan of extending the railway from Bosnia to Mitrovica in Kosovo, while the Serbian government announced plans to build a railway to reach the coast of Albania through Kosovo. Albanian leaders viewed these initiatives with hostility. At the beginning of July rumours spread fast throughout Kosovo (probably by Serb agitators and Young Turks) that Austria-Hungary was about to invade.[83] When it was announced that a special train, bringing students of the Austrian-German railway training school from Skopje would arrive, people started gathering in Ferizaj, thinking that it was the first step of an Austro-Hungarian invasion. On 5 July a large crowd of Albanians gathered in Ferizaj to protest.[84] Although initially there were some 5000 armed men gathered but by 23 July the number grew to 30,000.[85] This event was not linked with the insurrection in Manastir, which had started at the same time but created the effect which was aimed in Manastir.

Albanian leaders hurried to Ferizaj to hold an assembly which lasted more than two weeks. Among them was Isa Boletini, who had come back from Constantinople in March 1906 and had been rewarded the title of Bey and given land in Kosovo by the Sultan. Within two years, Isa Bey had become powerful and changed from a local leader to a conservative opposed to the Young Turks.[86] He left the meeting when he realized that his proposals would not pass. The meeting was also attended by Young Turks such as Nexhip Draga and Bajram Curri but though initially they were in the minority, this composition changed in favour of the Young Turks.

Galib Bey, the Albanian commander of the Ottoman troops in Skopje, received orders from Constantinople to disperse the Albanians in Ferizaj. He was happy to receive the order but would not execute it. Galip Bey, being a Young Turk, went to Ferizaj with his army to take part in the assembly and to push forward Young Turk proposals.[87] He was accompanied by other Albanian members of the Skopje branch and other personalities joined him from Prishitna.

More Albanian leaders and military personnel who were members of the Young Turk local committees from the region rushed to Ferizaj. They felt that this opportunity was simply perfect to initiate changes and come to power. Leaders of Albanian guerrilla groups also supported them. On 18 July the Young Turks, predominantly consisting of Albanian nationalists, outnumbered conservative Albanians who gathered there for a different matter and favoured different decisions.[88] This created high tensions in the mosque where the meeting of the leaders of the two parties was held. Eventually, on

20 July, all the Albanian leaders decided to support the Young Turks,[89] but only after the Young Turks promised that, once in power, they would implement a programme of Albanian language in schools. The Young Turks promised many more national rights, including privileges they enjoyed before and for a long time. Then, the Kosovo leaders addressed the masses, telling them they had achieved all their objectives including the 'abolition of prisons, the cancellation of all innovations and reforms'.[90]

On 21 July, after receiving the support of the masses, the Young Turks sent a telegram to Constantinople asking the Sultan to reinstate the constitution. The Sultan did not reply as he was busy taking steps to consolidate his power. But the Grand Vezier, Ferid Pasha, replied by sending a telegram to congratulate the leaders of the assembly for the good work. The telegram was even written in Albanian. That same day the Grand Vezier in confidence told the British ambassador that the Sultan has received several telegrams from his army officers in Macedonia and Kosovo informing about the dangerous situation.[91]

The Sultan ordered Ferid Pasha to act against the Albanians and calm the situation in Kosovo and Macedonia. The Pasha told the Sultan that this was not the duty of the Grand Vizier and resigned on the evening of 22 July.[92] The Albanian Grand Vizier could not keep his *Besa* as he 'failed' to maintain the Albanian's loyalty to the Sultan. In Constantinople it was said that the Grand Vizier was a Young Turk and a relative of Ismail Bey. Austro-Hungarian diplomats in Constantinople spoke about the Grand Vizier's support for the Albanian nationalist movement in Macedonia.[93]

As the Sultan did not respond to the first telegram, another was sent on 22 July. This time the Sultan was threatened. He was told that 30,000 armed Albanians would be joined by more Albanians in Macedonia and Ottoman troops stationed in Manastir and Salonika, and they would march to Constantinople. The Sultan gathered the Council of Ministers and discussed the issue in long and difficult meetings. Some of the ministers and advisers suggested 'half measures', but the majority succeeded in persuading the Sultan that resistance would be useless since movements like the one in Ferizaj were expected elsewhere in the empire and in other sections of the army. Describing the moment the decision was taken, the British ambassador wrote that 'the fact that the Albanians had declared themselves in favour of the Constitution, made the Sultan listen to counsels of moderation'.[94]

At midnight on 23/24 July 1908, the Sultan approved the constitution and allowed the formation of an Ottoman Parliament. Unprecedented jubilation followed all over Albania and in Manastir a military parade was organized. Nijazi Bey entered the town triumphantly, together with Çerçiz Topulli, the Albanian guerrilla leader and Apostol Mihajlovski, a Macedonian guerrilla leader[95] to symbolize the Albanian-Macedonian co-operation in the Revolution. The city of Salonika was illuminated and received with enthusiasm Enver Bey, who had gone north to Macedonia to organize Young Turk bands and now returned in triumph. He addressed a large crowd, telling them 'we are all brothers'. Europe no longer has a mandate over the Ottoman Empire and the state now does not belong to the Sultan but to its citizens, he told the cheering crowd.[96] However, within a few months joy turned into huge disappointment for Albanians and other ethnicities in Macedonia who had believed in the Young Turk promises and in the Revolution. To the Albanians, the Young Turks would prove to be nothing of what they appeared to be in Ferizaj.

5

Against the Young Turks, 1908–10

The British attitude towards the Young Turks

With the departure of Disraeli and his pro-Ottoman policies in 1880, relations between Britain and the Ottoman Empire took a worsening turn. The new British Liberal policy, which was introduced by Gladstone, was considered by the Porte as unfavourable towards the Balkans. The Macedonian question had caused further deterioration in relations between Britain and the Porte. During this period the Sultan was attracted by the ascendancy of Germany and its growing economic and military power, thus giving the German government an opportunity to replace British influence in Constantinople. At the beginning of 1908 there was no hope that the Anglo-Ottoman relationship would improve soon. About a month before the Young Turk Revolution took place, Fitzmaurice[1] sent a private letter to Tyrell[2] to explain the British policy in Constantinople. He wrote:

> During the last few years our policy, if I may so call it, in Turkey has been, and for some time to come will be, to attempt the impossible task of furthering our commercial interests while pursuing a course (in Macedonia, Armenia, Turco-Persian Boundary &c.) which the Sultan interprets as being pre-eminently hostile in aim and tendency. In a highly centralised theocracy like the Sultanate and caliphate combined, with its pre-economic conceptions, every big trade &c. concessions – is regarded as an Imperial favour to be bestowed on the seemingly friendly, a category in which, needless to say, we are not included.[3]

Fitzmaurice believed that the Porte's attitude would not change before the death of the Sultan or a change in the regime, which would come as a result of some unforeseen troubles. 'The next few years may see clouded times fraught with big events which one would not like to see spell disaster to British interests and prestige', predicted Fitzmaurice.[4] But significant changes arrived within a few weeks. When the Young Turks triumphed, the British press, public opinion and even the government were sceptical, but this soon changed and the new government in Constantinople started to receive compliments from London. The British government was convinced that the situation in the Balkans would change and the Macedonian reforms, together with the armed bands and the Albanian Question, would melt away once the problems were addressed properly by applying the constitution and elected government. This led British diplomats in Constantinople to justify their previous policy towards the Young Turks and one of the embassy's reports said that 'sympathy has always existed between the people of Great Britain and the population of Turkey', adding that 'grievances or misunderstandings of the British government were against the Turkish Government only'.[5]

Therefore, the change of government in Constantinople after the Revolution was quickly welcomed with enthusiasm by the British government. The Foreign Office issued a memorandum explaining that this enthusiasm stemmed from three reasons: 1. love of liberty; 2. the traditional friendship which began when Russia was traditional enemy; 3. the belief that the Muslim population of India is particularly loyal to England and can be still propitiated by kindness to Turkey.[6]

The third point of the memorandum alludes to both the satisfaction and concern held by the British about the outcome of the Revolution. If the Young Turks, with the help of the British government, were able to create a strong government and a strong empire, then the Muslims of India and other parts of the British dominions might appreciate Britain's help. Yet there was also a possibility that this could inspire the Indian Muslims to create their own government and constitution, something the British did not want. The situation could also have an effect on Egypt and it was for this reason that Grey told his ambassador Gerald Lowther: 'I should say as little as possible to the Khedive about a constitution for Egypt'. If the Young Turks could create a strong government, this reality 'must have a great effect in Egypt and upon our policy there', wrote Grey.[7]

Despite these concerns, the British were optimistic about the new Ottoman government, hoping to reassert their influence which had been overtaken by the Germans. British diplomats in Constantinople, who were predominantly Gladstonians, were convinced that German diplomats were at great pains to prove the Young Turk Revolution was the result of British intrigues and, as such, was doomed to fail.[8]

While Grey believed in reforms, his diplomats in Constantinople expected British business to acquire parts of various economic projects throughout the Ottoman Empire. Grey emphasized that he was 'distressed' when he became foreign secretary because the British were 'ousted from commercial enterprises in Turkey and how apparently hopeless it was to get any footing there'.[9] With the old regime gone and the Young Turks in power, there were hopes in London that British businessmen and financiers would strengthen British interests and influence in the Ottoman Empire. However, British diplomats in Constantinople expressed some scepticism. The situation changed on 5 October 1908 when Bulgaria proclaimed independence, Austria-Hungary annexed Bosnia and Crete declared its unification with Greece. This was a serious blow to the Young Turks. In order to help the Porte, the British had taken a diplomatic lead before Bulgaria proclaimed independence. On 2 October 1908 the Foreign Office issued a circular urging the Powers to prevent the Bulgarian government from declaring independence. Most of the Powers, including Russia, agreed with the British and reminded the Bulgarian government about the dangers a declaration of independence would bring.[10]

Edward Grey, like the Ottoman government, pointed out to the Austro-Hungarians that with the annexation of Bosnia and Herzegovina, the Treaty of Berlin was violated. Vienna had also violated the Convention of 21 April 1879, which stated that the occupation of Bosnia and Herzegovina should not affect the rights of the sovereignty of the Sultan. This crisis brought Serbia into the international scene. Austria-Hungary had traditionally supported Serbia's aspirations against the Ottoman Empire. Serbia's growing nationalist ambitions had regarded Austria-Hungary as a protector and hoped to extend towards her neighbouring territories. But, the annexation turned Austria-Hungary from a protector into a potential enemy of Serbia and frustrated Serbia's nationalist aspirations. This brought Serbia closer to Russia, therefore making her a threat to Austria-Hungary and *vice versa*. As Russia got closer to Belgrade, Vienna felt that it was being pushed away from its spheres of interest in the Balkans.[11] After the annexation, Serbia mobilized its troops and launched a protest to the Powers, demanding an extension of its territory across the *Sanjak* of Novi Pazar, in order to reach the Albanian coast.[12]

The British ambassador in Belgrade, James Whitehead, sketched with sympathy the 'aspirations of the Servian Nation for eventual union with the people of the same race and language' who were under Ottoman or Austro-Hungarian rule.[13] He believed that the transfer of the territory of Bosnia and Herzegovina to Austria-Hungary was a 'crushing blow to the most cherished aspirations', leaving the Serbs to hope for an increase in territory towards Kosovo. As a result of the annexation, Russia, assisted by Britain and France, supported Serbia's aspirations against the Austro-Hungarian Empire, which was firmly backed by Germany. Russia was forced to back down, leaving Serbia deeply hostile towards Austria-Hungary, a situational which became an important feature of European politics in the lead-up to the First World War.[14]

As the situation in the Balkans was changing, the Foreign Office asked Fitzmaurice to prepare a memorandum which would examine the possibilities of Serbian and Montenegrin territorial extensions. Compensating Montenegro with Albanian territory was always difficult, as the Ulqin problem had shown in 1880 and could lead to repeat of armed Albanian resistance which the Foreign Office wanted to avoid. However, the extension of Serbia was more complicated. The memorandum explained why Serbia wanted part of Kosovo:

> They want it firstly on practical grounds, in order to improve their frontier, and for reasons connected with roads and railways; secondly, because it contains the so-called Amselfeld, or Field of Sparrows, where Servia lost her independence in 1389 and the united Christian armies were destroyed in 1448. [...] An appeal to the Battle of Kossovo invariably excites the Servian imagination. [...] The cession of this district to Servia, would probably be met with resistance by the Albanians; they would also resist the cession of the north-western part of the Vilayet to Montenegro, which would very much like to have it.[15]

The author of the memorandum, influenced by both Serbian propaganda and British Liberal thought, went on to explain that the majority of the population were once Christian Serbs but were converted into Muslim Albanians. However, if the Albanians were to resist Serbian territorial expansion into their lands, then Serbia could try to expand towards Bulgaria.[16] In the end, Fitzmaurice did not consider these suggestions helpful but the Foreign Office had no other proposal and so this memorandum became the document upon which British foreign policy regarding Serbia and its extensions towards Albania and Macedonia was based. As the memorandum illustrates, Britain was slowly taking the side of Serbia.

By the end of 1908, when the Ottoman Parliament was formed in Constantinople, the Young Turks received more support from the British government. At the same time, the honeymoon period between the Albanians and the Young Turks was over and both parties became fierce enemies. The British government, by supporting Serbia's future plans as well as the policies of the Young Turks, was not seen as a friend of the Albanians. On these two matters the British government was fully supported by the majority of the public at home. Just before Christmas of 1908, Edith Durham returned to England from Albania where she had witnessed the difficult situation between the Albanians and the Young Turks. She wrote:

> I arrived in London, and was amazed to find for the first time people who believed in the Young Turks. They would listen to no facts, and would not believe me when I said that the Turkish Empire, as it stood, would probably barely survive one Parliament.[17]

Durham's prophesy was almost exactly fulfilled. Disappointment with the Young Turks, which initially started in Albania, spread widely throughout the Ottoman Empire. On 3 April 1909 a counter-revolution against the Young Turks and the constitution broke out in Constantinople. The counter-revolution against the Young Turks created some controversies in British Ottoman relations. Some historians, such as Ahmad Feroz, have wrongly suggested that the British supported Ismail Bey and Kiamil Pasha's activities to bring down the Young Turks.[18]

Although the British attitude towards the Young Turks was supportive, it was suggested that Ahrar, led by Ismail Bey and supported by a section of the Albanian troops in the Ottoman army, succeeded in staging a counter-revolution because the British were behind him. The British were also suspected of having been involved in fomenting the counter-revolution and even supplying the opposition to the Young Turks with funds through their embassy in Constantinople. The British supposedly took this action because of their commitments to Russia, which originated in the Anglo-Russian Convention of 1907, and as such it was an anti-Ottoman policy.[19] In his memoirs, Ismail Bey Qemali alleged that it was he who had convinced Lowther to offer some support to the counter-revolution. On another occasion, when it became clear that the CUP was about to regain power, Ismail Bey asked Lowther for British intervention. It is not clear what exactly Ismail Bey meant by intervention, but his proposal was not considered by the Foreign Office.

It was known that Lowther did not have much sympathy for the Young Turks, a position he had expressed several times to Grey. There were other diplomats in the British embassy who did not agree with the Young Turks, Fitzmaurice being one of them. His influential role in British diplomatic circles, good connections with newspapers and being an important personality among the power-brokers of the

Ottoman world led some diplomats to indicate that he was in some part responsible for the counter-revolution.[20]

Aubrey Herbert, who supported the Albanian cause and had worked in the British embassy in Constantinople in 1904–5, blamed Fitzmaurice for leading an anti-Young Turk policy. Like many Albanian nationalists, Herbert too believed that there would be a solution for the Albanian Question under the Young Turk democratic rule. Herbert was a well-known supporter of the Young Turks and a friend of Enver Bey and other leading members of the organization, most of whom, including Talaat Pasha, regarded Fitzmaurice as being hostile to the CUP.[21] However, none of these suspicions or allegations were true and there are no documents to support the involvement of the British in the counter revolution.

Ismail Bey Qemali seemed to have exaggerated his role in the counter-revolution because, as a politician, he wanted to portray himself as being important and having the British behind him. As a matter of fact the British embassy helped him to escape from Constantinople after his plan failed, but that was all they did for him. There is further evidence to show that Ismail Bey was not fully supported by the British. Lowther had told Grey that he did not trust Ismail Bey and when Ismail Bey went to the Foreign Office in autumn 1909, Grey did not meet him but rather was met by Tyrrell (Grey's secretary).[22] These facts demonstrate that Ismail Bey was not a trusted person of the British for a venture such as bringing the Young Turks down from the power.

After all, there was no reason for the British to turn their backs on the Young Turks. With the Young Turks in power, British diplomats saw themselves as once more becoming an important factor in Constantinople. The Foreign Office continued to support the Young Turks even after they promulgated the Law of Association in August 1909 which intended to abolish national differences in the Ottoman Empire. It was with these intentions that the Young Turks had organized the Congress of Dibra in July of that year, seeking to suppress Albanian nationalism by attacking the language and its Latin alphabet. The Congress, which was supposed to convince the Albanians to drop their idea of a Latin alphabet, had failed because all the Albanian leaders and intellectuals boycotted the event. Yet Grey supported the Young Turk idea of Ottomanizing the Albanians and other nationalities. On this matter he wrote to the Russian diplomat, Count Izvolski, expressing his support for the actions undertaken by the Young Turks.[23]

The Young Turks were also supported by the British press. When the Albanians rose against the Young Turks in April 1910, *The Times* published a communication which was sent to them from the Ottoman Embassy in London. The readers could only get the official view which stated that the Albanians in the *vilayet* of Kosovo rose against the empire 'because they did not want justice, liberty, equality, schools'.[24] As a matter of fact, the Albanians wanted exactly that.

There were only a few people in Britain who knew or cared about the true cause of the Albanian rebellions and insurrections against the Young Turks. George Frederick Abbott[25] explained that information from Albania was missing because the public and the government, being on the side of the Young Turks, were not interested in knowing the truth. 'There is a bewildering confusion regarding the true causes of the Albanian insurrection' wrote Abbott and added that the Young Turk government was worse than any that had come before it. He considered their governance in Albania 'military despotism'. Explaining the situation further, he added that Young Turk officers had only one idea in their heads: 'the reconstruction of the Great Ottoman Empire and the triumph of Islam', but 'the Albanians will not be Ottomanized'. Abbott also pointed out that the desire for autonomy was the main reason for the conflict between the Albanians and the Young Turks.[26]

However, at this point the Foreign Office was ignoring the Albanian Question and was not interested in understanding the cause of the conflict. Yet there were cases when the British diplomats in Constantinople had given some importance to the Albanian Question. At the beginning of 1909 Mansuell, an army officer and former military attaché in Constantinople, recommended the formation of an independent Albania and a greater Bulgaria in order to create an obstacle to Austro-Hungarian and German expansion in the Balkans.[27] But Lowther, even by 1910, still believed that the 'thorny Albanian Question' could be solved by bribing, decorating or by granting land to the Albanian leaders. This method of rule in Albania was applied by the Sultan himself but was about to collapse. Fitzmaurice's reports began to be read with more interest by Grey, Morley and even Prime Minister Asquith. Fitzmaurice, in more than one report, warned that discontent in Macedonia and Albania would cause the disintegration of the Ottoman Empire.[28] The Foreign Office disregarded such warnings and continued to believe in the Young Turks' policy.

Unifying the language and the nation

The reinstatement of the constitution in Constantinople was regarded as an Albanian triumph in northern Albania. Regarding the atmosphere in Shkodra Durham wrote that 'all North Albania was wild in joy' and 'it was believed the Europe had intervened, and the Turk would rule no more'.[29]

Elsewhere in Albania, as in Shkodër, the meaning of the constitution was rather misunderstood. The majority of the population were illiterate and had lived for a long time under Ottoman rule which prohibited education in the Albanian language. They had little idea what the constitution really meant. However, the constitution introduced a considerable degree of liberty which made some Albanian intellectuals return home from exile. The first question they hurried to address was opening new schools in order to educate the population. Immediately after the proclamation of the constitution Albanian intellectuals started establishing national clubs throughout Albania and elsewhere in the Ottoman Empire or abroad where they resided. Through national clubs they aimed to raise the national awareness of Albanians through the education. The first club Bashkimi (Unity) was established in Manastir on 31 July 1908. Fehim Zavalani, who came back from the exile, became a president with Gjergj Qiriazi as his deputy while Naum Naçi became secretary.[30] Within a short time Bashkimi sent emissaries to propagate the Albanian cause and spread its branches throughout Albania. Within few months sixty-six clubs were established and started to spread ideas of education and nationalism.[31] The result was noted by a British diplomat:

More important in that connection [nationalist] is the educational activity which displayed itself throughout Southern Albania immediately after the proclamation of the constitution. Early in August an Albanian school, founded and supported by voluntarily contributions, in subscribing to which the population displayed a remarkable liberality, was established in Elbassan [Elbasan], two schools in Korytza [Korça], which had been closed under the old regime, were reopened, and the example of these two places was rapidly followed by all the principal towns throughout the south.[32]

To a lesser degree schools were also established in northern parts of Albania. The national and cultural awakening Rilindja (Rebirth) was entering the last phase and scoring positive results. Albanian intellectuals were giving the last push to the idea of uniting Albanian people into one linguistic identity, one culture and one nation living in one territory.[33]

The Albanian writing was first mentioned in 1332 when a priest called Brochart presented a report to the king of France, Philippe de Valois. Brochart visited Albania and reported that the Albanians speak a very different language from Latin but they use Latin letters in their books. Writing in Albanian started in the northern parts of Albania and was closely linked with the Catholic clergy. The first known record, dating from 8 November 1462, is a simple sentence which says: *Unte paghesont premenit Atit et birit et spertit senit* (I baptize you in the name of the Father and the Son and the Holy Ghost). The sentence is known as *Formula e Pagëzimit* (Baptismal Formula) and was written by Pal Engjëlli (1417-70), the Archbishop of Durrës, who was also known as a close friend and advisor of Skenderbeg (1405-68). The first known book was published in Albanian in 1555, titled as *Meshari* (The Missal). It was written by a Catholic priest called Gjon Buzuku (1499-1577). In 188 pages the book has 154,000 words containing liturgical texts and parts from Old and New Testament. *Meshari* did not make an immediate effect as a book of prayers or in any other way. For almost two centuries after its publication, it was not known to have existed. Because of the anti-Reformation measures the Catholic Church had taken at the Council of Trent in 1545, *Meshari* ended up within the index of banned books.[34] It was considered that it was written in an 'unknown language' and became a subject for the Inquisition. In 1740 it was discovered in the library of the *College of the Propaganda Fide* by Gjon Nikollë Kazazi (1702-52), an Albanian Catholic priest and the Archbishop of Skopje. Kazazi has suggested that the book was published in hundreds of copies in Rome during 1555.[35] However, at the eighteenth century it was noted that only one copy existed and was found among rare collections of Cardinal Stephen Borgia and later was catalogued among the books of the Vatican Library.[36]

The most important writer of this period was Pjetër Bogdani (1630-89). While the work of previous priests was mainly translations, Bogdani's work was mostly original. Bogdani, as many Albanian priests, including Pjetër Budi and Frang Bardhi, was educated at *the Illyrian College of Loretto* in Italy which was established in 1574 in order to educate Albanian and Slav Catholic priests. Until 1746, when the College was closed, 193 students had graduated and had taken posts in Albania, Serbia and Montenegro. The *Illyrian College* did not only train the Albanian priests in religious matters but also played an important role in shaping their minds on ethnic grounds. Bogdani is best known for his treaties on theology, *Çeta e Profetëve* or *Cuneus Profetarum* (The Band of Prophets), published in both Albanian and Italian in Padua in 1686. Bogdani is often considered as the father of Albanian prose. He contributed to organize a force of 6000 Albanian soldiers and joined the Austrian Army under the command of Enea Piccolomini and clashed with the Ottoman Army in Kosovo and Macedonia during the Great Turkish War of 1683–99. Bogdani and Piccolomini, as many Austrian and Albanian soldiers, died from the plague.[37] However, the Ottomans triumphed but Bogdani entered the Albanian history as a writer and a patriot and also as a martyr of the Catholic Church.

The above priests wrote religious books but they established the basis of Albanian literature written with Latin letters and created the sense of an Albanian separate ethnicity. The Albanian history does not see the early writers as simply clerics nor their work as exclusively religious. From the fact that Budi and Bogdani were involved in organizing Albanians to fight against the Ottoman Empire, a political and patriotic dimension was added to their work and their personalities. The Ottoman occupation which begun in 1358 and completed by end the fifteenth century, divided Albanian lands in three cultural spheres: Islamic, Orthodox and Catholic. While Islamic culture was in rise, Orthodox and Catholic culture declined.

However, establishing Albanian schools proved to be a difficult task. Until 1908 schools were organized according to religious division of the Albanians: Muslim, Orthodox and Catholic. Muslims were taught in Ottoman (Turkish) with Arabic letters, the Orthodox went to Greek schools while Catholics used the Latin alphabet and Italian language. Therefore, these schools nurtured Ottoman feelings for the Muslims, pro-Greek sentiments for the Orthodox and pro-Italian or pro-Austria – Hungarian tendencies for Catholics. Another problem was the lack of text books and teachers for new established schools which started in August 1908.[38]

This division had produced Albanian Muslim writers who used the Ottoman alphabet (combination of Arabic and Persian), which continued for over two centuries (seventeenth and eighteenth), and their work is called *Literature of the Bejtexhinj*. While the works of Catholic writers were exclusively religious, the subject matter of the Muslim writers was mainly secular. However, religious themes were not absent and they often derived from Sunni spirituality, mystical Sufism and the liberal Bektashi pantheism.[39] Albanian Muslim writers, as Catholic priests before, considered themselves belonging to a separate ethnicity and took pride of their language.

Nezim Frakulla (1680–1760) was the major poet among the *Bejtexhinj* who also composed an Albanian-Ottoman dictionary in verse form and a *divan* in Albanian.[40] In his writings, for the first time, we see the Albanian language being praised. The author also praised himself for using the language or rather saving it:

Who made a *divan* speak in Albanian?
It was Nezim who made it known.
Who made elegance speak in Albanian?
It was Nezim who made it noble.

This language was in ruins,
Veiled in suffering and much shame.
Proof enough is this book
That Nezim made it rejoice.[41]

Bejtexhinj were replaced by the romantic nationalist literature of the Rilindja when Latin alphabet returned again. The veining of this literature is linked with the decay of the Ottoman Empire and rise of the Albanian nationalist movement during which the Albanians started turning their back to the Ottoman Empire and all things which were related with orientalism.[42]

The teaching of Albanian language became a patriotic duty and this brought in view the need of creating a unified alphabet. Albanian linguists started preparations to organize a congress and take a decision on this matter. This initiative disturbed conservative Albanians, most of whom were conservative Muslim clerics, who declared that their official language should remain 'Turkish'. This group was soon to be supported by Young Turks who saw the Albanian language as an important element of Albanian nationalism, and, as such, contrary to their idea of Ottomanism. The Greek Orthodox Church feared losing its influence over southern Albania and kept threatening Albanians, especially students in Greek schools, with excommunication.[43] Catholics, Austria-Hungary and Italy, to a degree, felt insecure but not threatened as there were signs that the new Albanian unified alphabet was going to be with Latin letters. Apart from religious and political complications there were also practical obstacles which were soon to be imposed by the Young Turks.

In the nineteenth century the role of the language became important in the development of the nationalists movements in the Balkans. In the Balkan peninsula, same as in Central Europe, an enlightenment interest in language and culture was manifested widely. Same as Catholics in the Austria-Hungary, the Orthodox Christians and the Muslims in the Ottoman Empire have used the language for their national affirmation. The Orthodox Slavs of the Ottoman Empire belonged to the same religion but the language made them to differ from each other. The national elites have deliberately highlighted and promoted differences between their own national language and those of others.[44]

The nineteenth-century nationalisms of Serbs, Greeks and Bulgarians can be explained by perennial theory which maintains that the nation as category and historical community is eternal and its origin can be 'traced to human biology, but which manifested itself as a specific type of socio-cultural community'.[45] Based on this theory, the Balkan Christians included religion (Orthodox Christianity) and the rebirth of the past culture (glorious age) as two essential characteristics of building their new nations. The development of the Albanian nationalism of the nineteenth century took a different path. Instead of the common religion and 'glorious past' Albanian national ideologists took common language as basis of their ethnic and national identity.[46]

Therefore, perennial theory cannot be applied in explaining the development of the Albanian nationalism during the period of the nineteenth century. However, the basis of perennial theory, as we have seen earlier, was laid by the end of the nineteenth century by Sami Frashëri. This theory was adopted by Albanian historians and sociologists after 1912 when Albania became independent and specifically after 1945 when the country came under communist regime. Therefore, today Albanian history refers to the Illyrian origins of the Albanians and considers the medieval hero Skanderbeg and occasionally Ali Pasha as important figures who played a significant role in the nation building process. Although both had ruled semi-independently and never claiming to have established an Albanian state, they became important during the national awakening period and specifically after 1912.[47]

However, during the nineteenth century the Albanian nationalists were aware that they could not rely much in this ethnic understanding and that was the reason why they made efforts to use priorities that were offered by language which became an important tool for advancing their national ideology. Thus, explaining the nineteenth-century development of the Albanian nationalism one should refer to another theory which regarded language as the main element of the national identity.

Adamantios Korais (1748–1833), one of the first language reformers in modern Europe, made links between language and national identity and developed his theory which fits more closely with the Albanian case. He held that language was one of the most important possessions of a nation.[48] Eric Hobsbawm (1917–2012) has also given an important place to the language in defining the nation. According to him, in most of the cases, nations are defined by language and ethnicity. Language is 'the very essence of what distinguishes one people from another, "us" from "them", real human beings from the barbarians'.[49]

Korais developed his theory during the pre-revolution period of Greece and became the most important exponent of the Greek Enlightenment. Speaking about Greece he did not give any importance to religion. He concluded that 'the character of a whole nation is known by its language' or 'the language is the nation itself'.[50] Another Greek philologist at the University of Sorbonne, Ioannis Psykharis (1854–1929), supported strongly Korais' theory. Psykharis, like Korais, proclaimed: 'Language and fatherland are identical. To fight for one's fatherland or one's language, the fight is one and the same.'[51]

Although Korais' studies were based on the situation of Greece, if we analyse closely his theory, we may see that it does not fit properly to the Greek case. In this regard Mackridge noted that Korais saw the language as a 'mother tongue' and ignored the fact that another language was spoken in Greece: Albanian.[52]

However, Korais exercised an enormous influence over the ideologists of other Balkan nations, including Albanians. Albanian awakeners of the nineteenth century considered language both as a means of enlightenment and unification and as a factor of national identity. Belonging to three religions they became aware of the language being powerful bond for the union of all those who spoke Albanian. Their language was different from the languages of their neighbours and of their rulers. Albanian awakeners worked to unite their dialects into a common language and were aware that this would strengthen their national identity.[53] Therefore, Korais' theory was entirely applicable in the Albanian case. Developing the language, with no regard for religion, was not only creating a grammar and text books. It was also an effort of establishing or legalizing Albanian schools and language which was a national programme and which was led entirely by nationalist intellectuals. During the National Rebirth (Rilindja Kombëtare), language was the nation and developing the language (mother tongue) meant fighting for the motherland.

Although the religion of the Albanians did not play any important role in constructing or defining national ideals, there was always a contact with religion. The contact consisted the fear from the Greek Orthodox Church which tended to Hellenize Albanian Orthodox Christians. The conflict between the Church and Albanian nationalists, in many ways, became a pushing force behind Albanian national movement.[54] The fight of the Albanian nationalists was about excluding the Greek Orthodox Church from their national programme and not including it which was the case of other Balkan nations.

The signs of the Albanian Rebirth came into the view when some of the Balkan countries became independent or autonomous at the beginning of the nineteenth century. This made an impact on Albanians who wanted to follow the same path and speed up the process of creating their own state. However, sparks of cultural awakening emerged earlier, in the second half of the eighteenth century, with the establishment of several schools that started functioning in South Albania.[55]

Significant support for the emergence of the Albanian national awakening came from the Arbëresh – the Albanians of Italy. Migration to Italy had begun in 1272 but settlements were mainly created during the fifteenth century as a result of the exodus that followed the Ottoman invasion and particularly after the death of Skanderbeg in 1468. In 1889 Lucien Bonaparte, Napoleon's nephew, who studied their dialect, noted that Albanian was still spoken in sixty-nine provinces of 'Terra d'Otranto'.[56] With their attempts to discover their roots, the Arbëresh gave a significant push to the Albanian cultural and national awakening.

There was also another help or influence which came from abroad. Such help, given particularly to the development of the Albanian language, and later nationalism, was rooted in Great Britain and connected with the Bible. The idea of translating the Bible into Albanian came from Jernej Bartolomeu Kopitar (1780–1844), a Slovenian linguist and philologist who worked for the British and Foreign Bible Society (BFBC). Kopitar considered that the translation of the Bible into Eastern European languages would help the process of national revival among the Slav nations. He included Albanians in this group, although he knew they were not Slavs.[57] A BFBC project, presented to Prince Metternich in Vienna in August 1816, said that the Albanians have no 'portion of the word of God' written in their language. Therefore, the 'dissemination of the Holy Scripture' would have done much good.[58] The BFBC considered Albanians as a 'nation which occupies a great part of ancient Illyricum and Epirus, and speaks a language which seems to have no grammatical affinity with the Slavonian, Turkish, Greek, or Latin languages'. Therefore, the society, with 'most zealous efforts,' decided to give to the Albanians a New Testament in their tongue.[59] Although this was done primarily for religious purposes the BFBC, as a British organization, became instrumental in helping the Albanian national movement to spread its national awareness.

After many difficulties, 500 copies of the book of Matthew were published in 1824. Finally, in 1827, the whole New Testament was published in British-ruled Corfu and 2,000 copies were printed.[60] Although the Greek Orthodox Church tried to prevent its distribution, this version of the Bible became popular and until the end of the nineteenth century it saw several further publications. The Bible Society continued to regard Albania seriously and believed that 'furnishing the Albanians with the Bible was a worthy work'.[61] Translations continued with Konstandin Kristoforidhi (1827–95), who worked for the BFBC and translated the New Testament into both the Toskë and Gegë Albanian dialects. His Bible translations served as the basis for the modern Albanian language.[62] By 1858 BFBC published 4,000 copies of the New Testament printed in Albanian parallel with the Greek translation. The work continued, and between 1866 and 1872 around 15,000 copies were published in Albanian.[63]

This contribution was also noted by British diplomats in the region. In 1893 Vice-consul Shipley wrote from Manastir to Consul General Blunt in Salonika acknowledging the important role that the Bible played in developing the Albanian language as well as national and spiritual revival of the Albanians.[64] 'The Albanian was invaluable to the Bible Society, and the Bible Society was invaluable to the Albanians', wrote Durham in 1904 while she was employed in distributing the Bible. At that time the Porte had banned the distribution of books in Albanian, but the Bible was distributed from the main depot in Manastir, which was practically in Albanian hands.[65]

The Bible was even bought by Albanian Ottoman soldiers, Albanian Muslims who served in the Ottoman administration and Muslim school boys. The Bible became popular simply because it was a book in Albanian. Durham travelled throughout Albania with the colporteurs and observed that the Albanian nationalist movement was spreading. Their leaders welcomed the Bible and supported its distribution because they saw this as a help against the influence of the Greek Orthodox Church and, as such, part of developing their national cause.[66]

Another foreign support to the Albanian language and national movement came also from the nineteenth-century British travellers, such as William Leake, who published dictionaries or vocabularies. Leake, as most of the travellers of the nineteenth century, held that Albanian originates from Illyrian but he also explained why he and other British travellers were interested or should be interested in Albania and the Albanian language. It was because the place where the Albanian was spoken had contacts with British enemies which in reality were European countries, such as France, seeking a road to Greece through Albania. Therefore, as he explained, this was the reason to study the language of the Albanians which were a nation of 'uncivilized savages' but with extraordinary ability to fight for freedom and resist foreign occupation, 'a virtue that many civilised European nations did not possess'.[67]

Foreign travellers and academics offered characteristics which created a cultural image of Albanians. An image containing ancient and autochthonous elements with a language which stood close to ancient and civilized nations. This heritage played the same role in boosting national pride among Albanian intellectuals and national ideologists as did the similar links to the classical past among Greeks or Romanians. As a result, among the Albanians, particularly among the Albanians in Italy and foreign scholars, the study of Albanian language, history and folklore became more popular in Europe.[68] Albanian language was placed with Greek and Latin in one group: Indo-European. This showed the antiquity of the Albanians and their language. Therefore, it was widely welcomed by the Rilindja writers and ideologists like Sami Frashëri and Vaso Pasha.[69]

Yet the cultivation of the Albanian language and the advancement of the national movement could not go far without schools. As Hroch noted, schools of the nineteenth century were important in developing a national identity for two reasons: they provided room for the transfer of nationally formative information to the wider population and paved the way for a strong communication network by being an essential tool for attaining literacy.[70]

As the Porte did not envisage any ideas for Albanian schools, the first initiatives to open Albanian secular schools were taken during the 1830s by a group of Albanian intellectuals. They tried to establish schools in urbanized centres of northern Albania, including Kosovo. Several small private schools were set up in Shkodra and were financially supported by local businesses, but could not last long because of insufficient funds and the negative attitude of the local Ottoman administration. These schools revealed the concept of the national character which aimed to unite Albanians by excluding religious or regional distinctions.[71]

However, opportunities to open schools grew with the formation of the Albanian League in 1878. On 12 October 1879, a number of leading Albanian intellectuals called the Istanbul Society gathered in Constantinople to launch an organization they called *Shoqëria e të Shtypurit Shkronja Shqip* (Society for Printing Albanian Books). They adopted a plan which consisted of twenty-five points.[72] This was the first Albanian national organization to have ever been registered legally in the Ottoman Empire. The goal of the Society was to establish a standard language and publish books, journals and newspapers to be used and understood by all and to be distributed throughout Albania. The Society also aimed to translate important books into Albanian.[73]

If we add other activities, such as preparing teachers and opening new schools which were sanctioned in the Society's constitution, then we may conclude that this organization acted as the Ministry of Education of the Albanian League. The Istanbul Society was not under the dependency of the Albanian League in Prizren though they shared the same interest in education. Frashëri wrote that the work of politically unifying Albania was the duty of the League while the Society's work aimed to develop and refine the Albanian language, unify dialects and enlighten the nation.[74]

Unifying dialects, printing books and opening schools are a primarily cultural activity, but in the Albanian case it was also a political matter of national interest. However, the activities of the Istanbul Society were short-lived and ended after 1881 when the Porte subdued the Albanian League and all other nationalistic activities. Among the immediate measures taken was the banning of literature from entering Albania. Then, the Ottoman authorities turned against the Istanbul Society and disbanded it. Many members were prosecuted, some were interned in other places in the empire and some escaped punishment. The Patriarchate supported the actions of the Porte against the Albanian movement and through local churches in Albania, cursed and considered as heretics those Orthodox Albanians who used books in the Albanian language. On several occasions the Patriarchate had warned the Porte about the 'dangers' the leaders of the Istanbul Society were creating for the empire.[75]

With these measures, hopes of establishing Albanian schools that were once raised high were now lowered. The situation worsened after the brutal intervention of Dervish Pasha in northern Albania to subdue the Albanian League. *Drita* (Light) newspaper, which was published in Sofia, wrote:

> When he [Dervish Pasha] returned to Istanbul, he said to the Sultan: If permission is given to Albanians to learn their language together with the Christians, then not only shall Albanians and Albania escape from your hand, but Istanbul, too, is in danger. Not only must the Albanian language not be written and read, but every memory of this nation must also be erased and forgotten.[76]

It is hard to confirm if these were the exact words of Dervish Pasha spoken to the Sultan, but it is certain that this was how Rilindja activists wanted his actions to be perceived by Albanians. After 1881 the right to use and teach the language became a more nationalistic goal and therefore took a more aggressive attitude towards the Porte and neighbouring countries. At the same time the Albanians, their language and history were praised by Albanian writers. These writings were mainly poetry praising the Albanians as fighters for their freedom and out of love for their country. Vaso Pasha and Naim Frashëri were among the many poets who aimed to raise the national feeling and love for Albania.[77]

The Albanian school in Korça which was opened in 1887 was a result of many efforts by the Albanian intellectuals in Constantinople. It was soon followed as an example in some towns of south and central Albania. In the north it was not easy to open new schools before 1889, when only one was established in Prizren. However, the Austro Hungarians took a step that satisfied, to a degree, the leaders of the Albanian national movement. On the initiative of Theodor Anton Ippen (1861–1935), the Austro-Hungarian consul in Shkodra, Vienna took over all of the elementary schools and replaced the Italian language with Albanian.[78] Lajos Thallóczy, an adviser on the Balkans in the Austro-Hungarian court, wrote to the Minister of Finance Béni Kállay and proposed to cover the expenses for a project of Albanian education. The project aimed to print a new alphabet book, a series of books and to fund a newspaper. This plan aimed to diminish Italian influence and establish a firm Austro-Hungarian feeling among the Albanians. Other plans were also proposed and some were approved by the Austro-Hungarian government.[79]

In 1891 the brothers Naim and Sami Frashëri managed to get another licence from the Ottoman government for the opening of Shkolla e Vashave (School for Girls) in Korça. The Frashëri brothers also mentored and supported the education of future nationalist teachers such as Sevasti Qiriazi (1871–1949) who graduated from Robert College in Constantinople in 1891. On her graduation day, she wrote in her diary to describe herself and her feelings using nationalist vocabulary:

> I am an Albanian. This is the most important fact in my life. It is more important than my family because the conscience of this fact had awoken within me ideas, it taught me what to do and gave me the meaning of life.[80]

When the School for Girls was opened, Sevasti became a director. This was probably the most important school in the long history of Albanian education and was the only school which was not closed down by the Porte in 1904 when the Sultan, alarmed by the rise of Albanian nationalism, ordered the closure of all other schools. In 1909 the Young Turks again tried to close it down but did not succeed.[81] The School for Girls was supported financially and morally by British and American Protestant Missions and it is likely this fact which induced the Porte to leave it open. But the school was closed by the Greeks when in 1912 their army invaded Albania.

Most of the Rilindja writers agreed with Sami Frashëri and held that the origin of the Albanian language and the Albanians was Illyrian. Most of them had written on Skanderbeg and agreed in their regard for him as a national hero.[82] In only a decade the education system and national movements had made an impact on a considerable number of the urban population, but more remote rural areas remained untouched. Yet still this was some progress. By now a network of writers, readers, educational and political activists had been created not only in Albania but throughout the Ottoman Empire and European countries where Albanians resided. However, one major problem remained unresolved. Schools, although functioning, were using different alphabets. Regional and religious divisions were also obstacles which made the national movement slow. The reinstating of the constitution in 1908 offered a chance to the Albanian national movement to narrow these differences and standardize the alphabet. For a long time, the alphabet was a concrete expression of Albanian nationhood, while schools were regarded as an appropriate place for taming differences between groups.[83]

On 14 November 1908 hundreds of writers, journalists, teachers, language experts, publicists and clerics gathered in Manastir to take part in discussions about the Albanian alphabet. There were also students and ordinary members of the public who were interested in influencing the decision making process. During the first and second days of the meeting, which rather resembled a big assembly, many participants gave speeches but they spoke little about language or the alphabet. In their patriotic speeches, all expressed the need to create unity between the north and the south, Gegë and Toskë, Muslim and Christian, in order to create a single culture. This served the nationalist idea of one nation, one language and one alphabet. The meeting was opened by a Franciscan priest, pater Gjergj Fishta (1871–1940) who was a fierce nationalist. Pater Fishta had, until then, written extensively on national themes aiming to awaken Albanian nationalist feelings and was to become the 'national poet of Albania' or the 'Albanian Homer'. He gave an 'artistic expression to the searching soul of the Albanian nation'.[84] Because of these qualities, Fishta was chosen to give the opening speech which was, as expected, predominantly nationalistic.[85]

Of course, the alphabet was not an issue which was to be decided by the masses, yet even among the experts discussions were of a nationalist tone. The object and the importance of the congress were noted by a British diplomat:

> In November an Albanian National Congress assembled at Monastir, attended by fifty delegates, representing every section of the Albanian people – Musulman, Catholic and Orthodox. The ostensible object of the meeting was apparently elementary one of agreeing upon the adoption of a common alphabet, and the discussions were mainly literary; but the importance of the subject from a nationalist point of view is incontestable, the passion of a common medium of inter-communication being absolutely essential to the formation of a real national sentiment.[86]

As the report noted, the importance of the congress was not only to be seen in the context of education. It also had the political effect of further forging the bond of unity among Albanians and advancing their nationalist aims. The fact that the town of Manastir was chosen for the congress was political and laden with nationalist meaning. With this, the organizers of the congress wanted to transmit a message to Bulgarians, Macedonians and others that the town and the region was Albanian. The same message was sent to the Greeks when it was announced that the Second Congress of Alphabet would take place in Janina in 1910. The other importance was that during the congress participants also held secret meetings in order to organize against the Porte and those neighbouring countries that had territorial pretensions in Albania. In secret sessions, a national programme of eighteen points was approved. Shahin Kolonja, who was elected a member of the Ottoman Parliament, presented a programme for the autonomy of Albania which was widely supported by participants of the congress and intended to be presented to the Ottoman Parliament.[87]

The political achievement of the congress was arguably more important than its linguistic purpose and was in fact the primary goal of all participants who held nationalist ideas. However, this was not what the Young Turks expected nor desired. The Latin alphabet which was adopted by the Congress of Manastir caused new confrontations between Albanian nationalists and the Young Turks.

Counter-Revolution: Albanian nationalism vs Young Turkish nationalism

The Congress of Manastir initiated a conflict between Albanian nationalists and the Young Turks, who saw the activity around the development of the Albanian language as a way of advancing Albanian nationalism. From now on Albanian nationalists were not only struggling against Ottomanism but were faced with a new nationalism in the form of Turkism.

From the start the Young Turk ottomanist movement showed some presence of Turkish nationalist idea and for this reason some Albanian nationalists, including Ismail Bey Qemali, never fully cooperated with this organization. Turkish nationalists gained the upper hand in the movement after the Congress of Paris in 1902. Ahmed Riza, the CUP leader, increasingly replaced the term 'Ottoman' with 'Turk' and this further shifted attention from Ottoman to Turkish nationalism. By the end of 1908 the Young Turk movement had undergone this transformation and, in the process, changed its policies and even its symbols become increasingly Turkish.[88]

As a result of this increase in Turkism, Sami Frashëri's work on defining the nation as an 'ethno linguistic category based on historic primordial races' became increasingly attractive for Albanian nationalists. Frashëri called for the revival of the literary works that were written, using the Latin alphabet, between the fifteenth and seventeenth centuries by Albanian priests. In this vein he characterized Pjetër Bogdani's work as important and described it as 'written in a very clean literary language' which should be considered as the basis of the Albanian language.[89]

Frashëri seems to have influenced Yusuf Akçura (1876–1939) who was working on developing Turkish nationalism. Akçura called for abandoning Ottomanism as a failed state ideology of the Tanzimat era, strengthening Turkish nationalism or Pan-Turkism and making Islam subservient to Turkism. He was convinced that Islam should not to be abandoned but used as a strong link between nationalities of the empire.[90] Thus, Frashëri and Akçura believed that multiple ethno-linguistic nations were in conflict with each other and must fight for their survival. This theory, which was based on 'proto-Darwinian understanding,' rejected Ottomanism as an outdated ideology.[91] Contributing further to the theory of national ideology in ethno-linguistic terms, Licursi wrote:

> Akçura and Sami advocated for a more exclusive notion of national identity, than ever conceived in Ottomanism, because for them it was the only foreseeable option in the face of structural ideological trends and the acute threat of nationalist movements on their borders. That is, both to keep up with Europe and the ever-encroaching nationalisms on Ottoman borderlands, both Albanians and Turks needed to adopt similar nationalist strategies for their survival as nations, even if that meant abandoning Ottomanism and the Empire, as such.[92]

Although it is likely that Frashëri and Akçura wanted a peaceful relationship between Albanians and Turks, their ideas led to an inevitable confrontation between the two nationalities. However, there was a point on which both thinkers disagreed. Frashëri advocated for an autonomous or independent Albania, while Akçura insisted that the Turks could fit into the Ottoman state by applying Turkist aims and ideas without rejecting Islam. Since religion was not a unifying factor for Albanians, Frashëri promoted a secular Albanian nationalism but both ideologies went on to undermine the idea of Ottomanism.[93]

It is not clear if Akçura and other Turkish ideologists regarded Albanians as a nationality that could embrace their pan Turkish ideology, but it was obvious that Albanian nationalists were not going to entertain such ideas. This theoretical development had an impact on the relationship between Albanian nationalists and Ottoman or Turkish nationalists, which came into view in the debates of the Ottoman parliament. Even before the elections and the Congress of Manastir took place, relations between the Albanians and the Young Turks had started to deteriorate.

The Young Turk Revolution created a strong shift in the organization of elites from many ethnic groups or nationalities in the Ottoman Empire. The Albanian conservative elite had benefitted from the Sultan's regime. However, the Young Turk Revolution changed this situation by replacing conservatives with an intellectual nationalist elite with leaders such as Hasan Prishtina (1873–1933), Mufid Libohova, Nexhib Draga and many others. Regarding this change, Hanioğlu noted:

> All of these aimed at uniting Albanians of three different faiths under the flag of Skënderbeu [Skanderbeg] and called for reforms for the benefit of all Albanians.[94]

The Albanian nationalism and the Young Turk movement were elitist ideologies and did not make a fast or significant impact on the masses. The unrest in northern Albania started immediately after the Young Turk Revolution and had little to do with nationalism. A British diplomatic report noted that the restored constitution was not a 'fortnight old' when the Porte had to dispatch the army to Kosovo in order to suppress the 'reactionary movement' of Isa Boletini.[95] Boletini, along with a group of conservatives, was committed to fighting the Young Turks out of fear that they would lose benefits and privileges given by the Sultan. Albanian nationalists took the side of the Porte or the Young Turks because they wanted to get rid of conservatives such as Boletini, who was becoming an obstacle not only to the Porte but also to the Albanian nationalist idea. Boletini, along with other conservatives such as Hasan Budakova, Hasan Shllaku and Rrustem Kabashi, rose again against the Young Turks in November 1908. They expelled the judicial authorities, the police and the rest of the administration and announced that they would not accept the constitution. A considerable force was sent against them and their movement was promptly suppressed.[96]

Isa Boletini, although a conservative and a fierce Ottomanist, was becoming a hero simply because he was seen as a fighter against the Young Turks who had turned against Albanian nationalism. Where Albanian nationalists and Young Turks could not 'sell' their ideas because the population was widely illiterate, Isa Boletini could raise an army against the Porte. Therefore, Albanian nationalist leaders had no choice other than to co-opt Boletini for their own aims and bring him into their midst. In the years to come, Boletini became the commander of the Albanian army that fought for autonomy and later independence, with Kosovo and Macedonia as the battle ground.

For Albanians in Shkodra, Esat Pasha Toptani was one of the many reasons they became disappointed with the Young Turks. Esat turned out to be a secret member of the Young Turk movement and maintained the position of the commander of the gendarmerie. There was no change of local functionaries and all hopes and faith of Shkodra inhabitants in the new regime were shattered. A Shkodranes told Edith Durham: 'The Young Turks are the sons of the old ones.'[97] On another occasion, on the subject of the new regime of the Young Turks, Durham was also told that 'the Turk is always a Turk'.[98]

The situation in the *vilayet* of Shkodra led an Albanian delegation, composed of both Muslims and Christians, to travel to Salonika to confer with the CUP leaders but there was no mutual understanding in their discussion of the situation. There were also problems with those Albanian Young Turks who returned from exile. Ibrahim Temo, the Young Turk Number One, was surprised when he returned home and was told by a Young Turk activist, Ahmet Cemal Bey (1872–1922) that the CUP had changed and was creating a society which was not something he had worked for abroad.[99] When Dervish Hima, also a well-known nationalist intellectual and a Young Turk, returned from exile, he delivered a nationalist speech at a banquet given in his honour by the Young Turk Committee. In his speech he said that 'the Albanians would never unite with the Turks'. The next day he was arrested.[100]

Meanwhile, national problems in Macedonia resurfaced again. The Bulgarian Internal Organisation of the *vilayet* of Manastir held a congress to demand 'autonomy for Macedonia as a whole' but proclaimed to respect the integrity of the Ottoman Empire.[101] The Bulgarian initiative caused worries among Albanian leaders because they were not seen as an important element in Macedonia. Difficulties were mounting and the Young Turks, as well as Albanian nationalists, were hoping that their problems would be solved by the parliament in a democratic way.

In September 1908 a British army officer, together with two Albanian Young Turk heroes, Enver and Nijazi Bey, toured the city of Salonika in a coach followed by a huge cheering crowd. Being aware of the serious problems that the ethnic groups or nationalities were facing in Macedonia, Enver Bey asked the crowd to aid the CUP by not putting obstacles in their way and 'awaiting the assembly of the parliament to settle their grievances'. He added that the 'CUP was one body'.[102]

Elections and the parliament would prove that this was not the case. Before the elections were held, the CUP revealed its political programme which appeared to be committed to Ottomanism but in reality was further promoting Turkism. Their political programme revealed that Turkish would become the official language of the empire,[103] a plan which had a negative impact on Albanians and led their language to be attacked by the CUP.

The debates of the first sessions of the Ottoman parliament brought into view the efforts of deputies who wanted to differentiate themselves from other nationalities or ethnicities by language, culture, religion and historical importance. They saw this act as a way of advancing their nationalist ideology as it was important for nationalist representatives of the Albanians, Greeks, Bulgarians and Macedonians to prove that they were not only different from each other but moreover that they were not Turks. Thus, the Ottoman parliament became a venue in which the nationalist movements of the empire expressed themselves.[104]

The fiercest debates fought and the harshest language used in the parliament were between Albanians and those who regarded themselves as Ottomans or Turks. Mufid Bey Libohova (1876-1927), later to become foreign minister of Albania, mentioned the word *Arnavutlar* (Albanians) while speaking in the parliament.[105] At that moment Ahmed Riza, the president of the parliament, interrupted Libohova by shouting: *Arnavutlar Yok. Hepimiz Osmanliyiz* (There are no Albanians. We are all Ottomans). '*Var, efendem, var!*' (There are, Sir, there are!), answered Libohova, together with other Albanian deputies who rose from their seats to protest against Riza. The phrase 'There are, Sir, there are!' became popular and was used by Albanian nationalists as a slogan.[106]

At the beginning of 1909, the Young Turks started to act against the result of the Congress of Manastir. The Young Turks took actions to try to convince the Albanians to retain Ottoman letters. On 4 February 1909, the Young Turks organized an assembly in a Bektashi monastery in Tepelena, southern Albania. In order to gain Albanian support, the CUP portrayed itself as a guarantor of Albanian territorial integrity against Greek expansionist intentions. To the surprise of the Young Turks, the only question the Albanian leaders wanted to discuss was the autonomy of the four Albanian *vilayets*. In the end, the organizers of the assembly did not endorse the proposal. The assembly was conducted in secret and so the British, who had no diplomatic representation in south Albania, had no information about the agenda and outcome of the meeting. Lamb, the British consul in Salonika, asked Stranieri, the

Italian consul at Prevesa, for information. When Lamb was informed, he interpreted Albanian actions as nationalistic. He added:

> They [Albanians] are working by every means in their power, including the formation of bands, to affect the 'Albanianisation' of the Christian population.[107]

It is not clear what Lamb meant by the 'Albanianization' of the Christians but one may presume that he wanted to explain that Albanian nationalists were working against the process of Hellenization of the Albanian Orthodox population. However, it was obvious that the Assembly of Tepelana had shown, yet again, the problem which existed between the Albanians and the Young Turks. The political position of the Albanian leaders 'diluted Young Turk illusions' and brought back 'the implications and particularities of the Albanian Question'.[108]

The Ottoman parliamentary democracy was barely three months old when dissatisfaction against the Young Turks in Constantinople became public and increased significantly. Of all the nationalities the most dissatisfied were the Albanians, who now became a target of the Young Turk's anti-Albanian policies. The press campaigns for and against the Young Turks increased rapidly. One of the fiercest enemies of the Young Turks was the newspaper *Serbesti*. The editor in chief was an Albanian called Hasan Fehmi Bey (1874–1909) who was killed on 6 April by a Young Turk officer acting on behalf of the CUP.[109] Fehmi Bey was assassinated under similar circumstances and most likely for the same reason as another Albanian nationalist, Ismail Mahir Pasha. More than 5000 mourners took part in Fehmi Bey's funeral and expressed their anger at the CUP's efforts to restrict the liberty of the press. Among them were not only Albanians but many liberal deputies, Muslim clerics and a great number of theological students. The agitation did not end with the funeral but continued to manifest indignation with the new regime.[110] Many mourners wanted revenge and this served as a cause of important upcoming events. Fehmi Bey's work against the CUP may have been the result of the anti-Albanian policy of the Young Turks, but his death was taken by a wide population of Constantinople, mostly conservative and religious, as cause to launch a counter-revolution.

The CUP also showed open hostility towards Ismail Bey and other Albanian deputies. Acting out of fear of the Albanians, the CUP dismissed the Albanian Imperial Guard. The CUP declared that they had to take such a decision as they had information that the Guard was plotting to kill Ahmed Riza and his supporters.[111] In reality the CUP wanted to strip the Sultan of his powers and simultaneously to weaken Albanian influence in the Palace. The Imperial Guard had been an important Albanian institution in Constantinople so their dismissal came as a big blow to the Albanians and contributed as another reason for the Albanians to join the counter-revolutionary movement which had already begun.

On 13 April a unit of Albanian soldiers and officers, probably acting at the request of Ismail Bey Qemali, seized the House of Parliament. A group of deputies, dominated by liberals of the Ahrar Party and religious exponents, which also became known as the Counter Revolutionary Group, gathered in the parliament and, headed by Ismail Bey, issued a six-point demand. Points 3 and 4 were of essential importance: 3. Ahmed

Riza, President of the Chamber, should be dismissed and replaced by Ismail Bey; 4. The expulsion of leading members of the CUP from Constantinople.[112]

However, it was time for Enver and Nijazi Bey to protect their regime and the constitution they had contributed to reinstating a few months earlier. They mobilized Albanian troops and volunteers and joined the commander of the Third Army based in Salonika, Mahmud Shevket Pasha, the former *vali* (governor) of Kosovo. The constitutional army of 20,000 regulars and 15,000 volunteers entered Constantinople on 24 April and easily secured the city. As Ismail Bey had played a prominent role in the counter-revolution, the CUP accused him of being 'privy and accessory to the reactionary movement' and demanded his head. As before, Ismail Bey turned to his friends, the British embassy and the Khedive dynasty, for help. He was swiftly evacuated to Greece but returned within a few weeks when the parliament reassembled and resumed the role of leading the opposition.[113]

The counter-revolution and the evacuation of Ismail Bey to Greece exposed a problem which existed between Albanian conservative and nationalist leaders and which was noted by British diplomats who monitored Ismail Bey's activities. The British consul in Salonika reported that a delegation of Albanian conservatives had travelled to the city to confer with CUP leaders when it became known that the counter-revolution was about to fail. Albanian conservatives demanded assurances that no harm would be caused to the Sultan and to Ismail Qemali's liberals who had led the counter-revolution.[114] On the other side, Albanian nationalists and Young Turks members, who opposed the counter-revolution, feared that Ismail Bey was about to travel to south Albania to organize an insurrection. Political activists of the Bashkimi Club in Manastir sent telegrams to all the clubs in south Albania asking Albanian patriots to be aware of Ismail Bey's activities and not to entertain his suggestions. The British consul wrote that Albanian nationalist leaders regarded Ismail Bey as a 'noxious abominable individual who has associated himself with enemies of his country'. Furthermore, from Lamb's dispatches it can be seen that Ismail Bey tried to cross into Albania from Greece but gave up, probably because of fear of reinforced Ottoman troops and Albanian nationalists who mobilized to block his activities.[115]

However, in Constantinople the Sultan was probably delighted with the short-lived result of the counter-revolution. He was at the centre of the conflict and the Young Turks, being aware of this fact, decided to take drastic measures against him. On 27 April the CUP took the decision to dethrone the Sultan. A group of four CUP members was sent to inform the Sultan about the decision: two Albanians, a Jew and an Armenian.[116] One of the Albanians was Esat Pasha, who had found a way to enter the group and even managed to be appointed as the one who would communicate the bad news to the Sultan. Finally, Esat Pasha found himself in front of the terrified Sultan and spoke the words: 'Abdul, the nation hath pronounced thee deposed'.[117] No other Albanian had benefitted from the Sultan more than Esat Pasha and his Toptani family. Terrified and betrayed, the Sultan was heard whispering 'you are a wicked man'.[118] The Sultan's policy of ruling Albania by favouring powerful Albanian families proved to be a failure.

In a hasty ceremony and in extreme simplicity, Mahmud V (Abdul Hamid's brother) was appointed the new Sultan. The street the Sultan passed from the place of the ceremony to the Palace was lined with a battalion of Albanian soldiers, commanded by Nijazi Bey,[119] who wanted to show that Albanians still mattered in Constantinople. In reality, with the departure of Abdul Hamid II, the Albanians had lost their power and influence in the Ottoman Empire for ever. Abdul Hamid was sent into exile with his family to Salonika.[120] However, Albanian conservatives made plans to rescue and return him to power.

Only a few days after Abdul Hamid was deposed at the end of April 1909, the Young Turks turned against the Albanians in Kosovo. The Albanians had rebelled against the Young Turks and armed men gathered in Ferizaj to demand the abolition of the new taxes. As the Young Turks had broken their promises, Albanians took the decision to fight their regime.[121] A force of 5,000 Ottoman soldiers was sent to pacify them under the command of Cavit Pasha. After two months of fierce fighting and the destruction of many villages, Cavit declared a victory. In reality he had not achieved his goal and as such a new campaign was started in September. The resistance of armed Albanians grew intensively and he was forced to retreat from Kosovo.[122]

The Albanians were rejecting the Young Turks whom they had helped come to power, a fact which caused some confusion and worry among British diplomats. The British ambassador in Vienna, Fairfax Cartwright, asked the Greek diplomat Manos for information regarding the 'attitude' the Albanians had adopted against the Porte. Manos told Cartwright that his government was monitoring Albania with great interest. He added that Albanians had no sympathy for the Young Turks and the Albanian movement for autonomy 'would spread like wildfire throughout that Province'.[123]

The Greek diplomat hoped that the Albanians would turn towards Greece and favour the creation of an autonomous government under the personal suzerainty of the Greek king. He also told Cartwright that the Greek government, through their schools, 'has built a strong link of sympathy between the two countries'. The Greek diplomat expressed the view of his government and pointed out that the autonomy of Albania was to become a serious problem for Greece and other Balkan countries. This information did not seem to have been taken seriously by Cartwright or Grey. Cartwright even wrote that the 'Greeks open their mouths wide'.[124]

However, in Kosovo and Macedonia the campaign of Cavit Pasha caused the majority of Albanians to stop believing in the Young Turk's policy. Yet at the same time, the Young Turks strengthened their relations with the Serbs, their new ally in Kosovo. In 1908 in Skopje, under the leadership of Bogdan Radenković (1874–1917) and with Young Turk approval, the Serbs established the Organisation of Ottoman Serbs. This organization spread its branches in Macedonia and Kosovo and also published a newspaper named *Vardar* with the purpose of supporting the Young Turks. *Vardar* unconditionally supported the Young Turk policy against the Albanian Latin alphabet. The Organisation of Ottoman Serbs kept an open relationship with Serbian paramilitary forces[125] and in August 1908 the Austro-Hungarian consul in Prizren reported that the local Serbs were actively taking part as members of Young Turk organizations in the town and the region.[126] Another report spoke of the Srpska Demokratska Liga (Serbian Democratic League) being formed in Skopje and spreading quickly throughout the *vilayet* of Kosovo.[127]

When the punitive mission of Cavit Pasha failed, another Ottoman force was sent to Kosovo in spring 1910 when a revolt broke out, again because of taxes, under leadership of Isa Boletini and Idriz Seferi (1847–1927) who had gathered 9,000 armed men. The Porte sent a strong army under the command of Shevket Durgut Pasha, which clashed with Albanian insurgents who had blocked the railway from Macedonia. But the biggest battle took place in Carraleva, central Kosovo, where the Ottoman army was repelled. In difficult moments, the Ottomans were helped by the local Serbs who knew a shortcut over the mountains which forced the Albanians to withdraw before becoming encircled.[128] Boletini and Seferi escaped capture but many thousands were killed, imprisoned and interned. Durgut Pasha, now with a force of 40,000, continued westwards to Shkodra to disarm the Albanians and subdue northern parts of Albania.[129]

When the campaign was over, the Young Turks proclaimed martial law. They closed down Albanian schools and prohibited publications in Albanian. With this, the Young Turks broke the last and most important promise they had made in Ferizaj two years earlier. This enraged the few remaining Albanians who might have still believed in Young Turk policies. The CUP annual congress was held in October 1910 in Salonika. No Albanian delegate was present.[130] With their absence, the Albanians demonstrated that reaching a peaceful agreement with the Young Turks was impossible.

The confrontation between the Young Turks and the Albanians brought to light a new problem which would result in major changes and bring into question the very existence of the Ottoman Empire. The growing and increasingly consolidated Albanian nationalism was now battling a new nationalism: Turkism. Therefore, disagreements between the Albanians and the Young Turks that started over language and initially manifested as confrontations in the press, parliament and other forums, culminated into armed conflict and produced consequences for the entire Balkan region.

6

From autonomy to independence

The insurrection of 1911

After the Congress of Berlin, the existence of the increasingly weak Ottoman Empire depended on the position that the European Powers took on the Eastern Question. The Porte had particularly counted on British support. Other nationalities, especially the Albanians, continued with efforts to win the British over to their side. Although for different reasons, both Ottoman officials and Albanian nationalists wanted British support. The Ottomans believed that British support would strengthen their empire. The Albanians maintained that with British support they would gain autonomy or independence, a fact which would weaken the Ottoman Empire and consequently would end the Porte's rule in Europe.

In January 1911, under the initiative of the Albanian nationalist writer Nikollë Ivanaj (1879–1951), an organization called the Albanian Republican Committee was formed in Podgorica, Montenegro. The aim of the Committee was to organize a general uprising which would include Albanian organizations abroad. Ivanaj moved to Bari in southern Italy to continue his attempts to attract the help of local Albanian communities and the support or sympathy of the Italian government. Hopes increased when another committee called Pro Albania was formed a few weeks later by Albanians and Italian supporters of the Albanian national cause. Ivanaj's initiative was supported by Italian Albanians and soon attracted the sympathy of republicans, socialists and other Italian politicians who joined Pro Albania, which was soon able to gather the backing of sixty members of the Italian Parliament. The Committee also collected money, arms and registered thousands of volunteers who expressed readiness to cross the Adriatic under the command of Ricciotti Garibaldi, Giuseppe Garibaldi's son, and help Albanian insurgents in the north. Albanians in Italy also lobbied for the support of the Italian government, but the initiative was cut short. The Italian government was planning an invasion of Libya and was not interested in helping anyone with the intention of intervening in Albania because it could jeopardize relations with Austria-Hungary. Therefore, within a short time, the Italian government ordered all activities of Pro Albania to be stopped.[1]

Meanwhile, Albanian leaders who resided in territories of the Ottoman Empire continued with preparations for a general uprising and attracting the attention of the Powers in order to involve them in solving the Albanian Question. Ismail

Qemali contacted European Powers to inform them about their plans.² The Powers, particularly Austria-Hungary, on whom Albanian leaders counted the most, were not pleased with this initiative. When it became clear that there would be no help from the Powers, Albanian leaders turned to their neighbouring countries. Ivanaj kept in touch with Garibaldi but moved to operate from Belgrade and tried to get support from the Serbian government.³ After a short time Ivanaj moved to Sofia, from where he tried to bring together the Albanian leaders. His intention was to revive Shoqënia e Zezë (the Black Society) which had been formed in 1878. From Sofia Ivanaj, together with five other activists, issued a declaration announcing the formation of the Komiteti Qendror i Shqipërisë (Central Committee of Albania) and asked other leaders to join.⁴ Throughout 1911 there were high levels of communication between many Albanian leaders but they did not succeed in creating a single body to represent the whole country as they had planned but rather acted in several small groups or individually.

Ismail Qemali contacted the Greek embassy in Constantinople and sent a message to the Greek government about the insurrection, which was expected to take place in the spring. The Greek government promised Qemali money, arms and ammunition.⁵ However, none of these were ever delivered to the Albanians.

Isa Boletini went to Montenegro and received Serbian delegations on several occasions with the aim of forming an alliance with Serbia, Montenegro and Greece. Boletini continually met Serbian officials and army officers until late August 1912 when he hosted a delegation headed by Colonel Apis who, a few months earlier, had formed the secret organization 'The Black Hand' (Crna Ruka). Apis was sent by Serbia's Prime Minister Nikola Pašić with the proposal that Serbia would fully support an Albanian insurrection against the Porte if they agreed to join Serbia after the region was liberated.⁶

The Serbian and Montenegrin governments agreed to supply the Albanian insurgents with a certain amount of arms, but no political agreement or military alliance was reached. Although they did not manage to secure the support of the Great Powers, the Albanians of Malësia (the northern mountains) began their insurrection in March 1911. Their proclaimed aims were self-government, for Albanian schools to be maintained by the Porte and for Albanian soldiers to serve only in Albania⁷ but the insurrection failed to spread across the country and as such did not achieve its goals. Although the Albanian leaders did not succeed in widening the insurrection, Serbia, Greece and Montenegro increasingly saw the Albanian efforts for autonomy as a threat to their own national aspirations. For this reason, these three governments saw the Albanian efforts for autonomy as a common problem and would soon take joint action.⁸

Since the insurrection did not engulf Kosovo and Macedonia, the Young Turks sought to show the Powers that the Porte was in control of its Balkan territories and the situation in most parts of Albania was peaceful. To such end, the Sultan visited these two regions in June 1911 in an effort to restore Ottoman prestige, stop the uprising and reach a reconciliation with the Albanians.⁹

The Sultan and the Young Turks were aware that the internationalization of the Albanian Question would create a problem for the Porte and they were therefore determined to demonstrate that the Macedonian and Albanian Questions were simply internal matters of the Porte. When the Sultan arrived in Skopje, he stated that the aim of the visit was to encourage a mutual understanding between ethnic groups in the region. He praised the Young Turks for their contribution to bringing ethnic groups closer. However, as was revealed in Skopje, the main aim of the Sultan's visit was to tend to the Albanians and the territories inhabited by them. The Sultan was pleased to see around 5000 Albanians cheering his visit in Skopje, yet the Young Turks made a considerable effort to 'engineer this Albanian enthusiasm'.[10]

The Young Turks had hoped to rebuild their damaged ties with the Albanians and reach a reconciliation with their leaders but none of the Albanian leaders attended the ceremony or wished to meet the Sultan. The Sultan's visit took place without incident, yet although according to the British Embassy in Constantinople it ended as 'an unqualified success'.[11]

Despite the political failings of the visit with regard to the Albanian Question, the Sultan and the Young Turks did manage to strengthen relations with the Serbs. Although it was expected that the visit would anger the Serbs, who considered Kosovo as sacred and important to their national identity, on this occasion they saw the Ottomans as friends and the Albanians as the source of danger.

Serbia publicly appeared as a friend of the Porte but secretly was preparing for war. Only a few months after the Sultan's visit to Macedonia and Kosovo, Serbia and Bulgaria reached a military agreement against the Ottoman and Austro-Hungarian empires. The mutual agreement, signed in March 1912, recognized Serbian interests in Kosovo and Albania, and Bulgarian interests in Thrace, demonstrating that interest in Macedonia and Albania was increasing. If the programme of autonomy for Macedonia was to fail, then both countries would partition the region. Bulgaria would take southern Macedonia while Serbia would take the north. Skopje, then the capital of the *vilayet* of Kosovo, was considered as a disputed zone on which the Russians would act as arbitrators.[12] This bilateral understanding was later supported by Montenegro and Greece and, after another series of agreements, the Balkan League was formed by the end of 1912.

From the perspective of the Young Turks, the uprising and the failure of the Sultan's visit made them consider the Albanian national requests more seriously. During the CUP Annual Congress, which was held in Salonika at the end of September and beginning of October 1911, the Young Turks made a secret decision regarding the Albanian Question. In the future the Albanians were to be allowed to use their language but it was also decided that a number of *hojas* (Muslim priests) would be sent to open schools in Albania and propagate against the Latin alphabet that the Albanians had adopted. The Young Turks decided to help strengthen Albanian nationalism but they only did this in order to weaken Greek nationalism, evidence of which can be seen through their decision to support Christian Orthodox Albanians wishing to separate from the Greek Church. Prayers in Albanian, which were not allowed in Greek Churches, were to be promoted. The list of decisions taken during the Congress regarding the Albanian Question was long and was regarded by a British diplomatic report as a way of 'fostering and spreading hatred' against the Greeks and their Orthodox Church.[13]

Although the Albanian leaders failed to organize a general uprising, their attempt alarmed the Powers and neighbouring states. The failure of the uprising demonstrated that the Albanians lacked a strong and united leadership but Albanian leaders did manage to draft and distribute their political programme to the international arena. On 23 June 1911 in Greça, a village in northern Albania, under the leadership of Ismail Qemali and Luigj Gurakuqi (1879–1925), a memorandum was distributed to the consular and diplomatic representatives of the Powers in Montenegro. Two of the main requests of the memorandum were autonomy and the recognition of Albanians as a nation.[14] The memorandum, which became known as the '12 Points Memorandum', had considerable resonance in the European and British press.

Changes in British and Austro-Hungarian policy

The British government continued to disregard Albanian efforts for their national ambitions and instead paid considerable attention to the situation which reappeared in Macedonia. Noel Baxton, the Chairman of the Balkan Committee, had visited Macedonia and in an interview published in the *Daily News* gave a grim outlook for the region. Baxton also published a letter with similar views in *The Times*.[15] As a result of several more articles of this nature, Macedonia came up as a matter to be discussed in the British Parliament. Macedonia was characterized as a dangerous place because of incidents that had happened between the armed bands that had reappeared after the Young Turk Revolution. Macedonia also became a subject matter between Ottoman, Austro-Hungarian and British diplomats in London. Although these incidents created a bad impression about the Porte's rule, Ottoman diplomats hoped that this would not change Britain's 'positive attitude towards the Sublime Porte'. The Ottomans also hoped that the situation would not give pretext to any of the powers wishing to 'exploit incidents' in Macedonia.[16] However, Albanians in Macedonia and their activity in northern Albania, where they were engaged in preparing an insurrection, were not seen as dangerous acts and, therefore, not discussed in the British Parliament nor by the diplomats.

In London, the press gave priority to British-Ottoman trade relations which were also of concern to the British government. After the Baghdad railway concessions were given to the Germans, Edward Grey was not happy but he expected a fair-trade treatment within the Ottoman Empire and to safeguard the dominant position in the Persian Gulf.[17] The British and Ottoman members of both parliaments believed that the two countries were nourishing a good relationship. In June 1911 an Ottoman parliamentary delegation led by two well-known politicians and intellectuals, Riza Tevfik Bey and Suleiman Bustani, took part in the Universal Races Congress held in London.[18] The guests were welcomed by Lord Weardale, chair of the Eastern Association, who said that they had every sympathy for the efforts being made to improve the Ottoman Empire and praised the work of the Young Turks. Admiral Fremantle spoke about the support that the British government had offered to the Ottomans during the past century and added that the Ottomans could still count on British assistance.[19]

Earlier, in mid-June 1911, a British parliamentary delegation had visited the Ottoman Parliament and both parties agreed that the Young Turk policy was on the right track. In the House of Commons, the British delegation reported that the Albanian Question 'ought to be dealt with promptly and in the spirit of conciliation'. The speaker of the House of Commons did not believe that the Albanians desired separation from the Ottoman government and 'under no circumstances could the [Ottoman] government submit to the dictation of others'. The Ottomans assured the British that the Albanian Question was not religious in nature since there was no fanaticism and Albanians were good Ottomans. When this sentence was heard in the House of Commons all members cheered loudly.[20] However, Lord Weardale, Admiral Fremantle and both parliamentary delegations were not aware that the Foreign Office and the British Government had started to change their policy towards the Porte. This change started to take root during the Albanian insurrection of 1911.

Initially, the Albanian insurrection of 1911 did not receive much attention in London. The reports that were sent to the Foreign Office from the British Embassy in Constantinople expressed hope or indeed confidence, that the Porte would be able to crush the Albanian insurgency. This view was similar to the one expressed in the Young Turk press which ignored the scale of the Albanian uprising.[21]

The British government did not take a stance on this matter because it waited to see the reactions of Austria-Hungary and Italy. However, in May 1911, when the uprising seemed to be spreading and reports began to appear in the press, the Foreign Office started to view the ability of the Porte with doubt and pessimism. The British view of Ottoman policy started to change, but not entirely in favour of the Albanians. The British government believed that the Young Turks should change their policy of Ottomanization out of fear that Albanian rejection of the policy could spread the insurrection to other regions. When the uprising spread further to northern Albania, the British government started to show more attention to the reports being sent to the Foreign Office by Edith Durham. Their attention grew further still when reports were published by newspapers, many of which caused some trouble within the Foreign Office when some officials expressed their belief that Durham was deliberately spreading 'Turcophobia'.[22]

After the '12 Point Memorandum'[23] had reached the Foreign Office at the end of June, Albanian insurgents sent a letter to Edward Grey, which was prepared by Durham and a French journalist. Two other dispatches that were sent to the Foreign Office from Montenegro by British diplomats earlier that month seemed to have put pressure on Edward Grey. Grey was informed that the Albanian insurgents, advised by Ismail Bey Qemali, would not surrender to the Porte without a guarantee from the Powers.[24] Other sources showed that the Montenegrin government was worried about the spread of the Albanian insurrection and did not favour the involvement of the British government. On this matter Grey pointed out that 'the alternative of doing nothing may lead to a situation in the Balkans that may be very disagreeable'.[25]

Therefore, Grey decided to act and deal with the Albanian request believing that the petition which had been addressed to the Foreign Office was public property; he saw no need to conceal it from the public. He maintained that the Ottoman government should express readiness to meet the wishes of the Albanians. Yet he also thought that it was possible that other Powers, specifically Austria-Hungary, may not be pleased by the fact that the Albanians had appealed to the British government for help. Hence, Grey felt that the British government should not deal with this matter on its own and so decided to involve all the Powers. He ordered his ambassadors in Vienna, Paris, St. Petersburg, Rome and Berlin to ask the respective governments for a joint representation to the Porte.[26] Ambassadors were also told to inform the foreign ministers of these Powers that the British government agreed with the Albanian request for limited autonomy, but in order to make things easier for the Powers, emphasized that the Albanians did not request independence.[27]

Surprisingly, the Russians supported Grey's plan. Neratow, the acting Russian foreign minister, told O'Beirne, the British ambassador in St. Petersburg, that he doubted whether the Albanians would be satisfied with less than full autonomy but agreed to join the British proposal. O'Beirne suggested that Vienna might take actions on its own if the Albanian insurrection continued because of the pressure which was being built by the Austro-Hungarian press. Neratow, claiming to have further information, assured O'Beirne that the Austro-Hungarians would not take up arms on behalf of the Albanians and would rather employ diplomatic means.[28]

While Austria-Hungary and Italy also joined Britain and Russia, this was not the case with Germany and France. The German government thought that Grey's proposal was based on 'good grounds tending to preserve peace' but felt that such a proposal constituted an interference in internal Ottoman affairs which would lead to a 'policy of intervention which died out with the old regime'. Thus, the Germans maintained that collective interventions would harm the Porte and would encourage 'unruly elements in Albania' and so the answer from Berlin was negative.[29]

The French rejected the proposal for the same reasons as the Germans and, in addition, maintained that there was little point supporting the British initiative if the Germans had already refused it. However, in Constantinople Lowther had reason to believe that the Germans had informed the Ottomans about Grey's initiative for Albanian autonomy, even though it was supposed to be secret.[30] Despite the fact that any joint representation of the Powers did not intend to request full autonomy for the Albanians, it was interpreted as a step towards such goal by the Porte and was therefore greeted with annoyance. More importantly, this moment was a pivotal step in the British government's abandonment of its friendly policy towards the Porte. The initiative on behalf of the Albanians led the Ottomans to have one more serious reason to distance themselves from the British and seek closer relations with the Germans.

Meanwhile, during the summer of 1911, when the insurrection was about to fail, some of the Albanian leaders, headed by Hasan Prishtina, did not give up their hope for British support. Hasan Prishtina, like all other Albanian leaders, was not aware of Grey's secret diplomatic efforts that had ended without success. Therefore, in late July, Prishtina approached the British consulate in Skopje for help telling vice consul Hugh that Albanian leaders were about to widen the insurrection and would listen to any advice the British government would offer.[31] According to the registered communication, Hugh informed Lowther about this meeting almost two months after it had taken place. By then, it was clear that Grey would not intervene in the Porte's affairs surrounding the Albanian insurrection. Therefore, the British advice for Hasan Prishtina was that the Albanian leaders should approach the Porte to address their problems by peaceful means. 'A general uprising,' as Lowther wrote, would be unfavourable to the Albanians.[32]

In autumn 1911 the chairman of the Macedonian Relief Fund, the well-known British journalist and war correspondent in the Balkans, Henry W. Nevinson, visited north Albania and published an article about the villages which had suffered under the latest Ottoman military intervention.[33] Articles, describing the difficult situation in north Albania and the mistreatment of Catholic Albanians by the Young Turk government, were numerous and seemed to have created an impact on governments.[34] The religious dimension of the situation was still considered important, following the longstanding trend of interpreting Balkan affairs through the prism of religion.

The Albanian uprising was not interpreted as an Ottoman or Albanian victory but it changed the British position towards the Near Eastern question. This change meant that, in the future, pessimistic reports about the Porte would become more acceptable by the British government[35] but such reports did not necessarily help the Albanian national movement. Apart from Durham's reports, there was other pessimistic information which originated in Serbia and was becoming more acceptable by the Foreign Office. One such example was the 'prognosis' of the Serbian Prime Minister Milovanović, who maintained that the break-up of the Ottoman Empire would come soon and from within.

Throughout 1909 Milovanović had developed an idea with regard to the 'Sanjak and the Albanian problem', as he called it, and had informed British diplomats about it on many occasions. On this subject Milovanović told Cartwright, the British ambassador in Vienna, that 'the Ottoman power has disappeared in Europe'. Milovanović was hoping to obtain the consent of Austria-Hungary to a cession to Serbia of the 'Sanjak with a strip of territory to the sea to the north of Albania'.[36] A year later, in 1910, Milovanović told Cartwright that public opinion in the Balkans was in a 'state of fermentation, and that a general restlessness existed among the various races'. Milovanović had also revealed a plan which was quite close to the war against the Ottoman Empire which was to take place two years later in the Balkans. On this Cartwright wrote:

> Milovanovitch's policy, if not very noble, is prudent. It consists in truckling to Turkey in spite of all the barbarity which the Turks may inflict on Servians in Macedonia, until the moment arrives when, Turkey being in difficulties with Greece, Servia with Bulgaria and perhaps Roumania, can fall on her flank and despoil her of Macedonia. He has no high opinion either of the Turkish army or of the new regime.[37]

In 1911 Milovanović went further by suggesting that the break-up of the Ottoman Empire should be followed by a general attack upon the European provinces. Arthur Nicolson, the Permanent Under-Secretary for Foreign Affairs, accepted Milovanović's 'prediction' and wrote to Lowther:

> I daresay it is not far from what may take place. Personally I should view with great equanimity the break-up of the Turkish regime and Turkish Empire in Europe. I have no desire to see either consolidated, for I consider that were they to become

strong they could be a menace to every Power with Muhamedan subjects, and specially to us who hold Egypt and India.[38]

As Heller pointed out, Nicolson was contributing greatly to the Foreign Office's rapid change of position by imposing the most pessimistic view about the future of the Ottoman Empire. Influenced by Milovanović, it was obvious who Nicolson and the Foreign Office would favour in the future. This change in British policy was also seen in September 1911 during the Italian invasion of Libya. Nicolson expressed the official British view in a private letter that he sent to Cartwright:

> It seems to me exceedingly foolish that we should displease a country with whom we have always been on the friendly terms and whose friendship to us is very great value, in order to keep well with Turkey, who has been a source of great annoyance to us and whose government is in one of the worst that can well be imagined. I should far prefer having Italy as a neighbour to Egypt than the Turks.[39]

Nicolson wrote that the British attitude towards the Italian invasion of Libya 'will be one of complete neutrality'. With such a step, he explained the intention of preserving Egypt as a dominion of the British. He considered it disastrous step if Italy or Austria-Hungary was to decide to land on the Albanian coast without mutual agreement. He did not want to speculate on such a situation because he felt that things were moving too fast and affecting the status quo in the Balkans.[40]

The change in policy was noted by the annual report issued at the end of 1911 by the British Embassy in Constantinople. According to the report the relationship between the Ottomans and the British during 1911 'was not a very friendly one'.[41] The report also recognized that the Baghdad railway and the Albanian Question were the two main issues that characterized relations between Great Britain and the Ottoman Empire. Regarding the troubles and brutalities that occurred during the insurrection in Albania, 'we were not slow to point them out, and, did not minimise them,' wrote Lowther. It seemed that Ottoman officials were not happy with the British, who criticized the manner in which the Porte had dealt with the Albanian uprising. 'It is difficult for Turks to understand that they cannot use their weapons they choose to exact taxation and to punish the rebellion', added Lowther.

Although Vienna was keeping its distance from the Albanian uprising, most of the European Powers, including the Balkan countries and specifically Serbia, expressed concerns about 'Austrian intrigue in Albania'. In September 1911 Milovanović told Edward Goschen, the British ambassador in Berlin, that he was convinced 'that Austria was at the bottom of the Albanian troubles'.[42] A few months later, Milovanović also told the British consul in Belgrade that Austria-Hungary was to be blamed for the uprising of the Albanians against the Porte. As a matter of fact, it was Serbia that was heavily involved in causing troubles around the border of Albania. Serbian officers were killed on many occasions at the border by Ottoman troops, but Milovanović denied the involvement of his government. A British diplomat, explaining Serbian involvement, wrote:

Servian authorities have connections with some of the leaders and there are many Servian emissaries at work in Old Servia [Kosovo]. The idea seems to be to prepare the ground and to establish relations with the bands and people in case events should lead to a Servian advance.[43]

Earlier, during the Macedonian crisis, the Serbian government had sponsored armed Serbian bands in Macedonia and Kosovo. However, the support that Serbia offered to the Serbs during 1912 was not only to create obstacles to reforms in Macedonia but also to prepare an invasion, as suggested by the above report.

Austro-Hungarian government did not support the Albanian insurrection of 1911 and this had angered the Albanians, particularly the Catholics. The Austro-Hungarian consul in Shkodra asked the Albanians to remain quiet and promised them that they would be free if they would wait for two more years. Although this promise was encouraging, in a letter which was delivered to the Foreign Office through Henry Nevinson, Durham noted that most of the Albanians had 'had enough of Austria'.[44] Even the Archbishop was very bitter with the Austro-Hungarian consul stationed in Shkodra because he believed that Vienna had betrayed the Albanian Catholics more than once.[45]

The diplomats in Cetinje and Shkodra were convinced that the Porte was trying to satisfy Albanian demands out of fear that they would appeal to Vienna for intervention.[46] In reality, at this stage, most of the Albanian leaders had ceased believing in Vienna. Furthermore, in the region of Shkodra, the arrival of many refugees from Bosnia led anti-Austro-Hungarian feelings to grow strong. However, the beginning of 1912 also brought changes in Austro-Hungarian policy, and Vienna would soon assume a supportive role towards the Albanians. Although it is likely that the changes came because, by the end of February 1912, it was becoming more evident that Albanians would soon renew conflict with the Porte, the plans of the Balkan League were arguably a more important factor in bringing about such changes.[47] Vienna believed that the Albanian Question was becoming an international issue and one in which they had to take part and play primary role.

In November 1897, Austria-Hungary and Italy had agreed, in principle, to support an autonomous or independent Albania if the Ottoman Empire collapsed.[48] Regarding this agreement, at the beginning of 1910 the British ambassador in Paris told Grey that there was 'some form of agreement between Austria and Italy relating to Albania' and added: 'It is, I believe, a self-denying protocol.'[49] Because of the importance of the Adriatic Sea, both powers were competing to prevent the other from gaining a dominant position in Albania. In this agreement they had reached an understanding not to occupy Albania and not to allow any other power to set foot on Albanian soil. Both governments agreed that if the Porte was to lose Macedonia, they would create an autonomous Albania under the sovereignty of the Porte or as an independent principality.[50]

The question was, when should Vienna and Rome consider that the Ottoman Empire was collapsing? Since the moment of collapse was not certain, neither Vienna nor Rome approached Albanian leaders to notify them about their agreement in support of an independent Albania. Until spring 1912 Austria-Hungary and Italy, as well as all other European Powers, did not think that the frequent rebellions of the Albanians would bring the collapse of Ottoman rule. They considered the Albanian insurrections to be local in character and directed only against taxes, despotic rule or changes of specific functionaries. The uprising of 1911 was viewed in the same way, even though the rebels' main request was autonomy.

From Taksim to Vlora

After the failure of the uprising of 1911, two of the most prominent Albanian leaders and members of the Ottoman Parliament, Hasan Prishtina and Ismail Bey Qemali, met secretly in Constantinople to discuss the situation. At the beginning of January 1912, they agreed to organize a general uprising against the Porte with the aim of securing autonomy for Albania. They also agreed to engage several Albanian personalities in drafting and implementing the plan.[51] Thus they invited Esat Pasha Toptani, Myfid Bey Libohova (1876-1927), Aziz Pasha Vrioni (1859-1919) and Syrja Bey Vlora (1860-1940) for a secret meeting which was held in Taksim in Constantinople. All were prominent Albanian personalities and, most importantly, they came from different parts of Albania so that through them the four Albanian *vilayets* were represented. They agreed to start a general uprising and all shared the role of finding money, buying arms, as well as forming and leading armed groups in their regions. Ismail Bey Qemali took the duty of presenting the Taksim decision diplomatically by contacting European governments and asking for support.[52]

The Ottoman government seemed to have discovered some aspects of this plan and, in order to diffuse the situation, sent Interior Minister, Kyoprolu, to Kosovo. Kyoprolu arrived in Skopje on 10 March 1912 but no Albanian leader came to meet him, nor did anyone receive him when he proceeded further north to Kosovo. The ottoman minister was mysteriously ambushed on three occasions on his way from Prizren to Shkodra and, though he survived all three attempts on his life, several of his armed escorts were killed.[53] However, the Young Turk press in Constantinople, as well as the Minister's telegrams, said that the Albanians had given him an excellent reception.[54]

After several other armed incidents occurred, the four leaders decided to publicize their plan and ask for foreign support. The first power to be approached was Britain. In April 1912, Hasan Prishtina went again to the British Consulate in Skopje and revealed the 'Taksim Agreement' to the British Consul who reported to London:

> He aspired to complete fiscal and military separation and to an Albanian republic whose connection with the Porte should be merely nominal.[55]

The British Consul received the new plan with scepticism. He reminded Prishtina that on previous occasions the Albanians of the north 'did not show much national cohesion', but Prishtina assured him that this time the situation was different and Albanians had come under 'complete organization from Shkodra to Janina'. To the consul's amazement, Hasan Prishtina also said that this time the Albanians were so well prepared that Kosovo and Macedonia would fall into their hands within weeks, while Salonika would follow within a month. This prophesy almost proved to be true, as Kosovo and most parts of Macedonia did fall under Albanian control by August 1912. However, Hasan Prishtina was wrong to predict international involvement in the plan and misread the intentions of the Powers and neighbouring countries. He had hoped that Montenegro, Serbia, Bulgaria and Austria-Hungary would abstain from interference by regarding the Albanian insurrection as an internal matter of the Porte. However, in the event that things went wrong, Hasan Prishtina said that Austro-Hungarian rule over Albania would be preferable but 'the most desirable of all would be British'.[56] As in many other cases before, Hasan Prishtina once again showed that Albanian leaders preferred British patronage over that of all other Powers.

Hasan Prishtina asked for political support from the British government and said that financial support would also be needed after the start of the uprising. He also told the consul that the Albanians would not start the uprising before they received an answer from London. A few days later the British government responded to Prishtina's request: 'England had no interest in Balkan issues.' In his memoires, Prishtina interpreted the British response as meaning that 'England was neither for nor against an Albanian uprising'.[57]

The meeting between Hasan Prishtina and the British consul took place almost a month after Serbia and Bulgaria had signed their secret treaty on 11–13 March 1912. Bax-Ironside, the British ambassador in Sofia, had warned the Foreign Office about secret talks between the two countries but the British government did not pay much attention to this information. For about a month, even Lowther in Constantinople had no information about this important event. Only in May 1912 did Nicolson, through the British Embassy in St Petersburg, discovered that the Bulgarian-Serbian treaty was a serious matter and that the two signatories intended to carve up Macedonia. Even then, Nicolson was confident that no trouble would occur in the Balkans in 1912,[58] an opinion which most likely contributed to his response to Hasan Prishtina that 'England had no interest in Balkan issues'.

It is hard to confirm whether the Albanian leaders knew about the details of the Bulgarian-Serbian alliance, but it is certain that they had some information because they hurried to start the insurrection in May 1912. *Yeni Asr*, a newspaper in Salonika, published a manifesto which was sent by Ismail Qemali who was active in helping to organize the insurgency in south Albania. The manifesto contained the demand for autonomy and was directed at the Ottoman government and at readers in Macedonia.[59]

At this point the Russian government supported the Albanian request for autonomy because it was seen as a good opportunity for introducing further reforms in Macedonia. The Russians even asked for the support of the British for a new scheme of reforms, hoping that this would keep Serbia and Bulgaria quiet. Grey did not agree to this proposal as he still believed that justice and good government were all that Macedonia needed. Although the British government had started to change its supportive policy towards the Porte, it still favoured a non-interventionist approach in Ottoman internal affairs.[60] The existing situation and the British government's position was further supported by the British press, with *The Times* and *The Spectator* praising the initiative to reorganize the gendarmerie in Macedonia and supporting the Porte's proposal to appoint five British officers who would contribute to keeping law and order. Furthermore, the British press ignored the Albanian uprising that started in 1912 and believed the uprising of the previous year to be highly exaggerated. According to the British press, it was only reforms that Albania and Macedonia needed.[61]

However, Albanian rebel forces, like all other Balkan nations, were not interested in reforms but in advancing their national aspirations. By that time, Kosovo had become the main battlefield, firstly because the majority of Ottoman troops were concentrated there and, secondly, because the entire *vilayet* of Kosovo and most of the *vilayet* of Manastir were marked by Albanian leaders as their territory and where the eastern border of the future Albanian state had to be placed.

In June 1912, a considerable part of Albania fell under the control of the Albanian insurgents. The leaders of the insurrection believed that it was time to further internationalize their cause by publicly explaining their aims to the Powers and the Balkan countries. They issued a memorandum and sent a copy to the British consulate in Manastir.[62]

The memorandum was signed by nineteen leaders, mainly from Kosovo, including Hasan Prishtina, Bajram Curri, Isa Boletini and Riza Gjakova. The aim was to show that not only Albania but the whole Ottoman Empire was facing an invasion by Balkan armies. The leaders, some still loyal to the Porte, used the term 'Fatherland' for the Ottoman Empire because they still needed political support from Constantinople and from the army stationed in Kosovo and Macedonia. By the end of June, desertions of Albanian soldiers and officers from the Ottoman army were rife in Kosovo. In Macedonia the majority of Ottoman officers may have not shared the Albanians' nationalistic views, but they supported Albania's demands. Sympathy for the Albanians within the army was growing steadily while morale was declining.[63]

Another memorandum followed from Shkodra, demanding an Albanian National Assembly and a government which would independently control its finances and its territorial (armed) force. With this, it looked like the Albanians had put forward three different sets of political demands, coming from three different organizations and different areas of Albania. But, the demands showed a degree of consistency among the Albanian nationalists in their request for autonomy. However, the leaders, being anti-Young Turk, had also accommodated requests from those conservatives who supported the Hamidian regime and, as requests, such as reinstituting old privileges, were in fact demands for reversing the situation. Lowther, explaining this 'confusion' to Grey, wrote:

> If, however, the unanimity of the purpose shown in the three sets of demands is illustrative of a real unity in Albanian nationalism, the divergences which exist between them are equally indicative of the different interpretations put upon the meaning of their nationality.[64]

While the insurrection was taking place in July, Grey wrote that in London Ismail Bey Qemali met Grujić, the Serbian *Charge d'Affaires*, whom he told that 'Albania was solid' and the Albanians were 'determined this time to see the thing through'. Grujić must have met Ismail Qemali elsewhere, as there is no evidence of Qemali visiting London or Britain in 1912. Nevertheless, Grujić told the Under Secretary of State for Foreign Affairs, Lord Onslow, that the Serbian government was not inclined to share Qemali's view. Grey added that the Serbs regarded the Albanian insurrection as a primarily anti-Young Turk movement and, therefore, they 'were not inclined to attach a great deal of importance to it'.[65] This was the line taken by Serbian diplomats in public who would not hesitate to deny the existence of the Albanian nationality, but in reality the Serbian government was seriously worried about the Albanian insurrection.

At the same time, the insurrection in Kosovo was spreading widely and with great speed. Since the leaders in Kosovo were playing the main role in the uprising, they were able to impose their own conservative views upon the movement, a factor which represented an obstacle for the nationalist majority. By the end of July, the town of Prishtina became the centre of the movement with a force of 30,000 armed Albanians led by Hasan Prishtina, Isa Boletini, Bajram Curri and Riza Gjakova. As they grew stronger, they put forward more demands, including the resignation of the Ottoman government and the dissolution of the Parliament. A section of the movement even demanded the abdication of the Sultan. By the beginning of August, most of Kosovo was controlled by the insurgents and out of sixty-seven Ottoman battalions stationed in the area, thirty-eight joined the insurgents. New Ottoman troops were brought from Asia but it was too late to change the situation, many began joining the Albanians or deserted.[66]

Under the pressure of events, the government in Constantinople resigned on 22 July 1912. The resignation proved that Albanian leaders were well organized and had achieved success. Explaining the effect of this successful organization, Lowther wrote:

> The 1912 rising is, moreover, exceptional, in that its conspicuous success was due to the fact that it was organised by men of far greater ability than were the leaders of former movements, by men who succeeded in affecting a combination with the military elements opposed to the Committee Cabinet – a combination which paralysed the action of the government and in the end effectively secured its fall.[67]

However, at this stage, the change of government in Constantinople did not mean much for the insurgents in Albania. Albanian autonomy was not considered an option even by the new government. The insurrection was also complicating the situation in Macedonia and this in turn caused worries in Vienna, leading the Austro-Hungarian foreign minister, Count Leopold Berchtold, to contact the British government and propose the 'political decentralization of Albania'. The British rejected the proposal and Grey, again, reaffirmed his position that Albania needed a 'good government with special arrangement'.[68]

The denial of autonomy led the insurgents to move southwards to Macedonia, to occupy more territory and intensify the pressure. On 11 August, a group of 200 Albanian fighters entered Skopje and occupied the main town square. There was no reaction from the Ottoman army or administration. By 15 August, the number of insurgents that had entered Skopje reached 30,000. The Ottoman army did not even come out of its barracks, meaning there was no opposition to the takeover. In the national history of Albania, 15 August 1912 has entered as the date of the liberation of Skopje.⁶⁹

This fact forced the Porte to endorse most of the Albanian terms which were known as the '14 Points Demand'. Macedonia was now at the mercy of the Albanian insurgents. There was nothing to stop them if they decided to move to Salonika since the Third Army stationed at Manastir, as well as other barracks on the way to Salonika, were ready to join the Albanians. But a major misunderstanding occurred between Albanian leaders, some of them, unsatisfied with autonomy, insisted on declaring independence, with Skopje as the capital. Conservatives such as Isa Boletini and Riza Gjakova insisted on proceeding to Salonika in order to occupy, release the deposed Sultan Abdul Hamid II from his house arrest, and march to Constantinople to change the government and the Sultan.⁷⁰ This was unacceptable for Hasan Prishtina and the majority of the leaders who believed the occupation of Salonika and the replacement of the Sultan were not national concerns. Hasan Prishtina, who became the main figure of the movement, and the remaining followers of the Taksim Group, reached a compromise: to accept the offer of the Porte for partial autonomy and meanwhile to work towards independence, which would be declared at a later date. The plan was to be better organized within three or four months, during which period some of the conservatives who were 'creating obstacles would be eliminated'.⁷¹ By 'eliminated', it is likely that Prishtina intended to isolate or remove the loyalists from influential positions. Meanwhile, the Albanian leaders were convinced that they would continue to build upon the partial autonomy offered by the Porte.

Meanwhile, in September 1912, Grey seemed ready to change his mind about Albanian autonomy but with one condition. He agreed that whatever autonomy the Ottoman government would grant to the Albanians, the same had to be applied to the Christian population in Macedonia.⁷² Other powers maintained the same position. Thus, the Ottoman Grand Vizier informed the Austro-Hungarian ambassador that the reforms granted to the Albanians would be 'extended to the Christian races' and his government would be encouraged to 'pursue this policy'.⁷³

Any form of autonomy meant a decentralization of power which was contrary to the political philosophy of the Young Turks, who aimed for a strong and centralized state.⁷⁴ Yet autonomy would satisfy, at least temporarily, most of the Albanian leadership who saw it as a compromise that would eventually lead to independence. As a matter of fact, this is what happened although in a manner contrary to the plans that were made in Taksim and Skopje. The plan had been to build autonomy in cooperation with the Porte and probably with the help of the Powers, while independence would come in the process. However, the situation in the Balkans developed unfavourably for the Albanians and the Porte, as there was no opportunity to start the process of autonomy because the neighbouring countries had different plans.⁷⁵ Serbia, Bulgaria, Greece and Montenegro intervened in the Porte and complained to the Powers about Albanian autonomy, arguing that their interests were endangered. Russia and France warned the Porte that there would be serious consequences if the borders of Albania were redrawn, with both countries emphasizing that they would not allow any Slavs to remain within any form or shape of Albania. Barclay, the British ambassador in Sofia, summed up the situation:

It is hardly necessary to point out the anxiety caused in Bulgaria as well, doubtless, as in Servia and Greece, by the success of the Albanian revolt, these three States would view the autonomy of Albania as a total blow to their aspirations. They wish to see Albania remain a thorn in the side of Turkey – a source of Weakness – and not become a semi-independent Mohammedan State, a strong pillar of the Empire.[76]

Barclay also noted that because of the situation in Macedonia, Albanian autonomy had caused considerable anxiety in the Bulgarian government. Albanians in Sofia were seen as acquiring an entirely new sphere of influence. Hence, the Bulgarian government maintained that such a development could produce 'grave consequences for the Macedonian peoples' who would not allow 'their national claims to be overridden by the Albanians in this way'.[77]

Even Austria-Hungary maintained that autonomy, as perceived by the Albanians, was not acceptable. Instead, Vienna urged the Porte to implement a plan for the decentralization of the Ottoman administration in a way which would address the needs of the ethnic distribution of the population. With these actions, Vienna was attempting to keep both the Albanians and the Porte happy and also prevent the intervention of the Balkan countries.[78]

By late August 1912, an atmosphere of war was felt everywhere in the Balkans, with Albanian autonomy being a key reason. Now Albania was to be defined territorially in an agreement with the Ottomans, according to which it was to include the four *vilayets* previously desired by the Albanian leaders. The governments of the neighbouring countries resolved to resist the creation of Albania along these lines, arguing that it was too large in size and 'would encroach heavily on their expectations'.[79] The neighbouring states believed that, if the Albanians were to achieve their national aspirations, it would help to stabilize the balance of power in the Balkans, a situation which was not desired under their national aspirations.[80] Historian Mark Mazower explains:

> The Albanian rebellion presaged radical changes in the balance of power in the Balkans. It showed that armed revolt against the Turkish authorities could succeed, spurring the Balkan states to assert their own claims to Ottoman territory. It marked the emergence of organised and militant Albanian nationalism, to the intense alarm of Serbia and Greece, both of which claimed territories with substantial Albanian-speaking populations. And it encouraged both Austria and Italy to dream of new footholds in southeastern Europe, which alarmed the Balkan states still more.[81]

Another reason for the atmosphere of war was the invasion of Libya by Italian forces. This meant that the Ottoman army was busy elsewhere and thus considerably weakened in its capacity to control the Balkan situation. Nazim Pasha, the war minister, contributed further to weakening the army by purging the Ottoman army of what he thought to be unreliable elements. He dismissed the troops in Macedonia which had completed their last year in active service. When the new mobilization took place in autumn 1912, it went at a slow pace and under low discipline. Around 50,000 untrained soldiers were called up to serve in Macedonia meaning that the Ottoman army was not ready to face new hostilities in the area. This fact would not have been difficult to note by those Balkan countries preparing for armed conflict.[82]

Albanian leaders also asked the Porte to provide 50,000 rifles for their people with the pretext of defending their borders, but the Porte provided no arms. However, arms were entering Kosovo from Serbia, some of which were given to Albanians in the area of Gjilani (east Kosovo) even though most were intended for the local Serbs. The Serbian consul in Skopje denied the involvement of his government and maintained that Belgrade had no power to stop this traffic of arms. No matter the Serbian consul's official stance, everyone knew the purpose of such supply. As confirmed by a British diplomat, Serbia was perusing the favourite Balkan policy of encouraging outrages in order to secure European intervention or provide a *casus belli*.[83]

The Serbian consulate in Skopje also distributed a memorandum to all the diplomatic missions in the city. The content of the memorandum detailed mistreatment of the Serbs by the Ottoman regime and particularly by the Albanians in Kosovo. Although some cases of such mistreatment were true, as the British vice-consul explained 'it was possible that the Serbs might invent outrages to act as a counterbalance to the Bulgarian atrocities at Kochana'.[84]

Hopes for the autonomy of Albania were shattered on 8 October 1912 when Montenegro declared war on the Ottoman Empire. The aim of the Montenegrin army was to occupy Shkodra, the biggest and most prosperous Albanian city in the region at that time. Montenegro had started the war and Serbia, which was making final preparations close to the borders of Kosovo, would soon join in. In March 1912, Vojislav Tankosić, a Serbian army officer and a member of the 'Black Hand', was transferred to the headquarters of the border troops near Kosovo with the task of training Serbian volunteers. On the eve of the First Balkan War, a young man called Gavrilo Princip (1894–1918) arrived at the recruiting centre as a volunteer but was refused on medical grounds being 'too weak and small'.[85] Because of his physical appearance and ill health, he was mocked by other recruiters. He was sensitive and felt humiliated that he had not been given a chance to fight for the Serbian national cause within 'comitadjis' ranks, the irregular Serbian military force which was commanded by 'Black Hand' officers.[86] However, this humiliation did not prevent him from continuing with other nationalist activities and further radicalization. Princip's war was yet to come.[87]

The Serbian army attacked northern Kosovo on 14 October at Merdare. The disorganized Ottoman army withdrew and left the battlefield but Albanian resistance continued. On 18 October 1912, four days after the Serbian army entered Kosovo, King Petar of Serbia, in accordance with Article 23 of the Treaty of Berlin, issued a declaration 'To the Serbian People', proclaiming:

> Things got so far out of hand that no one was satisfied with the situation in Turkey in Europe. It became unbearable for the Serbs, the Greeks and for the Albanians, too. By the grace of God, I have therefore ordered my brave army to join in the Holy War to free our brethren and to ensure a better future.[88]

This was in effect a declaration of war. Albanians continued to offer resistance in several other areas but they were no match for the well-armed Serbian army. On 24 October the territory of what is today Kosovo was occupied by the Serbian army.[89] The Serbian First Army continued towards Macedonia, while the Third Army moved across Kosovo towards north Albania in order to reach the Albanian coast. Albanian leaders such as Hasan Prishtina, Nexhip Draga and Bajram Curri issued a declaration to explain to the Powers that the Albanians had joined the Ottoman army to protect the land which was inhabited by Albanians and not the Ottoman Empire.[90] The decision to join the Ottoman army was taken on 14 October in Skopje by Albanian leaders who were organized within a patriotic society called *Shoqëria e Zezë për Shpëtim* (Black Society for Salvation).[91] Before the meeting in Skopje took place, the newspaper *Liri e Shqipërisë* (Freedom of Albania), published in Bulgaria, called upon all Albanians to take up arms to defend the borders of Albania and raise the Albanian flag as a symbol of claiming national rights. These developments led Austro-Hungarian diplomats to report to Vienna that the Albanians had decided to serve on the fronts of the Balkan War.[92]

Between spring 1908 and August 1912, the Ottoman army and Albanian insurgents had exhausted each other in continuous clashes. Yet now Albanians and Ottomans were allies once again. However, the battle of Kumanovo ended after two days (23–24 October 1912) and the Ottoman army was heavily defeated.[93] With the victory at Kumanovo, the Serbs took control of northern Macedonia and were in a position to move south, towards Manastir, and west towards inland Albania and the Adriatic Sea. The Ottomans also suffered defeat elsewhere in Macedonia by the Bulgarian and Greek armies.[94] The Ottoman army, on whose protection the Albanians counted and relied, was practically destroyed. Some Ottoman and Albanian army units continued to resist the Balkan armies moving towards Albania, but to no avail. The moment the Albanian leaders feared most had come. There was no force to protect their country or their people.

However, Albanian leaders still hoped to save the prospect of autonomy. As agreed in Taksim, Ismail Bey Qemali continued to visit European foreign ministries. When the Balkan War started, he went to meet Austro-Hungarian officials and ask for their support. Vienna's policy had regarded the Porte as the main factor in the Balkans but the swift victory of the Balkan armies had ruined this policy, leaving Vienna forced to make changes and abandon its old attitude. The new Serbian territorial gains in Macedonia were acceptable, to a degree, by Vienna which insisted that Belgrade was not to move towards any Albanian port in the Adriatic.[95]

This was a vague policy of Vienna, but within it, there was hope for the future of an Albanian state. After all, Vienna and Italy had already agreed to an independent Albania to be recognized only when the Ottoman Empire collapsed. Now that the collapse had finally arrived Ismail Bey Qemali was about to remind Vienna of this fact. Before visiting Vienna, Ismail Bey Qemali stopped at Bucharest, where a large and influential Albanian colony existed. He held a meeting with prominent members of the community and revealed his plan to declare Albanian independence. Some decided to accompany Ismail Bey Qemali on his tour of Europe and to return to Albania. He also telegraphed to all important cities in Albania and asked for delegates to be sent to the convention where independence would be declared.[96]

On 10 November 1912 Ismail Bey Qemali met Count Berchtold, the Austro-Hungarian Foreign Minister. In his memoirs Ismail Bey Qemali wrote:

> His Excellency approved my views on the national question, and readily granted the sole request which I made him, namely, to place at my disposal a vessel which would enable me to reach the first Albanian port before the arrival of the Serbian Army.[97]

That was all he wrote about the meeting and, as seen above, he did not explain his views on the 'national question' nor the answer of Count Berchtold. As it became known later, Count Berchtold told Ismail Bey Qemali that Vienna supported autonomy and not the independence of Albania. It is also not known what answer Ismail Bey Qemali offered in return but his actions, which were taken a few days later, showed that he considered independence to be the only answer. Qemali also visited Trieste, Italy, and proceeded to his birthplace, the Adriatic town of Vlora.[98] The Austro-Hungarian vessel could not approach Vlora as the port was blockaded by Greek warships so instead, on 21 November, he disembarked in Durrës only to find the town and the area in chaos. The population, deceived by the Ottoman authorities, believed that the Ottoman army had been victorious in the war. 'They did not even know that the Serbs were at their very gates', wrote Ismail Bey Qemali.[99]

The Ottoman authorities still showed hostility to the idea of Albanian independence being declared in Durrës. Therefore, Ismail Bey and his group of notable supporters, which grew again in Durrës, took the land road to Vlora which was being held by armed Albanians. Before the Serbian, Montenegrin and Greek armies invaded the Albanian territory without encountering any serious resistance, some of the Albanian cities proclaimed independence and elected their delegates to attend a national convention which was announced by Ismail Bey from Bucharest.[100]

On 28 November 1912, eighty-three delegates, representing most of the towns of Kosovo, Macedonia and what was later to become Albania, opened the first Albanian National Assembly. Most of the delegates were intellectuals, politicians or diplomats who until then had served the Ottoman Empire.[101] The time to end their service to the empire and raise the Albanian flag had finally come. After signing the Declaration of Independence, the formalities were over. They formed a provisional government to be headed by Ismail Bey Qemali while the ministers (two Catholics, three Orthodox and five Muslims) were chosen according to the principle of national distribution and covering the four *vilayet*s they believed belonged to Albania.[102]

The very first duty of the government was to send telegrams to the European Powers and neighbouring Balkan countries in order to inform them that Albania, from now on, was independent and had taken a neutral stance in the Balkan War. The first day of work of the first Albanian government had ended, and this was in fact all they could do for some time in the future. The government had no army and the territory they controlled did not extend far beyond the surroundings of the town of Vlora, which itself was besieged and blockaded by the invading Greek army.[103] This was a very different Albania from what Albanian leaders had envisaged in Taksim and Skopje. The provisional government appealed for international recognition or for any form of help and to such ends a telegram was sent to the 'Government of His Britannic Majesty to recognise the change of the political life of the Albanian nation'.[104] London did not respond.

The British government avoided any contact with the Albanian provisional government as it still regarded the area as an Ottoman dominion. However, the relationship between the British government and the Porte had by now had gone through significant changes. At the end of 1912, British diplomats in Constantinople confirmed that the attitude of the British Government towards the Porte throughout that year was 'one of reserve' and caused a 'feeling of profound disappointment' among Ottoman politicians. The Ottoman officials, in moments of crisis, had traditionally looked to the British government for help but it would no longer offer assistance to the Porte. British diplomats believed that Ottoman officials had 'completely closed their eyes' to the fact that London had changed its policy towards and modified relations with Russia. A decade later Talaat Pasha, a prominent Young Turk and by then a Grand Vizier, spoke about this matter. He told Aubrey Herbert that the Young Turks had made a big mistake in not decentralizing the empire and in not granting autonomy to the Albanians when they came to power.[105] Talaat Pasha also blamed the policies made in London and the British embassy in Constantinople for worsening Ottoman–British relations. He told Herbert:

> There was nothing in those days which we would not have given if you had asked it from us. But you wanted nothing of us, and gratitude cannot live on air. The Ambassador [Lowther] was cold; Fitzmaurice was hostile; we had to find means to live. But even after our estrangement, we still tried to regain your friendship. We accepted Kiamil Pasha, our determined opponent, as Grand Vizier, to please you. You drove us into the arms of Germany. We had no alternative: anything else was political death and partition.[106]

Talaat Pasha also hinted that autonomy would have been granted to the Albanians if the British had pressurized the Porte. This information came in 1921. Herbert has explained the dependency of the Ottoman Empire from the West, particularly from Britain:

> The East depended upon the West and in the past an Englishman in Turkey who was a disinterested friend of any of the nationalities within the Ottoman Empire really had his own unassailable niche. All the people in Turkey, including the Turk, were in chronic state of shipwreck; the English were in permanent possession of the lifeboat, though often that boat could not put out to sea.[107]

However, in 1912 London had made it known that the Porte could not rely on British assistance nor on their sympathy any longer. This was made clear on 9 November 1912 when the Prime Minister Herbert Asquith spoke at Guildhall. Speaking about the Balkan War and having in mind the progress of the Balkan armies into Ottoman territories, he confirmed that 'the victors were not to be robbed of the fruits which cost them so dear'.[108] This was not good news for Albania, either. Asquith declared that the British government was to recognize the occupation of Macedonia, Kosovo and Albania by the armies of the Balkan League. A few days later, Winston Churchill, then a First Lord of the Admiralty, confirmed the success of the Balkan League which, to him, was in line with Gladstonian Liberal ideas and thus a satisfactory outcome. On 30 November 1912 in his speech at the Eighty Club, Churchill praised Gladstone 'that great man who predicted the course of events in extraordinary precision and detail'.[109] An international conference was soon to be held in London to deal with the Albanian Question which was entirely internationalized, albeit in a manner contrary to that which the Albanian leaders had worked and hoped for.

The beginning of the First Balkan War showed that the British were not interested in the Ottoman Empire. This also meant that the British were no longer neutral, as they made no attempts to deny the advance of the Balkan armies or build any obstacles to their future military operations in the remaining European parts of the Ottoman Empire. Before any international peace conference took place, Prime Minister Asquith had confirmed the British position which favoured the Allied Balkan countries who had occupied Macedonia and Albania.[110]

In doing so, the British government applied the Gladstonian or Liberal approach to events in the Balkans. In London, the Balkan League's military engagement against the Porte was considered as a reasonable act. Grey declared that the cause of the war was just and as such it was seen as the 'emancipation of the Christian subjects of Turkey in South-East Europe'.[111] However, Albania had become a dangerous spot with the potential of spreading into a wider Balkan and even European conflict, and as such could not be ignored any longer.

7

The Balkans for the Balkan people

Edith Durham's Liberal view on the Balkans and Albania

Edith Durham arrived in the Balkans for the first time in 1900. By 1908 she had 'gone native' and in an 'Albanian manner' she celebrated the promulgation of the Ottoman Constitution reinstated following the Young Turk Revolution. On this occasion, she wrote:

> The Constitution was proclaimed, Scutari [Shkodra] was wild with joy. Thousands of mountain men in finest array marched into the town, were feted and feasted. We fired revolvers (I had one in each hand) into the air till not a cartridge was left. Not an accident nor disorder occurred.[1]

Edith Durham was born in London to Arthur and Mary Durham and was the eldest of nine children. Her father was a senior consulting surgeon at Guy's Hospital in London. Her mother was the daughter of the well-known economist William Ellis, a close friend and colleague of John Stuart Mill. Ellis was also known as a pioneer of technical schools in England and as a friend of Giuseppe Garibaldi, whom he helped in early clandestine work towards the unification of Italy. She attended Bedford College (1878–82) and later studied art at the Royal Academy of Arts in London. Until 1900 Durham exhibited her drawings and illustrated publications, including a volume of the *Cambridge Natural History* published in 1899.[2]

Aged thirty-seven, Durham went to Montenegro, as advised by her doctor, to spend some time in a warm-climate country. She arrived in Cetinje, the capital of Montenegro, where she discovered taste for Balkan life that would have great impact on her future.[3] At first, Durham did not like Montenegro, a small country of around 100,000 inhabitants. Cetinje seemed to her like a village yet strangely, the tiny capital housed consular representatives of the Powers, leading Durham to wonder why they had found an interest in this small country. She wrote to her mother to describe the strangeness of Montenegro 'as Gilbert and Sullivan opera'.[4]

Durham also described this unusual situation in an unpublished story titled *International Episode*. Together foreign diplomats dined in a two-storey hotel in Maligrad (Smallville), as she named Cetinje in this story. The hotel symbolically represents Montenegro, while the waiter represents the government or the ruler of the country. The dominant diplomat is the Austro-Hungarian representative, a character so important that the waiter must always apologize to him, even for the delay of food which he did not order. Montenegro, a country which cannot protect itself, should serve, with a smiling face, the Ministers Plenipotentiary whose business it is to plan its 'absorption'.[5] At the dining table, England, as a 'non-annexing Power,' is an ordinary guest and happy with the Austro-Hungarian representative who offers him information as to the 'advisability of firmness in dealing with semi-civilised people'.[6] Furthermore, the representatives of Austria-Hungary, Italy and France observe developments in Albania. Russia, in turn, keeps an eye on Austria-Hungary, Italy and France. This was the local and international situation in Montenegro as Durham viewed it in 1900.

Durham used Montenegro as base from which she travelled to Serbia, Bosnia, Albania and Macedonia. In 1902 she visited Serbia and wrote *Through the Land of the Serbs* in which she gave an account of the situation in the country, emphasizing that it was full of military personnel and everyone spoke about expansion towards the south, an area which was still part of the Ottoman Empire. She sent the manuscript to many publishers but none of them were interested in publishing it since the Balkans, and particularly Serbia, was not considered an interesting topic at that time. Above all, Durham was a woman and had no prior published books. Unexpectedly a historic event helped her situation. In 1903 King Alexandar and Queen Draga Obrenović of Serbia were assassinated and replaced by Petar Karađorđević. The assassination was executed with a merciless barbarity which had culminated after a long rivalry between the Karađorđević and Obrenović families for the Serbian throne.[7] A few years later, Durham would write about this subject on many occasions.[8] The British and European public were shocked by the regicide in Belgrade and the British government, in protest of such barbarity, withdrew its diplomatic mission from Belgrade. Suddenly, interest in Serbia grew in Britain and Durham found a publisher for her first book.[9]

In *Through the Land of the Serbs*, Durham exposed her belief in the doctrine of the Gladstonian Liberals which was optimistic about the future of the Balkans but showed little regard for its Muslim population. Based on this doctrine, Durham believed that the Balkan people should be left to work out their separate destinies but soon discovered that this doctrine was 'unworkable and inappropriate'. Based on experiences she had gained in Serbia and later in Macedonia, Albania, Bosnia and Montenegro, she was convinced that the borders, which had been imposed by the Treaty of Berlin, were artificial and creating ethnic tensions. In another unpublished manuscript, Durham described how the Powers met in Berlin to settle the Near Eastern question and make peace, yet practically each Power was there only 'to out-wit the other'.[10] The land was there to be divided for the benefit of the dividers and with no respect for ethnic lines. Her story was about *Gornji Bunar and Donji Bunar* (Upper and Lower Well) in which the village was given to Montenegro but the well was given to the Austro-Hungarian Empire. 'Three men had died and undying hatred had been born'. She added that 'the truth had died and many more people would die, because of the united wisdom and the split differences of the Berlin Congress'.[11]

However, the published book *Through the Land of the Serbs* did make an impact. Durham warned that the Balkan system, imposed by the Powers at the Congress of Berlin, was about to collapse together with the Ottoman Empire.[12] The book strengthened the perceptions of those who believed the Treaty of Berlin had failed to satisfy the Balkan states' demands and further encouraged British Liberals to continue lobbying against it. However, Durham, at this stage, appeared as a supporter of the Serbian national cause.

With her first book and the many other articles she published consequently about the Balkans, Durham joined the ranks of other Balkan experts and, in early 1904, was sent to Macedonia by the newly formed Macedonian Relief Committee to help with humanitarian work.[13] In Macedonia, Durham equipped herself with knowledge and experience about the region. Although she greatly disliked the regime of the Porte, she maintained that demonizing the Ottomans unreasonably, as other Liberals did, was not something she would support. As a result of her family background, she did not give much consideration to religion, an attitude very different to that of most Gladstonians. Divisions between her and other Liberals of the *Balkan Committee* widened but at that time she was not strong enough to enter in direct conflict with them. After all it was the Liberals who had enabled her to go and work in Macedonia. However, as time passed, she began to enter into fierce conflict with Committee members such as Henry Noel Brailsford and R. W. Seton-Watson, who were known supporters of the Bulgarian and Serbian national cause. Durham strongly supported her own opinions which were based on the principle of 'the Balkans for the Balkan people' and, because of this, she made many other enemies among Balkan specialists, academics and politicians in Britain.[14] Within the idea of 'the Balkans for the Balkan people' Durham believed it possible to apply the principle of nationality which, as time passed, brought her close to the Albanian national cause.

Soon after her arrival in Macedonia in 1904 was disappointed by the difficult situation she found there and was underwhelmed by the Christian people of Slav origin. In one of her first articles on Macedonia she characterized the peasants of this region as backward, 'slow-minded, ignorant, and inferior to any other race of the Balkans', adding that they had no hope for the future. Durham blamed Ottoman rule and neglect by Europe for the difficulties in Macedonia, urging that the region be put under a 'Christian ruler' with the supervision of the Powers.[15]

Durham also sought to explain the source of tensions which led to the Balkan Wars. She pointed out that Western ideas, which were forced upon the Balkan states, were incompatible with the reality that she saw on the ground. She also dismissed the idea, which was widely maintained in Britain and other European countries, that religion was the main factor causing the conflicts in the Balkans. She explained that it was in fact nationalism which was causing conflicts and which, ultimately, would end Ottoman rule in Europe.[16] In holding such a view, Durham had already started to distance herself from mainstream Gladstonian Liberalism.

Becoming more familiar with the Albanian national cause, Durham discovered that the principle 'the Balkans for the Balkan people' was not as inclusive as most British Liberals believed. This principle excluded the Albanians from the future of the Balkans which was envisaged once free from Ottoman rule. She criticized the Powers, particularly Britain, for not supporting the Albanian national cause which, according to her, was central to the Balkan problem. However, supporting the Albanians did not mean that she abandoned her support or sympathy for other Balkan nations. 'I should like each of the Balkan peoples to be left to work out its own salvation in its own national way, with fair play and no favour,'[17] she wrote in her book *The Burden of the Balkans* in 1905. The publication of this book received wide and fair reviews in the British press, but all reviews noted and concentrated upon the difficult situation of the Balkan Christians under Ottoman rule. Although Durham's aim was to present the Macedonian conflict as a product of nationalist movements, and not as a question of religion as presumed,[18] the press failed to see the principle of 'the Balkans for the Balkan people' as the book had intended.

In 1904 Durham was employed by the British Foreign Bible Society which was based in Manastir, Macedonia and journeyed to Albania to sell Bibles. There she came to know the Albanian population encountering intellectuals who were mostly nationalist and hoped to find a solution to their national cause within the principle of the 'Balkans for the Balkan people'. Durham was fascinated with Albania, particularly with its northern part. Albanians too were fascinated by this foreign woman who liked them, respected their heritage, helped them and who was travelling, on most occasions, alone through Albania. It was not long before she was approached by some of the Albanian leaders and asked to advocate on behalf of their national movement to the British, European Powers and the press. In some ways she had already taken such a role before being asked to do so.[19]

After 1905 a picturesque Albania and idyllic Albanians were not only the subject of her watercolour drawings but she gradually started to show more intensive support for the Albanian national cause. However, from the Liberal perspective she had chosen to support the 'wrong' people. Durham's efforts to present the Albanians in the same manner as all other Balkan peoples caused trouble among Gladstonian Liberals in Britain. However, with strong determination, great experience and knowledge, Durham secured a respectable place among the members of the *Balkan Committee*, academics and the Foreign Office. Decades later, A.J.P. Taylor thought that 'Intelligent people with interest in foreign affairs would read Miss M. E. Durham on Albania'.[20]

By 1905 she had written books and published articles in the British press which acted as a good reason why the foreign consuls and diplomats in Cetinje and Shkodra wanted to talk and dine with her. Her reputation also grew in London among diplomats in the Foreign Office and the press. In 1908 Durham was asked by the Royal Anthropological Institute to speak on the Balkans at Fitzwilliam College in Cambridge. After an impressive lecture, the Institute also asked her to visit north Albania and conduct anthropological research there. After she spent a considerable time among the mountaineers of northern Albania, the book *High Albania* came out in 1909.[21]

High Albania was reviewed by a dozen or so British newspapers and magazines. Probably the best review which explained Durham's work and intentions was published in *Pall Mall Gazette*. The position of Albania was explained as a result of Austrian intrigue and Italian ambition. It was also noted that the Albanian efforts 'to receive reconsideration at the hands of Great Britain' would be dangerous as it would 'be accompanied by interminable complications'.[22] The ambition of the Albanians for autonomy was regarded as 'an experiment which would be provocative and even more disastrous'. The book, apart from its political message, also contained studies on the customs and folklore of Albania. Therefore, the reviewer suggested that 'the unofficial character of this book will be clear to the Albanians themselves'²³ and would 'appeal to a limited circle' of readers. The angle taken by the review was close to the official position held by the British government on Albania at that time and, as such, did not achieve Durham's purpose of making the Albanian Question popular among the government and public. This was a disappointment for Durham but did not discourage her from developing further her interest in and support for Albanians, nor from trying to win British support for their cause.

Nevertheless, her continuous work confirmed Durham's authority on the Albanian Question in Britain. By 1910 she had also become widely known and popular in Albania where she was recognized as their 'protector' in the West who worked tirelessly to publicize their cause and get support. Therefore, the mountaineers of the north 'proclaimed' her as 'Krajlica e Malevet' (Mountain Queen). This honorary title gave her the will and authority to represent them before the world.²⁴ Durham also became popular among the Albanian diaspora in Europe and the United States. In August 1911, Durham received a letter from a group of Albanians in the United States, saying that the Albanian colony there holds her in high regard and informing her that she should be 'enshrined in history as the Albanian Joan of Arc'.²⁵

As a Liberal, Durham supported the Albanian rebellions against the Porte, including the insurrection of 1911. Before the insurrection started, she wrote to the Foreign Office with the aim of gaining British support. She was aware that the British government still believed the Young Turk government to be democratic, and as such, able to deal with the Albanian Question. She wrote that Albanians, Catholic and Muslim, were resolved to act together against the Young Turk regime because they saw in it no hope for the progress and development for Albania. Explaining the Ottoman state institutions which were run by the Young Turks she wrote:

> He [the Ottoman] is a good soldier and nothing more. Parliament is merely a piece of European goods stuck in the front window to hide what is going on behind. The government is really a military tyranny. The Turkish pretence that the Albanians do not wish for law and order is false.²⁶

As Austria-Hungary and Italy were not interested in helping Albanians preparing the insurrection of 1911, she suggested that the British government should offer help. To this end she wrote to the Foreign Office to show her readiness to help the Albanians and to express her thoughts about the future of Ottoman rule in the Balkans:

> The whole thing now is in ferment. I am afraid I am no longer strong enough to go and help shoot Turks myself, but I certainly hope to live to see them cease to rule in Europe.²⁷

The governments of Britain and the other Powers were not pleased with such a move by the Albanians. Their response worried Durham, who wished to see London and Vienna applying the principle of 'the Balkans for the Balkan people' together and supporting the Albanian national cause. After the insurrection of 1911 Durham was the only authority to whom Albanian leaders would turn for help and advice.

Austria-Hungary was not happy with the 'leeway it had lost', a point Durham noted when she wrote that the mountaineers came to her for advice 'in preference to the Austrian consul'. She added that the Austro-Hungarian consul 'used to be king; but they [the Albanians] call me Queen'.[28] By now she was gaining wide popularity among the Albanians thanks to her personality and the fact that she was British. As a result of her work and activity, the popularity of Great Britain grew among the Albanians. She wrote to the Foreign Office, emphasizing her importance and hoping to gain sympathy for Albania.[29]

King Nikola of Montenegro knew that Durham was an important woman because she was writing for *The Times* and *The Manchester Guardian*. Though Durham had no direct links with the British government, it was not farfetched to presume that some of her reports would end up on the desks of the Foreign Office. For this reason, the Montenegrin king showed hospitality to her and sought to use Durham's prestige among the Albanians; he had tried to use the influence she had over the Albanians but she had refused to get engaged in such a relationship.[30]

In March 1912, signs of general insurrection for autonomy appeared in Kosovo and Macedonia about which Durham, being in contact with Albanian leaders, had information. During that time Durham was in Shkodra and observed attempts by foreign diplomats to find out what exactly was happening. These diplomats knew that no one was better informed about Albania than Durham and so approached her for information. She wrote: 'they ask me, and I say I don't know'.[31] This may show that she was determined to provide the diplomats with only the information she regarded as useful for the Albanian cause. Despite this, there were two British diplomats with whom she established very close cooperation and to whom she did provide information.

Durham often wrote to the British Consul in Shkodra and to others who served in Macedonia to keep them informed about and influence their opinion on Albanian matters. One of the consuls she targeted was Harry Lamb (1857–1948) who served as General Consul in Salonika, the main consular centre in Macedonia. When Lamb was transferred to Durrës and Vlora in Albania in 1912, Durham intensified her letters to him and she despatched many of these letters to the Foreign Office. In one report he told Grey that Durham's 'interest in and knowledge of Albanian affairs is well known'.[32] In the same letter, Lamb wrote that 'after consultation with myself' Durham had gone to Vlora in order to form a reliable estimate about the situation and 'work out a possibility of relieving it'.[33] Decades later in a letter Durham sent to her friend Edward Boyle,[34] who at that time was the chairman of the *Balkan Committee*, spoke about another cooperation between her and Lamb. 'I was in a spying mission' she wrote about one of the journeys she made during the summer of 1914 to south Albania. She described the 'Greek invasion and the savage devastation' and added 'I spied the position of the Greek Army and of the relief work I undertook at Sir Harry Lamb's request.'[35]

Likely as a result of frequent meetings with Durham, Lamb adopted a more positive approach towards the Albanian Question in many of his reports to the Foreign Office and also reported to the Foreign Office about the atrocities of the First Balkan War. As a matter of fact, Lamb was not alone in reporting on this matter. Other disturbing reports reached the Foreign Office from British diplomats in Macedonia, mainly from Charles Greig's despatches from Manastir, though the Foreign Office seems initially to have believed and endorsed only the reports sent from Belgrade by Dayrell Crackenthorpe, who was as 'a man of pronounced Serbophile sentiment'.[36] It was only when the number of reports grew and the international and British press published details of the atrocities that the Foreign Office was persuaded to act. The British contacted the Serbian Prime Minister, Nikola Pašić, about the atrocities that the Serbian army had committed in the area of Manastir. Pašić replied by saying that he had no comment because 'he did not know the prefect there personally'.[37]

Lamb went further than reporting about atrocities that were committed throughout Kosovo and Macedonia. He criticized the Foreign Office for lacking courage and dignity and for not warning the Balkan League about the atrocities they had committed. He maintained that it was not proper for the British government to conceal the bitter reality of atrocities out of fear of the reaction of the Muslims in India and other dominions.[38]

In her efforts to win British diplomats to her side, Durham also befriended Count de Salis, a prominent British diplomat who served in the Foreign Office in London from 1901 to 1906 and in several diplomatic missions as ambassador, including to Germany and the Vatican. De Salis also served as the British representative in Montenegro from 1911 to 1916 as 'Envoy Extraordinary and Minister Plenipotentiary'. It was during this period that Durham established contact with de Salis and maintained a friendly relationship until his death in 1939. When de Salis died, Durham revealed her close cooperation with him:

> A more upright, honest and clean minded man never existed. I always felt that Foreign Office did not make so much or such good use of him as it should have. And as we had lot of men sent out there I paid no particular attention to him at first. But the Count when he found out I had been long in the Balkans asked me for information and at last used to entrust me with the task of finding out for him various things; what was going on up country; who was so & so, etc. When the Balkan War broke out I was continually in touch with him and giving all the facts I could get.[39]

De Salis and Durham held identical views on the Balkans and from their correspondence it could be concluded that Durham had some influence on him. During and after the Balkan Wars they both rejected Pan-Slavism, Serbia's expansionist policy and disliked R. W. Seton- Watson. De Salis' views about the Balkans are to be seen from the official reports he sent from Montenegro to the Foreign Office[40] and from his private correspondence with Lord Onslow.[41] De Salis, like Durham, maintained that the region of Shkodra and the town itself was Albanian and was unjustly attacked by the Serbian and Montenegrin armies. De Salis suggested that the idea of the Serbs and Montenegrins to rule over Albanians should not be approved.[42] In 1924 de Salis told Durham: 'I hold no brief for Orthodoxy'. He regarded R. W. Seton-Watson and others who supported Serbia, and later Yugoslavia, as a 'pro Juggo tribe'.[43]

Durham also befriended Sir Maurice de Bunsen, another prominent diplomat who served as British ambassador in Vienna during the Balkan Wars and the beginning of the First World War. De Bunsen had informed Grey that Austria-Hungary was preparing a plan to attack Serbia but, according to Durham, Grey did not take de Bunsen's reports seriously. However, both de Salis and de Bunsen continued to support Durham morally. After the First World War they urged Durham to 'work out Serb guilt & publish it'.[44] On her side, Durham also urged de Salis and de Bunsen to publish their experiences or memoirs about the Balkan Wars and the First World War which would have exposed Serbia's guilt of aggression towards Albania and their 'responsibility for the Sarajevo crime'. Both abstained from expressing their opinions and experiences publicly out of 'some idea of loyalty to the FO [Foreign Office]'. To this Durham added: 'And now what might have been a very important book will never be written.'[45]

However, Harry Lamb and de Salis had played an important role in alarming the Foreign Office about the situation in Albania at the beginning of the Balkan Wars. When the Conference of Ambassadors was convened in London in December 1912, Albania was the subject about which Edward Grey was well informed and was urged to find a solution. However, it was through the British press that Durham preferred to inform the public at home and influence politicians. Being aware of the lack of knowledge on Albania in Britain, Durham was ready to speak to the people in any sort of conferences or meetings and continued to do so well after the Balkan Wars had ended.[46]

Observing closely the developments in Montenegro during autumn 1912, Durham could predict that the outbreak of war was a matter of days away. She believed that Albanians had no leader like Giuseppe Garibaldi to unite them against the threats of their neighbours. As a result of many other factors Durham changed her previous position on the Ottoman Empire in relation to Albania and just before the outbreak of the Balkan Wars, she started to think that the immediate expulsion of the Ottomans from Europe was not necessary. When the Ottomans considered granting autonomy to Albania in August 1912, Durham suggested that the presence of the Ottoman regime should be continued for few more years. Within that suggested period, the Porte would have served 'as a kind of protective incubator' for the new Albanian state.[47] Only a year earlier Durham had criticized the Young Turks for exiling and imprisoning the majority of the best Albanian political activists and intellectuals and now, when educated Albanians were needed even by the Young Turks, they were not available.[48]

The Balkan Wars and the rejection of the principle of nationality

With the start of the Balkan Wars, Durham discovered that the countries of the Balkan League had no intention of applying the principle of nationality or implementing notions of 'the Balkans for the Balkan people'. Until this point Durham had supported the Balkan League as she wished to see all Balkan nations freed from Ottoman rule. Durham was, most probably, the first female war reporter and in this capacity, she witnessed the very start of the Balkan War, when the Montenegrin artillery fired towards Albania. The First Balkan War had begun and Durham hurried off to send the news to England and made headlines for *The Manchester Guardian* and *The Chronicle*.[49]

As a Liberal she held an anti-Ottoman view and sided with Montenegro. She wrote that 'Gladstone was right when he said that, bag and baggage, the Turk must go'.[50] On

15 October 1912 she went again as a reporter with the Montenegrin Army to witness the fall of Tuzi, an Albanian border town. She even congratulated Prince Danilo of Montenegro on the speedy victory which was achieved by his army. During the late afternoon, after the battle and war formalities between the Montenegrins and the Ottomans were over, Durham observed the sun going down and compared the end of the day with the end of the Ottoman Empire in Europe:

> Then the slender crescent moon shone softly in the heavens – the only crescent now above the land, for the Turkish emblem has been howled down, we hope for ever.[51]

That evening she went back to Cetinje seated courteously in one of the government cars reserved for Montenegrin royalties and state functionaries. The day had ended in complete satisfaction for the Liberal Gladstonian that she was. To explain her feelings further, she added:

> For many years I have given all my energy to the task – as far as one woman can help it – of releasing the European peoples from the Turkish yoke, and it seems that at last the goal is in sight.[52]

From the start of the Balkan Wars, Durham was also engaged in humanitarian relief work with the Montenegrin Red Cross, where she came to know about atrocities committed during the war. This marked a turning point in Durham's beliefs and political activities in the Balkans. In December 1912 she explained that Albania was the reason for the eruption of the Balkan War. By giving testimonies of Serb actions, she also explained that atrocities were announced before the war had started.[53]

Durham did not seem to believe in such 'announcements'. When the war started, she was working as a nurse helping the Montenegrin army but subsequently left with many foreign doctors serving with the Red Cross. She believed that her work prolonged the unjust war and gave the Montenegrin army reinforcements from the cured soldiers. The intentions of the wounded soldiers and the thoughts and actions of the Montenegrin and Serbian establishment made her change her opinion of the situation. In a long and unpublished report about her relief work, she wrote:

> The man of this last batch wanted only to be sufficiently cured to be able to be present at the looting of Scutari [...] The Montenegrin doctor under whom I was working said that he considered they were justified in cutting the throats of every woman and child in Scutari [Shkodra]. The King's cousin told me that in two years they would have stamped out the Albanian language. The Catholic Albanians resident in Podgoritza were continually insulted and threatened with the torments that would be shortly inflicted on their relatives in Scutari. It became the race of life and death to make the Powers realize the truth of the situation and intervene before it was too late.[54]

Durham was terrified when a Serbian officer told her about his 'heroism' in Kosovo and 'nearly choked with laughter' as he told how he had bayoneted the women and children of Luma. Other officers told her that within a short time 'no one would dare speak that dirty language [Albanian]' in the newly occupied lands. They openly spoke about the violence which was being used in converting Muslim and Catholic Albanians into Christian Orthodox. Durham was also told that 'in one generation we shall thus Serbize the lot'.[55]

The mutilated bodies of the Ottoman soldiers terrified her. She reported this problem to the Montenegrin authorities with some strong comments. As a result, all newspaper correspondents were prohibited from going to Tuzi. After she made this discovery, the attitude of the Montenegrin authorities towards her changed. She saw many other unacceptable cases in hospitals. She wrote that 'the war was to be one of the terrorism and extermination'. It was not the liberation of the Balkan people she had expected but rather a war underpinned with religious character that she had believed would not happen. On this she wrote:

> Tsar Ferdinand spoke the truth when he said the war was one of Cross vs Crescent. The Orthodox Cross drips red with blood of victims. They are not all Muslims. Orthodox fanaticism has not spared the Roman Catholics.[56]

Not long before the start of the First Balkan War, Durham was approached by Serbian diplomats in Montenegro who hoped to win her over to their side. She received a letter from the Serbian Legation which considered her as 'the greatest hope of the Serbs, the dearest, the darling and a lot more such stuff'.[57] She thought that the Serbs wanted to use her as a 'cat's paw for Serbia's ambitions'. She told Edward Boyle:

> So I made no reply and never again communicated with that Legation. I was glad I did so, as the Serb atrocities in that war opened my eyes to what they were really up to with their Velika Srbija [Great Serbia].[58]

Durham did not approve of this policy which directly contradicted and violated the principle of 'the Balkans for the Balkan people' in which she believed and on which her activity was based. She finally broke with Gladstonian Liberalism which, according to her, had helped to produce the violence in the Balkans. On this, Durham wrote:

> What a humbug all that talk about 'freeing Xtians from the Turkish youke was!' that fanatic old Gladstone started in England. Never having lived out there he did not know what he was talking about.[59]

Defending this principle, she would soon change her mind about Austria-Hungary and the Balkan League. Vienna, aiming to check the territorial expansion of Serbia, proposed to create an independent Albania which would include most of the territory of what is today Kosovo.[60] This also meant that Greece, Serbia and Montenegro would not be able to divide Albania in the way they wished. Austria-Hungary kept insisting for the continuation of its established policy in the region under the principle of 'the

Balkans for the Balkan people'. Vienna used this policy as a 'back-up for the interdiction of a Serbian land-grab on the Adriatic', which meant that Serbia would not be allowed to keep a port in the middle of a country inhabited by Albanians.[61]

Finally, the principle of 'the Balkans for the Balkan people' brought together Durham and the Austro-Hungarians. Strangely and unexpectedly, Durham's idea also received the support of R. W. Seton-Watson and a few other Gladstonians. A day before the declaration of Albanian independence (27 November 1912), R. W. Seton-Watson expressed disapproval with the Serbian government which was seeking a port at Durrës or Shën Gjin on the Albanian coast. In this regard, R. W. Seton-Watson wrote that 'the Balkans for Balkan people' was his 'reason for approving of this war' but he disapproved of the Serbian occupation of the Albanian coast 'because it would make Albanian independence impossible'.[62] R. W. Seton-Watson added that the Albanians should be counted as a Balkan people who deserved independence.[63]

However, this did not mean that Durham and R. W. Seton-Watson became friends. The very first disagreement between them was about the geographical size of independent Albania. Disagreements continued because R. W. Seton-Watson could not abandon his commitment to the pro-Serb or pro-Slav policies which Durham considered to be anti-Albanian. R. W. Seton-Watson's support for the Serbian government was shown in the correspondence he kept with a Serbian diplomat Stanoje Mihajlović. Mihajlović thanked R. W. Seton-Watson 'in the name of the Serbian people' for his supportive writings in the British press during the Balkan Wars, in which Serbian aims were 'explained properly'.[64]

When the Balkan War was over and peace was temporarily restored, the national question of the Balkan countries came up again for discussion among Gladstonians of the Balkan Committee. This discussion continued even after the First World War was over. Durham still supported the 'principle of nationality' and the ethnic distribution of Albanians which led the conflict with R. W. Seton-Watson to continue. In the Albanian case, R. W. Seton-Watson and Brailsford were in favour of applying the 'principle of civilization' but differed in their reasons for supporting such an approach. Brailsford supported independence for Albania because he was convinced that the Albanians were 'equipped with a sufficient foundation of civilisation', yet R. W. Seton-Watson, supporting the national cause of the Slavs under Austro-Hungarian rule, maintained that Albanians should not enjoy more rights than the 'civilized subjects of Austria-Hungary'.[65]

Lobbying for Albania

Durham's commitment to the principle of 'the Balkans for the Balkan people' distanced her from the Montenegrins and the Serbs because she did not approve of their disregard for this principle and the violence that they applied against the Albanians. The 'liberation' turned into the occupation of Albania and this made Durham strengthen her support for her principle. Because of this principle, Durham decided to end her friendship with the Montenegrin and Serbian regimes. In October 1913, she packed up the Gold Medal which was given to her by King Nikola of

Montenegro and returned it to him. She did the same with the medal that was given to her by King Petar of Serbia.[66]

From this point on, Durham's work can be characterized as lobbying on behalf of Albania. Lobbying was underpinned with efforts to publicize atrocities that were committed against the Albanians. The Carnegie Report, produced by the International Commission to inquire into the causes and conduct of the Balkan Wars which came out in 1914, confirmed the objectivity of Durham's writing on this subject. The Report proved that the Albanian civil population and their property suffered severely at the hands of the Serbian army.[67] Soon after this report, Durham wrote in *The Struggle for Scutari* that 'the destruction of the whole Albanian race was the avowed intention of both Serb and Montenegrin'.[68]

This led the Albanian leaders to use Durham's writings as strong proof to reinforce their nationalist discourse and argue against the violence of the invading or occupying armies. When the war was over, King Nikola of Montenegro, with whom Durham had ended a long friendship without any regret or hesitation, delivered a speech to his returned soldiers:

> With blood your hands are, my blessed soldiers, because you have broken the chains of slavery to your dearest brothers. The hopes of millions of living and dead Serbs are realised. [...] You took revenge for the failure in Kosovo and brought back and raised the honour of the Serbian arms. [...] Let us not forget that Europe took Shkodra from our hands [and] after 20 days we captured and lowered our flag there. We have not given away Shkodra because we do not give away our historic rights.[69]

The Montenegrins were angered with Britain since the international force which forced them to leave Shkodra was composed mainly of Britons and commanded by Vice Admiral Cecil Burney (1858–1929). Burney, at the request of the London Conference, had blockaded the Montenegrin coastline and threatened to attack the Montenegrin army. The threat produced an effect and the Montenegrins left Shkodra[70] but hatred against Austria-Hungary and Albania only rose in Montenegro. The Russian, French and Italian diplomats in Cetinje expressed similar feelings.[71]

Durham went on to underline that the Serbs and Montenegrins were dissatisfied and angry with the result of the Balkan Wars because they did not get enough territory from Albania, and Austria-Hungary was to be blamed. According to Durham, Albania, which became independent during the Balkan Wars, also became a prelude to another big war which would start within a year. When the First Balkan War ended, Durham's belief in the principle of 'the Balkans for the Balkan people' was shattered. The war had produced a result she had never imagined:

> And miseria is the price of war. 'The Balkan land for the Balkan people'. But the Balkan lands were but sparsely populated, and the victims are innumerable.[72]

When the armies of Montenegro and Serbia retreated from Shkodra in April 1913, an international force of nearly 2000 soldiers and marines was dispatched to occupy the town. Vice Admiral Burney was appointed President of a Provisional Administration whose jurisdiction extended only 6 miles around Shkodra.[73] In October that year Burney was replaced by General George Fraser Phillips (1863–1921). Durham was quick to establish contact with Phillips and also discovered that her pro-Albanian friend Dr Cunningham was also a friend of Phillips. After exchanging a few letters, Cunningham told Durham that General Phillips had 'changed his mind about the Serbs' and now 'we should stick out for complete independence under international guarantee'.[74] In one of her letters sent to Herbert, Durham wrote that 'Phillips had taken a much more helpful view of the situation'.[75] This meant that Phillips was supporting the Albanians, at least regarding the Shkodra issue. Until many years later Durham kept sending her books to Phillips and included other relevant books, such as Byron's works on Albania and Brailsford's on Macedonia.[76]

The importance of Harry Lamb grew when he was appointed as representative of the British government in the International Commission of Control, which was established on 29 July 1913 by the London Treaty of the Conference of Ambassadors. The headquarters of the Commission were based in Vlora and its aim was to take care of the administration of Albania until permanent political and administrative institutions were established. Harry Lamb pressured the Foreign Office on three points: 1. Nominating a civil governor for Shkodra; 2. Recognizing the Albanian Provisional Government; and 3. Considering an economic plan for the future of Albania. Lamb made this proposal with the purpose of exercising control or influence over the Albanian Provisional Government and improving the British position which, according to Lamb, was 'beginning to suffer loss of prestige'. By the end of October 1913, the Foreign Office had expressed its consent on all three points. 'I was from the beginning of [the] opinion that we ought to enter into official relation with Ismail Kemal as the "Autorité Existante" at Valona [Vlora]', wrote Lamb.[77]

Having in mind these developments, it could be concluded that the British policy was slowly taking a positive stance on Albania and Durham had certainly played an important role in this change. In spring of 1914 Albania was still in a state of devastation that was brought about by the Balkan Wars, but there was hope that things would be improved with the help of considerable British engagement. However, this situation was soon to change.

On Sunday, 28 June 1914, Harry Lamb had invited Durham for afternoon tea. Admiral Troubridge (1862–1926), commander of the international fleet in Adriatic, came later (uninvited) to the consul's residence in Durrës. The Admiral came to tell the consul that his navy wireless had just 'picked up a bit of a message'. The Archduke Franz Ferdinand was murdered in Sarajevo. 'Just that!', said the Admiral. Durham was not greatly surprised by the information and said to Lamb: 'this means war.' Lamb was surprised by Durham and replied: 'Not necessarily.'[78]

It did mean war and, under these circumstances, Durham was left with no possibility of continuing her humanitarian work. She left Albania in August 1914, a few days after the First World War had started. The way that the war had begun was against Durham's principles and all her expectations.[79]

The situation in Albania was now similar to that of October 1912, when the First Balkan War had begun. Although greatly disappointed, she started again the same activity of saving Albania as the situation was reversed. To Durham this was a repeated episode of the Balkan Wars on which she wrote:

> I hoped that when once Albania's independence was gained in 1913 I should never again have to wallow in these dirty Balkan politics. Then came the war of 1914–18 & it all had to be fought again.[80]

Durham refused to take part directly in the state forming process of the new Albania. She disliked Ismail Qemali, the founder of the Albanian state and never wanted to meet King Zog of Albania who she considered as both undemocratic and immoral. After she left in 1914 she visited Albania only once, in 1921. 'Tired. Don't feel as if my Albania existed any more', she wrote during the visit.[81] Durham's Albania was to include all Albanians in one state but she felt that the principle 'the Balkans for the Balkan people' was only partially applied in this case. In London, defending this principle and on behalf of Albania, she never stopped debating with supporters of Serbia and later Yugoslavia, usually with R. W. Seton-Watson, Wickham Steed, Rebecca West and other Gladstonian Liberals.

Although the Balkan Wars and the First World War were over, the debate about the causes and conduct of the war intensified in the British press between Durham on one side and R. W. Seton-Watson[82] and Henry Wickham Steed, a foreign correspondent from Vienna and foreign editor for *The Times*, on the other side. Albania and Serbia, and particularly the role of the Serbian state in atrocities against Albanians and the assassination of Franz Ferdinand, were the key themes of the debate. Seton-Watson and his friend Steed were better placed in the academic world, the press and British politics but Durham was far more knowledgeable than the two about the Balkans. Durham couldn't win the fight against them but the debate helped her to keep the subject of Albania alive.[83] Debating Seton-Watson and Wickham Steed, Durham is remembered to have invented a jingle about them which became popular and she was very keen of using it often when writing on this matter:

> SW, WS.
> The two of them made
> the hell of a mess![84]

Durham, Seton-Watson and Steed continued to be members of the Balkan Committee despite the fact that they had different opinions on countries in this part of Europe. She held them responsible for the events that had taken a wrong turn during the Balkan Wars and First World War. She considered that they contributed to spreading the flame of war:

> Seton-Watson & Wickham Steed were like children who played with matches, throughout they had made a nice blaze and burned the house down.[85]

The debate continued and Durham used all opportunities to put Albania in the centre of it, emphasizing that the principle of nationality was not applied to Albanians and as a result the Balkans will remain destabilized.[86] However, Durham is today far less known for her humanitarian work, another principle that she applied to all victims of war. Even when she wrote articles of a political nature she was keen to emphasize that she was also engaged in humanitarian work in the Balkans and asked for donations.

Durham's work showed that Liberal Gladstonians had artificially constructed an idea about the Balkans which was based on religion and, as such, reflected negatively on the Albanians. The Liberal's idea of 'illuminating' and liberating the Christians was not acceptable for her. Durham was among rare experts, travel writers and political activists who recognized that the conflict in the Balkans was in fact of a nationalist character. Therefore, the essence of her work was to correct this misguided approach of the Liberals. Her approach was inclusive as she insisted that both Christians and non-Christians should be supported in their efforts to liberate themselves from Ottoman rule. Of all the British experts and travel writers on the Balkans of the twentieth century, Durham became the most important one. As a woman but also through her work, she made a great impact on the countries she came to know and love. The expansionist policies of the countries of the Balkan League, the violence and the policy of the Powers were the reasons that made Durham change her mind and her support for differing Balkan nations.[87]

8

Refuting Gladstonian liberalism

Aubrey Herbert and the Albanian statehood

In 1913 Aubrey Herbert went to Vlora, the seat of the Albanian Provisional Government. There was a large crowd of people gathered in front of the house where he was staying and cheered for Great Britain. Herbert gave a speech and explained to them the work of the Albanian Committee, the organization he had formed in London to lobby on behalf of Albania. They cheered again, saluted and called him the 'Paladin of Liberty'. This scenario 'resembled Seton-Watson's triumphal voyage' a year earlier, in Dalmatia, Croatia, where he was saluted and cheered for representing the Slavs in Great Britain.[1]

Aubrey Herbert was born in 1889, in the midst of the general election that brought Gladstone into power for the second time.[2] Aubrey, as the second son of Henry Herbert, 4th Earl of Carnarvon, would follow the tradition of aristocratic and rich English families by serving in British diplomacy while his elder brother, George Edward Stanhope Molyneux Herbert (1866–1923) would retain the title of 5th Earl of Carnarvon. Their father, Henry Howard Molyneux Herbert, had twice served as Colonial Secretary as well as Lord-Lieutenant of Ireland and was also known as a classical scholar.[3] The Carnarvon family became famous worldwide when in 1923, under the expedition of the 5th Earl of Carnarvon, archaeologist Howard Carter discovered the tomb of Pharaoh Tutankhamun in the Valley of the Kings in Egypt.

Coming from the British ruling class and with a wide circle of important friends, Herbert was guaranteed to have a bright future. John Buchan, the author of *Thirty-Nine Steps*, used Herbert's autobiography *Ben Kendim* to construct *Greenmantle*, a famous novel published in 1916, in which Herbert is understood to be Sandy, the main character.[4] The structure of *Greenmantle* was also based on Herbert's activities as described in his war diaries, the first of which was written in a hospital in Mons, the second focused on the Dardanelles and Gallipoli and the third dealt with the fall of Kut.[5]

In 1904, after spending a few months at the British Embassy in Tokyo and visiting Cyprus and Athens, Herbert reached Salonika, a multi-national city that he liked and where he met 'a wild Albanian highlander' named Kiazim [Qazim] Kukeli. Herbert employed Kukeli as a bodyguard and servant. Kukeli became Herbert's long-term companion, instilling in Herbert an interest in Albania through his 'edifying stories' about Albanian *komitadjis* (rebels or guerrillas).[6]

In Salonika Herbert enjoyed spending time with Ottoman intellectuals, including Riza Tewfik Bey (1869–1949), an Albanian poet, philosopher and statesman who liked discussing John Stuart Mill. While in Greece and Crete, Herbert had held anti-Turkish prejudices, but began to change his opinion while travelling in Macedonia. Herbert wrote to his mother from Macedonia saying that Christians were unattractive and inferior compared to 'the genial, polished Turk'.[7] Herbert, like Durham, despised Macedonian Christians but was convinced that they were put to this position as a result of the cruelty and injustice of the Ottoman regime.[8]

In Constantinople, as honorary attaché, Herbert was quick to make friends in high Ottoman society and was even presented to the Sultan. Herbert found Constantinople a very pleasant place and liked the Turks, but told his mother that he can't understand anyone being a Turcophile. In 1908 he supported the Young Turks and their Revolution, hoping that they would bring changes in the Ottoman Empire. Despite his forays into Ottoman and Albanian society, Macedonia remained Herbert's primary interest at this time. From early on Herbert understood that the problem in Macedonia was not the religion, as Liberals had consistently argued, but was of a nationalist character.[9]

This insight was reflected in Herbert's involvement with the Balkan Committee, where he held an opinion different to those Liberal Gladstonians who constituted the vast majority of members. Almost a decade later, during the Balkan Wars, his position on the Balkans and the Ottoman Empire at large was completely changed and had become broadly anti-Liberal. This change could be seen in a note he wrote to his brother, Mervyn, in July 1913:

> Ten years ago I went to Turkey, strongly anti-Turk, ready in fact to write pamphlets on its government in Macedonia, and it was only the fact that I was able to compare, in the archives of the Embassy, the way in which Turks and Bulgars behaved in Macedonia that completely changed my sympathies. For the Turk is the one man in the Balkans whom I have known who is a gentleman.[10]

As a traveller and journalist, Herbert had visited the Albanian part of the Balkans in 1907 and acquired further knowledge about the place and its people. After witnessing the solemn opening of the new Ottoman Parliament in December 1908, Herbert travelled through Macedonia to Kosovo, a visit that would bring him close to the Albanian national cause. In January 1909 he went to Mitrovica and discovered that many Albanians who had supported the Revolution were now expressing doubts about its success. In June 1909 he went to south Albania and published a few articles under his pen name *Ben Kendim*. Most of his articles from that time, dedicated to the British public, contained basic informative knowledge about Albania and the Albanians. However, there was an article with a political message which he titled 'Southern Albania and Epirus'.[11] As seen from the title, Herbert sought to distinguish the Albanian part of the south from Greek Epirus or northern Greece. This was done deliberately in order to reject the term Epirus, with which the Greeks had named the entire area of what was later to become south Albania. For unknown reasons the article remained unpublished, but its significance in indicating where Herbert's sympathies lay is clear.[12]

By 1910, British politics and diplomacy were beginning to diverge from the views Herbert had formed about the Ottoman Europe and so he decided to play an active role in changing this course. In a by-election in November 1911, Herbert won the South Somerset seat for the Conservatives against the Liberal candidate Edward Strachey; and from 1918 to his death in 1923 he represented the Yeovil constituency. In his first speech to the House of Commons on 14 December 1911, Herbert criticized British policy towards Ottoman reforms for being 'stonily indifferent', adding that the Young Turk Revolution was 'an experiment that deserved more sympathy than it got from the Liberal Government'. He considered that the British policy was going wrong in regard of the Ottoman Empire and he made an appeal:

> I would appeal for a very cordial consideration of the whole Turkish question by His Majesty's Government. I appeal not only from motives of generosity and chivalry, not only from the motives of principle, but because His Majesty King George V rules over millions of Mussulman subjects whose spiritual allegiance turns towards the Sultan of Turkey. This cordiality of our relations with Turkey must always be a matter of the deepest and gravest concern to these people.[13]

Making such an appeal, Herbert's criticism of Liberal policy can be seen as indicative of his Conservative approach to the matters at hand. When speaking of troubles in the Ottoman Empire Herbert did not specifically mention Albania, seeing their question as part of the broader Balkan problem. However, Herbert did speak about the insurrection which had started in Albania in September 1911, for which he blamed the British government's apparent indifference to events. This gave Hugh Alexander Law (1872–1943), who represented the Irish constituencies of County Donegal, chance to speak and hail Herbert's speech 'extremely brilliant'. Law added that while it was true the British government reigned over many millions of Muslim subjects, it was also true that Great Britain was 'a great Christian country – a country which both naturally and by actual treaty obligations owes certain duties to the Christian subjects of the Turkish Empire'.[14] Although Herbert found some supporters for his views, the vast majority of the House shared Law's favouring of the Christians in the Ottoman Empire. However, the debate about Albania had started and Herbert was to bring more of it.

In August 1912, when the Albanian nationalist movement had successfully influenced Porte's attitude towards granting them autonomy, Herbert went to Kosovo. His aim was to collect information from Albanian leaders about their future intentions, coordinate plans with them and influence public discourse in Britain. He wrote about his journey to the *Sanjak* of Novi Pazar, a region which he called the 'Albanian borderland' in a bid to demonstrate to the British public the northern border of Albania, as he had done earlier with the southern border with Greece.[15] In private Herbert held a different opinion. In his diary he described Novi Pazar as a 'no man's land, occupied by the Turks, held precariously by the Albanians, ruled by none'.[16] He also emphasized that there were indications that 'with the growing feeling of nationality among the Albanians' the responsibility of Albanian leaders was taking steps towards championing the cause of the Christians in this part of Albania. This fact was also recorded by Ottoman officials. A report sent from Kosovo to Constantinople noted that Isa Boletini was enlarging his group of Albanian fighters and was planning either to include Serbs among their ranks or to protect them.[17]

Herbert also explained the Albanians' belief that they needed foreign protection.[18] By now a Turcophile, it is likely that Herbert believed autonomy would satisfy Albanian nationalist needs and that they would feel comfortable within the new Young Turk regime. However, within less than a month, the First Balkan War of October 1912 markedly changed this situation and Herbert began to advocate for the independence of Albania as opposed to autonomy. One of his immediate actions was to distance himself completely from the Balkan Committee, which he believed was only looking after the national interests of the Christian Slavs and thus ignoring the Albanians.

The lack of interest in Albania shown by the Balkan Committee can be seen in its activities throughout the Balkan Wars. Towards the end of July 1913, the Balkan Committee issued a resolution asking the Powers to intervene for ending the conflict between the Balkan Allies and free the Christian population from Ottoman rule. The resolution stated that there was no other solution for the Balkans except the 'bag and baggage – the Turk out of Constantinople and the Turk out of Europe'. The resolution also stated that the Christian Allies should be permitted to 'reap fruits of their handsome victory' because 'they were not ashamed or afraid to appeal to force'.[19]

On 1 August 1913, the Balkan Committee sent a letter to the Foreign Office, regarding the 'recognition of nationalities', asking the Powers and the British government to recognize the occupation of Macedonia by the Allied armies. The Albanians of Macedonia were not mentioned at all. The Committee asked the British government, which had accepted the leadership of the Concert of Europe, to impose an active policy in 'promoting humane government'.[20] A few weeks later, Arthur Symonds, the Secretary of the Balkan Committee, wrote a letter to *The Times* criticizing the British press for publishing items about atrocities that the Allied armies committed against non-Christians: 'What good can come of repeating and publishing them?' asked Symonds.[21] The actions of the Balkan Committee, as a Liberal Gladstonian organization, can thus be seen as positioning themselves against the Ottoman Empire, favouring the Allies in the outcome of the First Balkan War, and ignoring the Albanian national question. Herbert, being simultaneously pro-Ottoman and pro-Albanian, could not continue being a member of this Liberal organization. He therefore resigned from the Committee, stating its support for the claims of the Balkan Allies, the Serbian massacres committed against Albanians and the Bulgarian massacres committed against Muslims, none of which were condemned by the Committee, as his reasons.[22]

The Albanian Committee

When the First Balkan War started, Herbert was concerned that Albanian lands would be partitioned. As a result, he decided to campaign against the occupation of territories by the Allied armies and formed an alternative organization to the Balkan Committee designed to support the Albanian national cause. On 9 December 1912 Herbert sent invitations informing interested personalities that:

The question of Albanian Autonomy differs considerably from the questions of other Balkan States, as it is one of nationality, not of religion. The Albanians, as an ancient race (the original Macedonians), are surrounded to-day by people who threatened their national ideals with destruction. As Albania may be sacrificed at any moment to the exigencies of diplomacy, an immediate effort is called for. In view of the urgency of the Albanian Question and the importance of the Anglo-Muhammedan situation, the Committee, which has no party ties, invites you to join it.[23]

On 17 December 1912, the same day that the Conference of Ambassadors convened in London to decide about Albania's future, Herbert held a meeting with those who answered his call and agreed to form the Albanian Committee.[24] All became members of this new organization, although the reasons for their decision to join varied widely. Many were more interested in opposing the new situation in the Balkans created by the advance of the Allied armies than solving the Albanian Question specifically. Some were Turcophiles and as such against any enemies of the Ottoman Empire. Some were supporters of the principle of self-determination and wanted this principle to be applied to Albania as it was to other Balkan nations. The Albanian Committee also attracted Muslims and British imperialists who were concerned about the reaction of the Muslim dominions of the British Empire. The Committee was particularly attractive to Jews, whose brethren had suffered persecution at the hands of the Allied armies and who hoped for tolerance in the future Albanian state. Hostility towards Russia, the force behind the Allied armies, also brought to the Committee the ideological heirs of Disraeli as well as radicals and socialists who opposed Russia's pan=Slav policy. There were also members of various pressure groups who favoured the independence of small countries, many of whom had no previous knowledge or connection with the Albanian national cause but now showed an interest in seeing Albania as an independent country. Above all, the Albanian Committee brought together all those who held anti-Liberal views and who opposed the effects of this policy in the Balkans. Those who took principal interest in the work of the Committee were C. F. Ryder, Mark H. Judge, J. C. Paget and Major Paget. Herbert recalled later that it was only he and Major Paget who had lived in Shkodra and who had 'actual acquaintance' with Albania, while 'the others were prompted by a generous love for freedom'.[25] Two other important personalities, Edith Durham and Captain MacRury, joined the Committee later.

Aubrey Herbert was elected President of the Albanian Committee, while Lord Lamington (1860–1940), a Conservative MP and former Governor of Queensland and Bombay, was elected Vice President. Mark H. Judge (1847–1927), founder of the University Extension Guild and chairman of the British Constitutional Association, was elected Treasurer while John C. Paget, also from the British Constitutional Association, was elected Honourable Secretary. The Executive Committee included personalities such as Dr Moses Gaster (1856–1949), Chief Rabbi of the Sephardic Jews in Britain and a well-known British intellectual.[26] Gaster joined the Albanian Committee in search of a solution for the Jews in Macedonia, but he also had an interest in Albania as a scholar linguist and known collector of books on Albania.

Other Jewish members of the Committee shared Gaster's search for a solution for the Jewish population of Macedonia who were opposed to the Greek and Bulgarian rule. They increasingly pushed the idea of an autonomous Macedonia which coincided with Herbert's aims, albeit for different reasons. Although Herbert's aim was to focus the Committee's activity on the Albanian Question, the influence of the Jews grew so great that Herbert told his wife 'they have made a desperate effort to get hold of the Albanian Committee'.[27]

The Liberal policy of supporting only Christian groups in the Balkans had contributed to worsening inter-religious relations in the region. Though the aim of the Albanian Committee was to assist in the establishment of an autonomous Albania, their members also identified the lack of knowledge about the Balkans as an obstacle to their future activities. Therefore, the Committee also aimed to 'develop a wider knowledge of the Balkan problem and to promote a good understanding' between Christians and Muslims. Mark H. Judge believed that the Committee should 'send a much-needed message of good will' to the Muslims of the world and assure the Muslims of the British Empire that the British still 'upheld the principle of freedom as necessary for the maintenance of the Empire'.[28]

The counter-Liberal view of the Committee was manifested by all members including Gaster who maintained that Muslims and Jews were ignored by the British government and the public. He elaborated the Committee's views:

> The Committee believes that settlement of the Balkan question, to be lasting, must bring freedom to all, and as this freedom can only be established on an ethnical basis, no nationality should be forced to forgo its natural heritage of language or faith: The Committee urges that the claims of the Albanians and Kutzo-Vlachs, in union, to political and religious autonomy should now be conceded, while at the same time the rights of Muslims and Jews throughout the Balkans should receive full recognition and protection.[29]

Gaster complained about the Greek suppression of stories detailing atrocities in their occupied territories, adding that the Greeks could not ignore the fact that the Albanians were most cruelly treated and this treatment should certainly be brought to the public knowledge.[30]

Most of the members maintained that it was necessary to win over the British public and government in order to reverse British Liberal policy, but winning such support proved problematic. The Committee prepared a report explaining the aims and sent it to most of the newspapers in Britain. None of the newspapers published it. The future state of Albania, with a Muslim majority and Christian and Jewish minorities, which would serve as an example of religious cooperation, was apparently not an interesting subject for the British press. The report did appear on the front page of *The Times* but only as an announcement paid for by the Committee. The Albanian Committee intensified the pressure for their cause, leveraging their impressive list of twelve MPs, a Lord Justice of Appeals, a Privy Councillor, two peers, a Chief Rabbi and many other dignitaries. Despite this list of influential figures, the group was not as powerful as the Balkan Committee which for a decade had cultivated the Gladstonian tradition.[31]

The Committee worked in close collaboration with the Albanian Provisional Government and organized a visit by an Albanian delegation, consisting of Filip Noga, Mehmet Bey Konitza and Rashit Bey Dino, which arrived in London in January 1913. Since the Albanian Provisional Government was not officially recognized, these delegates could not participate in the work of the London Conference. However, Herbert and other members of the Committee assisted the delegation in presenting a memorandum on Albanian claims to the Conference and the Foreign Office.[32] They also lobbied to influence British politicians and diplomats at the Conference, publicize the Albanian national cause, including a map of Albania[33], presented by the delegation and raise funds for refugees in Albania. In early May, Ismail Qemali attended a meeting of the Albanian Committee and told members that his government and the Albanian people 'have preserved the hope that the English nation would not forget us'.[34] Herbert made efforts to arrange meetings between Ismail Qemali and Edward Grey, though this ended without success because the British government still did not recognize the Albanian Provisional Government at this stage. The Foreign Office wrote to Ismail Qemali to explain 'with regret' that Grey was 'busy with parliamentarian work'.[35]

The press likewise continued to show no interest in the Albanian Question. The visit of the Albanian delegation led the Committee to intensify its work and find ways of reaching the British public. Gaster emphasized the need to 'stir up public opinion in order to make people realize the claims of the Albanians' whose aim was to 'establish themselves according to their race, faith and customs'.[36] Gaster believed that in order to do so reports of atrocities committed against Albanians should be made known to the British public, together with emphasizing the need to create an ethnic Albania. In the House of Commons, questions were asked about the atrocities but Gaster regarded the replies as unsatisfactory. Speaking further on this matter in a Committee meeting, he added that it was essential for the Albanians to be included within borders on ethnic basis and irrespective of religion.[37]

The Committee published several documents by May 1913 on the subject of influencing the public.[38] The *Plea of Albania* was one such work created on behalf of the Albanian Provisional Government and submitted to the London Conference to counter the Greek claim in southern Albania. This publication aimed to present the fact that, during the Conference, the Greek government did not distinguish between the question of religion and that of nationality.[39] Unwilling to recognize separate nationalities, the Greek government, like the Ottoman government, divided the Albanians into two distinct categories: Muslims and Christians. As a result of this ambiguity the number of inhabitants and the percentage of Greeks and Albanians in south Albania was grossly disputed by both sides.[40] The Committee believed that the Greek approach was a mistake and aimed to correct it.

The most important publication following Gaster's speech, *Albania for the Albanians*, was in the form of a letter to the press written by C. F. Ryder on behalf of the Albanian Committee. The letter was in fact a criticism of Liberal ideas in Britain and their impact on policy in the Balkans.[41] Ryder explained that the problem of the Albanian Question in Britain was primarily the result of a lack of knowledge about Albania on the part of the British public. He further explained that, if there was some knowledge on this matter, the problem was in fact even greater. Ryder believed that the religious prejudices held by the Powers, the British government and the public led them to ignore the Albanian Question on the grounds that they were a non-Christian population. Ryder criticized the Powers and the British government for supporting the 'stronger races over the weaker ones'. He pointed out that in the Albanian case, contrary to the position it had adopted in the case of Montenegro, the British public and government regarded the formation of the Albanian state along ethnic lines as impracticable. On this matter Ryder also criticized the press, politicians and, above all, intellectuals for not adopting the same position towards Albania as they did towards other Balkan nations.[42]

Furthermore, Ryder criticized the British establishment for 'being happy that England was fascinated by Russia', as he put it, and yet did nothing to promote the independence of 'one of the most ancient races in Europe'. Therefore, Ryder continued to make it known that the Albanian Committee was entitled to work towards establishing an Albanian state and preventing the Albanian nation from being sacrificed to the political intrigues of the Powers. 'Albania for some mysterious reason has no claim upon its good offices' added Ryder. He went on to explain the 'mysterious reason':

> The truth is, however, that with many freedom is cursed in Albania while it is blessed in Switzerland, because a large portion of Albanian people have the misfortune to belong, by the heritage of centuries, to the Muslem faith. Had these people been of any other religion or of non like so many of our rulers in England to-day, their misfeasance might have been overlooked, but since they are Muhammedans the prejudice of almost every ecclesiastic in the kingdom is against them.[43]

Ryder went further in examining the cause of this problem, seeing the religious prejudice which existed in Britain against Jews until the beginning of the twentieth century as a key factor. In this respect, he added that one great objective of the Albanian Committee was to 'mitigate this aversion and to ensure that no man shall be prejudiced by his religion in Albania any more than elsewhere'.[44]

Despite Ryder's letter, to Herbert's dissatisfaction, the press, the government and public opinion continued in their prejudice against Muslims. In February 1913, Herbert visited Constantinople and was disappointed to learn at the British Embassy there that the Powers continued to approach the Balkan Question 'very ignorantly' and that the ambassador was not consulted at all by London on the questions of the Ottoman Empire and Albania.[45] When Herbert returned to London he tried to publish his views on this matter, but anti-Turk feeling ran deep in the press and most newspapers would not publish his views. In anger and bitterness, Herbert expressed his views in a poem he wrote:

> Intrigues within, intrigues without, no man to trust,
> He [the Turk] feeds street dogs that starve with him; to friends who are his foe
> The Greeks and Bulgars in his lines, he flings a sudden crust
> The Turk who has to go.
>
> The Turk worked in the vineyard, others drunk the wine,
> The Jew who sold him plough shares kept an interest in his plough.

The Serb and Bulgar waited till King and Priest should sign,
Till Kings said 'kill, kill now'.

So now the twilight falls upon the twice betrayed,
The *Daily Mail* tells England and the *Daily News* tells God
That God and British Statesmen should make the Turk afraid
Who fight unfed, unshod.⁴⁶

The poem particularly emphasized the power that the media exercised over the public and politics, a fact which Herbert had experienced first-hand. Liberal public opinion and the press were strongly against Herbert's views and continued to have strong influence over the British position regarding the Ottoman Empire and the Balkans, a fact which was admitted by Edward Grey.⁴⁷

The British position on Albania and the London Conference of Ambassadors

When the First Balkan War started on 9 October 1912, the British government had no clear idea of how to deal with the situation. The Foreign Office hoped that none of the Allied armies would achieve a clear victory. 'The prospect of a Turkish "débâcle" and the complete victory of the Balkan States makes things more difficult', wrote Grey on 30 October 1912.⁴⁸ Contrary to the hopes of the British, the Ottoman army was defeated sooner than anyone could have imagined. The defeat of the Ottoman Empire and the massacres committed against its Muslim population by the Balkan armies, whose advance the British public had initially supported, caused worries among the British government. Their key consideration was the feelings of the Muslims in India and elsewhere in the empire about the treatment of their brothers in the Balkans.⁴⁹

By late November the situation was complicated even further when the Serbian, Montenegrin and Greek armies invaded Albania. The advance of the Balkan armies was supported by the British public and even cheered by most politicians. As seen earlier, Asquith expressed support for the Balkan armies in his Guildhall speech. A few days later, Winston Churchill made an even more extreme speech and praised Gladstone for predicting the course of events in the Balkans.⁵⁰ No matter the view of the British Liberal public and government and their disregard for the Albanian national question, Edward Grey believed that Albania was about to spark a European war. Whatever was to happen in the Balkans, the British made it clear during the Conference that they would remain neutral and would not go to war, and certainly not to 'secure an Adriatic seaport for Belgrade'.⁵¹ However the fact that all the Powers had interests in the Balkans meant that, in reality, none truly remained neutral.

The Conference of London, or the Conference of Ambassadors as it is known in Albania, started on 17 December 1912. In seeking a post-war settlement, 'the Conference was not of justice but of force', wrote Grey in his diary, adding that 'the point of friction and danger was Albania'.⁵² Most historians of the Balkan Wars, including Ernst Helmreich and Christopher Clark, have maintained that during the Conference the only Powers that supported the creation of Albania based on ethnic principles was Austria-Hungary and to some extent Italy. However, the German ambassador, Prince Lichnovsky, wrote in his memoirs that Germany also supported Albania in order to fall in line with the position prescribed by Vienna.[53] As a result, Germany took the side of Austria-Hungary and Italy on the problem of Shkodra, the Serbian port on the Adriatic and on the delimitation of the frontiers.

Despite German rhetorical support, it was only Austria-Hungary which gave signs of being prepared to go to war over Albania. Austria-Hungary also pushed for the new state to be as large as possible, a position Russia vehemently opposed. Under the banner of 'Albania for Albanians', Vienna was carrying out its policy of supporting Albanian nationalism and the creation of an Albanian state. The Austro-Hungarian ambassador managed to impose his proposal that Albania should border Greece in the south and Montenegro in the north. This ended the question of Serbian expansion to the Albanian Adriatic coast but introduced many border problems in the north-east and east of Albania.[54]

The British government was not concerned with the ethnographic form of independent Albania. Its primary concern was to protect its direct interests by maintaining the balance of power in the Adriatic and Mediterranean seas. Since Albania held a strategic location in this respect, it became a matter of concern for the British. The main aim of the British government was to ensure that the territories of the Ottoman and Austro-Hungarian empires, after their eventual dissolution, would not fall under Russian rule. Therefore, the British were ready to support the creation of an independent Albania or enlargements of existing Balkan states if this would help to achieve their objective, and if not the principle of compromise would be applied.[55] During the London Conference the British government declared that this policy was pursued in line with the principle of neutrality.

It was for this reason that Edward Grey insisted the British government had adopted a neutral role. In his public appearances and later in his memoirs, Grey was keen to emphasize that he had not taken sides in negotiations during the Conference because the settlement 'did not touch British interest'.[56] While it is true that Albania was not within the scope of direct British interests, Grey was not as neutral as he publicly declared. Regarding Grey's 'neutrality', Lichnovsky gave a conflicting account when he wrote that Grey 'supported our group in order not to give a pretext like the one a dead Archduke was to furnish later on'.[57]

At the beginning of the Balkan Wars, Grey was among the first European diplomats to recognize the need for Albania to become autonomous. Although this recognition was the result of strategic not ideological aims, it was nonetheless useful for the Albanian national cause and led Herbert to show respect and sympathy for Grey. On 28 October 1912 Grey told Edward Goschen, the British ambassador to Germany, that 'Albania could hardly be absorbed' because 'Albanians both Christian and Moslem would combine against the Serbs'.[58] Another letter Grey sent to Francis Bertie, the British ambassador to France, emphasized that British foreign policy would not go against British public opinion. This was fundamental to his policies, and his respecting for Liberal public opinion led to his support of the Balkan Allied armies. Speaking on this matter, Grey laid out the framework that he was to follow during the Conference:

Public opinion here will be dead against turning the Balkan States out of what they may show their ability to conquer by their own forces. If Russia and Austria do agree upon a settlement, public opinion here will not push its own views and force the Government to assert them. But if Austria were to attack the Balkan States, and Russia said "Hands off", it would be impossible for a British Government, even if it desired, to side diplomatically with Austria against Russia. I propose to work for agreement between Russia and Austria, but it will have to be with the limitation that Austria is reasonable.[59]

Grey also expressed the 'neutral position' of the British government to the Serbian *Charge d'Affaires*, who informed Grey that Serbia was claiming the *Vilayet* of Kosovo, the *Sanjak* of Novi Pazar, part of the *Vilayet* of Shkodra and the ports of Durrës and Shën Gjin. Grey repeated that it was public opinion which would not allow the British government to 'deprive the victors of the fruits of their victories'.[60] In doing so Grey indicated that the British government would not object totally to Serbian claims on Albania. However, Grey did not give in entirely to public opinion and acted between the pressure of this and the strategic interest of the British government. In taking this position Grey had partly satisfied Albanian nationalism, but also encouraged Serbian ambitions to continue their military advance and attempts to occupy as much Albanian land as possible.[61]

On 7 April 1913 Edward Grey made a statement about Albania in the House of Commons, claiming that the British government had maintained its neutrality. He told the House that an agreement, which was a compromise between the Powers, had been reached about the north-east borders of Albania. It was decided that most of the *Vilayet* of Kosovo would not be included in Albania but rather divided between Serbia and Montenegro. Grey also said that this agreement was essential for Europe as it was 'accomplished only just in time to preserve the peace between the Great Powers'.[62] Preserving the peace thus proved more important than applying the principle of nationality in the case of Albania.

The Albanian Committee had hoped for a better decision. However, in Albania the situation worsened as Montenegrin and Serbian forces ignored the decision of the Conference and continued to attack Shkodra.[63] Shkodra was eventually handed to the Montenegrins by Esat Pasha, but the London Conference, just before the start of the Second Balkan War, decided to return the city to Albania. On this occasion Herbert told the House of Commons that Shkodra was to remain within the borders of Albania 'thanks to great extent to England'. Yet Herbert also added that by and large the Conference had decided to give to Albania only 'rocks and gorges and mountain torrents' and stripped it of 'rivers and fertile plains'. Speaking about the territory that remained outside Albania, Herbert told the House:

Towns that are most Albanian and that she needs – like Ipek [Peja], like Dibra, which stands in the same relationship to Albania as Yorkshire does to England; or Prizren with its fertile plain and beautiful cypresses – have been taken from her.[64]

Herbert's view was supported by several conservative MPs, who criticized the 'neutrality' of the British government which they saw as an erroneous approach towards Albania. Since the war was not over, Herbert and another conservative MP, Walter Guinness, suggested that the British and other governments in Europe should adopt a different approach, applying the principle of 'Balkans for the Balkan people' in Albania and fully disclosing and condemning atrocities committed against the Albanians.[65]

Herbert was also supported by John Annan Bryce, a Liberal MP, but the number of MPs who supported Montenegro and Serbia was far greater. Though none objected to the Albanian right to statehood, they favoured the decisions taken thus far by the Conference and denied the number of Albanian refugees and atrocities which were committed by Allied armies.[66]

Although the decision of the Conference was regarded as unfavourable by the Committee and Albanians, Herbert saw the role of the British government and Grey as positive for Albania. On this matter Herbert said that the House of Commons ought to feel very proud to have a statesman like Grey, 'who throws his influence into the scales of justice on behalf of small nationalities'. It is likely that Herbert knew the situation would have been much worse for Albania without Grey's engagement in the Conference. The difficult situation in Albania was far from over and Herbert, as a cautious politician, had no intention of jeopardizing his relationship with Grey and closing the door to the British government. The Albanian Committee, and particularly Herbert, needed a good relationship with the British government as he might have had pretensions to the Albanian throne. Another reason Herbert needed Grey's support was his and the Committee's humanitarian engagement with Albania.

Herbert led several relief missions to help the refugees who had flooded Albania, escaping persecution from the lands which were given to Montenegro, Serbia and Greece. Largely thanks to the work of Herbert, these humanitarian activities were supported by Grey and the Chancellor of the Exchequer, Lloyd George.[67]

Herbert continued his fundraising through different events organized by the Committee and other British humanitarian organizations, among the donors to which there were royal family members. Filip Noga, a minister in Ismail Qemali's government, sent a telegram to thank Herbert and the Albanian Committee and also praised the British government for their humanitarian support.[68]

Grey maintained that the Conference had managed to avoid endangering the peace of Europe. He believed that 'the things that had threatened the relations between the Great Powers in 1912–13' had been successfully avoided.[69] However, the decision of the London Conference was met with fierce criticism in the British Parliament and the press by Herbert and members of the Albanian Committee. During the Conference, as Clark notes, Grey had adopted 'a latent pro-Serbian policy'. Clark maintains that Grey favoured 'Belgrade's claims over those of the new Albanian state, not because he supported the Great Serbian cause as such', but because he regarded Serbia as an important factor for the 'durability of Entente'.[70] As a result of Grey's 'neutrality', Clark added that over half of the Albanian territory and half of the population remained outside the newly created Kingdom and most of those who fell under Serb rule 'suffered persecution, deportation, mistreatment and massacres'.[71]

However, Grey's hopes for keeping Europe out of a wide armed conflict were not fulfilled. The First World War began less than a year after the Conference of

London had ended. One of the main reasons that peace did not last long after the Balkan settlement was that Serbia was not satisfied with the extent of its territorial expansion and its lack of access to the Albanian coast. The London Conference and British neutrality left Serbia with a desire for further expansion towards Bosnia and Herzegovina. Grey's aim during the Conference was to prevent the Powers from falling into two camps. R. W. Seton-Watson argued that if Grey had revived the Conference of Ambassadors in 1914, the great catastrophe would have been averted.[72]

However, in his memoirs, Herbert did not criticize the British press either:

> The Albanian Committee did not have to complain of the way in which it was treated by the Government or the Press. Those pre-War days were Christian, and the howling cannibals of 1919 had not yet been loosed upon the suffering world. [...] In spite of the intrigues of the Great Powers, the world was not too bad a place, and the Albanians, in England at any rate, received a fair hearing through the Albanian Committee, which tried to be, if not impartial, as moderate as possible. Very little was known about Albania. The general impression was that the Albanians were another branch of the Armenian family, and indeed, as far as massacres were concerned, this was most understandable, for the unarmed, pastoral Albanians of the South were massacred by the Greeks in 1913, while the Albanians of the North-West received the same treatment at the hands of the Serbs.[73]

Having in mind this situation, Herbert criticized the Powers but congratulated Grey for the part he played in the creation of the Albanian state. In this regard Herbert said that 'if Lord Byron and Garibaldi could have looked down upon this struggle', they would have helped Edward Grey. Herbert saw the efforts of the Powers in building an Albanian state as akin to 'starting a young man on his career with his legs amputated and his arms truncated, and the same time you pick his pockets'.[74] However, British officials went on to play an important and constructive role within the International Commission of Control, British Consulate and the international troops that occupied Shkodra.

The quest for a monarch of Albania

The London Conference of Ambassadors concluded its work on 11 August 1913. The Powers agreed to establish the International Commission of Control which would oversee the creation of the new Albanian state. The work of the Commission was to decide an outline of the borders between Albania and Greece. The Conference issued a final decision by which Albania was recognized as an independent, sovereign, neutral and hereditary principality. A monarch was to be designated by the Powers and all ties between Albania and the Porte were to be cut off. The Powers would organize a civil administration, police and military forces under the authority of the International Commission of Control with a mandate of ten years.[75]

When the Conference decided that Albania was to become a kingdom, many royal names from Europe were mentioned as potential candidates. Many Albanian leaders were in favour of a British sovereign. Herbert had become a hero and his humanitarian work and his political contribution to the establishment of the Albanian state was seen as second to none. Thus Ismail Qemali, on behalf of the Provisional Government, offered the Albanian throne to Herbert. Herbert could not decide to take the offer of the crown without the agreement and support of the British government.[76] He therefore put the proposal to Edward Grey, whom he met several times to discuss this matter. However, Grey and Prime Minister Asquith, although a close family friend, did not support Herbert's candidacy for King of Albania. The neutrality of the British government meant that none of its nationals should acquire such a high position, since appointing a British national as King of Albania meant that Great Britain would be expected to intervene in support if a crisis were to occur in the future.[77] The British government had no such plans to support the new Kingdom.

Another problem that Herbert saw in the offer was the Albanians themselves. From experience he knew that the Ottoman Empire had never managed to collect taxes from Albania and he believed that the Albanians were likely to continue with their resistance to such policies. Even if the Albanians were to pay taxes, they could not contribute much with a weak economy and a country destroyed during the war. Had Herbert been the eldest of Carnarvon's sons, he would have inherited the title of Earl and the money attached to such a position, which would probably have led him to accept the offer even without the support of the British government. 'If I had fifty thousand a year, I think I should take Albania', wrote Herbert to his brother, adding that there was 'quite a decent chance of making something of it, if it is properly treated'.[78]

Another British personality the Albanians considered for their throne was Colonel George Phillips (1863–1921), who was appointed President of the International Administration of Shkodra in 1913–14 and Head of the British Military Mission to Albania. Phillip became very important for the Albanians. Explaining this relationship Herbert wrote that Phillips had 'fallen completely under the spell of Albania and loves the people, with whom he gets on extremely well'.[79] Phillips' success as governor of Shkodra was remarkable, his influence extending beyond the assigned perimeter of Shkodra and his authority reaching the most remote parts of Albania in the north.

Among the major tasks of the international presence in Shkodra was to improve the infrastructure of the town and the region now they had returned to normal life. For this reason, the population respected Phillips, who also made efforts to organize cooperation between local authorities, elders and town councils and tried to rebuild local self-government. He also managed to create a harmonious relationship between the five military contingents of the International Force in Shkodra.[80]

Many Albanians increasingly saw Phillips as a just and able man who could solve their problems and his good reputation reached all parts of Albania. Therefore, a deputation of Albanian notables asked Phillips if he could assume the Crown of Albania. Phillips, knowing that he would lack the support of his government, preferred to continue his career with the British Army and refused the offer.[81]

Edith Durham has noted another option explored by the Albanians in order to find a Briton for their king. She wrote that Albanian leaders had explored the possibility of appointing Prince Arthur of Connaught (1850–1942), the third son of Queen Victoria, as King of Albania, but nothing came of this initiative.[82]

Meanwhile, the Powers were also looking for a suitable monarch for Albania. Herbert, being familiar with the situation in Albania and the Powers' attitude towards it, wrote to his younger brother, Mervyn:

> I don't think they are likely to get a good Prince. Any prince would be an ass to take it if he knew the difficulties and more of an ass if he didn't.[83]

Herbert's prediction was almost entirely true. Until October 1913 the Powers could not agree on an Albanian sovereign. The British did not want to play any part in this project but agreed that the Austro-Hungarians should take the initiative of recruiting a monarch. Vienna would not accept Italian or French candidates, nor a British prince or aristocrat. The Italians, who wanted to gain influence in Albania, preferred a Protestant king while Russians would object to a Catholic prince and favoured a Muslim. Muslim members of the Albanian Committee, such as Amir Ali – head of the All India Muslim League – and Dusé Mohamed Ali – a playwright, historian and journalist who also became known for his African nationalism – advocated for a Muslim monarch. They were in favour of the candidacy of Prince Ahmad Fuad of the Albanian Khedive dynasty of Egypt. However, most of the Albanian leaders rejected Muslim, Catholic or Orthodox candidates because each of these choices would have led to some part of the population being alienated. In light of these limitations and the fact that their desire for a British monarch could not be fulfilled, the only option seemed to be a Protestant king.[84]

By late October 1913, the Powers had narrowed their choice to one candidate called William Fredrick Henry of Wied (1872–1945). He came from minor German royalty, was a Protestant by religion and connected with the Rumanian, Dutch and Prussian royal families. William, later to become Prince Wied of Albania, was acceptable to all Powers. He was also acceptable to the Albanians, although they were not asked their opinion and played no role in the selection process. William initially hesitated in accepting the offer, but behind the scenes his wife Sophie and his aunt Queen Elisabeth of Rumania continuously strove to persuade him, while the Austro-Hungarian authorities insisted that he accept the offer. In November the Powers announced that William Fredrick Henry of Wied was selected to be the future sovereign of Albania. During the selection process the German government had not shown any interest at all in Wied, while the Austro-Hungarian Emperor was understood to be 'hostile to the whole adventure'. Prince Wied, supported by his uncle King Carol of Rumania, negotiated with the Powers a loan of 10 million francs but no military force was assigned to him. Finally, on 7 February 1914, Prince Wied wrote to the Powers to state that he would accept the throne of Albania.[85]

Before leaving for Albania, Prince Wied, on his tour of visiting the capitals of the Powers, went to London on 18 February and lunched at Buckingham Palace with the royal family. The British government and the Foreign Office did not show much interest in him. While in London, the Prince met Herbert and discussed the situation in Albania. The Prince thanked Herbert and the Albanian Committee for its work on behalf of Albania, and in return Herbert and the Committee expressed hope that Prince Wied would succeed in restoring peace and prosperity in Albania.[86]

When Prince Wied arrived in Albania on 9 March 1914 Harry Lamb was impressed by him but wrote that his courtiers and advisers, both European and local Albanian, were not of much use to him. Prince Wied's arrival in Albania was greeted with great enthusiasm by Albanians. A nationalist newspaper *Perlindja e Shqipëniës* (Albania's Rebirth), that supported the Albanian Provisional Government, used its front-page article to call Wied *Mbret i Shqipëtarëvet* (King of the Albanians) and published a poem titled *Salve Caesar*. The article went on to say that the dream of the Albanians was coming true and Wied's picture was published alongside Skanderbeg's portrait.[87]

Despite this initial enthusiasm the Albanians would soon become disappointed with their *Mbret* who was only a minor royal, had no army, little money and little knowledge on the country or his subjects. He had arrived in Albania eight months after the decision was taken by the London Conference and some political forces had already started to undermine his power. One of the first letters that Wied sent to Herbert from Albania revealed his lack of knowledge about the country. 'We feel almost like children learning geography and all sorts of things one has not learnt for centuries'.[88]

This lack of knowledge resulted in mistakes. On 18 March 1914 Prince Wied formed his new government, which consisted of powerful landlords and some other important personalities. He appointed Hasan Prishtina as a minister, the only politician to come from the well-known ranks of the nationalists. All other ministers and government functionaries were either born abroad or had lived there for a long time but had no real connection or feelings for Albania. Wied's private secretary, Duncan Heaton–Armstrong, wrote that the first meeting of the government was held in the Turkish language because some of the ministers could not even speak Albanian. For most of them Turkish was the most appropriate language because they had studied it or lived in Constantinople or elsewhere working as functionaries of the Ottoman Empire. This act enraged nationalists who were excluded from the government. The population did not accept such a government with its members who were regarded as 'foreigners'.[89] Wied's governance quickly resembled Abdul Hamid's failed strategy of ruling in Albania by relying heavily on Albanian *pashas* and *beys*, chief among who was Esat Pasha who he had chosen as Minister of Internal Affairs.

The Powers, including Britain, showed no serious intention of supporting the new principality of Albania. The Italians, through Esat Pasha, were active in undermining Wied's rule. As the unity of the Powers disintegrated with the onset of war, so did Wied's power and popularity. Lamb and Phillips made numerous appeals for help to the British government, but there was no positive response from London.[90]

Wied's rapidly deteriorating situation meant more international troops were required in Albania because, as Lamb explained, the British government had a 'responsibility to the Prince'.[91] Edward Grey refused Lamb's request.[92] The lack of will to help Albania was also seen on numerous other occasions, including when Phillips supported the initiative of the Powers' representatives in Shkodra on the training of an Albanian force. He proposed more support from the British government, but Grey warned that no force should be established if there was no money to pay the soldiers.[93]

This lack of money was a serious problem for Albania and one which Grey had addressed a few months earlier. In January 1914 the Italian ambassador to London had asked Grey if the British government would join the initiative in guaranteeing a loan for Albania. Grey said that the government had first to authorize such an initiative which required the consent of the Parliament. This process took a long time and the money was nowhere to be seen. In addition, Grey told the Italian diplomat:

> I could not feel quite the same attachment to Albania as some other Powers did; indeed, more than once we had all but parted from Albania.[94]

Grey was at least sincere in admitting this failure, but he also made it clear that his interest was only in the creation of the Albanian state and not its development. It is this creation of the Albanian state and his sincerity that were the things Herbert appreciated about Grey. In March 1914 the British government finally contributed £5000 to the cause, a quota that other Powers did not follow because they preferred to give a loan through a bank. Herbert argued that such a loan was a political act by the Powers which, as a consequence, would produce political requests and complications.[95]

Albania, an abandoned project

The British military staff, headed initially by Admiral Burney and later by Colonel Phillips, as well as the diplomatic staff in Albania, played an important and constructive role in the state-building process of the new country. They were committed to making Albania a successful project but their centre in London did not endorse the advice they passed on. Admiral Burney was largely unsuccessful in his difficult task because in Britain people knew very little about the Albanian Question and, as he wrote, they 'were chary of coming to decisions on a very thorny subject'.[96] In Shkodra, the Admiral had often asked his headquarters and the British government for more political and military support. He also proposed that in England more organizations and personalities such as the Lord Mayor of London should use their influence to obtain more money for Albania.[97]

Intending to improve the position of the Provisional Government and the economy of Albania, Herbert made efforts to establish a regular line between British and Albanian sea ports which would have established trade relations with Britain. He wrote to his friend Lloyd George, asking him and his office to study this matter and come up with a proposal. Trade experts studied possibilities and found out that none of the British lines were interested in Albania. 'It is perfectly clear that you will never succeed in introducing anyone to form a new line for Albanian trade' wrote Lloyd George to Herbert. George added that there was no need of export or import with Albania in Britain and advised Herbert that the Albanian goods are rather destined for Austrian or German market.[98]

The refusal of the British government for greater engagement in Albania marked a change in relations between Herbert and Grey. Since the arrival of Prince Wied, Herbert believed that Grey was ignoring the difficulties that the Greek government created in south Albania. Contrary to the decisions of the London Conference, the Greek government continued to keep its troops in the Albanian territory. After some pressure the Greek government announced that the troops were withdrawn but reports that Lamb sent from Albania showed that this was not entirely true. Even if the Greek army withdrew, they left behind bands of irregular forces to create trouble. Lamb reported that during 1914 both Christian and Muslim Albanians were 'subjected to persecution as they were during 1913'. Particularly, the Albanians of the border villages were treated with excessive severity. On many occasions the Serbian and more often the Greek army and irregulars attacked the Albanian Gendarmerie.[99] Lamb also reported that Greek officials exercised violence, particularly against the Albanian Muslim landowners of Çamëria.[100]

Francis Elliot, the British ambassador to Greece, painted a different picture of these events. He despatched mainly the Greek view and this meant that the Foreign Office was receiving conflicting reports about the situation in south Albania and the Albanian parts that were awarded to Greece. On 17 February 1914 the situation worsened when a group of Greeks in Gjirokastra, under the leadership of Christakis Zographos, announced the formation of the 'Provisional Government of Autonomous Epirus', a region that consisted of southern Albania.

The complication of the situation and Greek atrocities in southern Albania led Edward Grey to make a statement in the House of Commons:

Northern Epirus is, by international agreement, to form part of the new State of Albania; Greek authority, as far as it exists in that region, is based on military occupation of recent date, and will shortly be terminated by the withdrawal of the Greek forces there.[101]

This was an encouraging answer but the problem still remained acute as the Greek government was not withdrawing its forces and continued to commit atrocities against Albanians. As a result, Grey denied the involvement of the Greek government and accused Greek irregular forces. Using this situation, Herbert tried to initiate changes in the British policy. He exposed the problem that he thought the British policy was facing in the Mediterranean and the Balkans. He also criticized the government's policy and the press for not adopting a friendlier approach towards Balkan Muslims and for letting Serbia take Albanian land and Greece take Salonika where the vast majority of the inhabitants were Jews and Muslims and not Greeks or Christians. He believed that this attitude was the result of a wrong established policy which produced weaknesses for British power and influence in the Mediterranean. Hence, Herbert, supported by a good number of MPs, suggested that the British government should be present in the Mediterranean with a strong fleet. 'You cannot have a strong policy unless you have a strong Fleet', Herbert told the House and added: 'It is as important to us as Adriatic was to Venice, for it is by the Mediterranean that we feed London and that we hold India.'[102]

There is no doubt that Albania would have benefitted from the presence of a British fleet in the Mediterranean which could reach the Adriatic. That was one more reason why Herbert made this suggestion which would result in a change of the British policy. Grey admitted that some of the problems which were occurring within the territory of the Ottoman Empire were the result of the absence of a British fleet in the region. Therefore, Grey maintained that because of this absence, the Sultan in the past had adopted a violent approach towards these parts of his empire.[103] Although this caused anger, anxiety and 'loud indignation of British public opinion' in Britain and despite Herbert's suggestion, Grey had no intention of changing the existing policy.[104]

By the end of June 1914 Herbert proposed in the House of Commons to send a British consul to south Albania. Grey maintained that the Greek government was no party to the atrocities but admitted that Athens faced difficulties in exercising control. As a matter of fact, this was not true as numerous reports that Grey received from his consuls showed clearly the direct involvement of the Greek government. Herbert insisted on more active and practical involvement of the British government in Albania. After a fierce debate, Grey came to the point that he had been avoiding for months and told Herbert and the House that he was not going to send a British Consul to south Albania or Epirus. Grey concluded that the British government had 'taken the line that we are not prepared to send British troops into Albania'.[105]

Prince Wied had hoped that the Powers would send an international force to his assistance so Grey's refusal to send troops to Albania was not good news. However, Wied was soon to be further disappointed when Grey suggested that the Prince should apply to Austria-Hungary and Italy for support.[106]

Grey, explaining his position, revealed that the Powers were nowhere near to fulfilling their duties and the state-building process in Albania was going from bad to worse. Predicting the collapse of international involvement, Lamb decided to remind Grey 'without hoping to modify in any way the deliberate decisions of H. M. Government' but merely to explain the situation in Albania. Lamb explained the reason why he was insisting to 'impose' his point. He wrote that it was Grey who stated in his despatches that the Conference of Ambassadors had established Albania in order to protect this country from being partitioned by the neighbouring countries and from the interference of Austria-Hungary and Italy. Lamb considered the Albanians to be made by the Powers to create a 'legitimate grievance against Europe' which was to prevent Austria-Hungary and Italy from quarrelling about dividing the Albanian coast. In this respect, according to Lamb, the Powers were not fulfilling their duty.[107]

Lamb maintained that Albania, 'in the opinion of all who reason objectively', was being made a source of conflict. Therefore, he suggested that the Powers and Britain should adopt a just policy which would be in interest of Albania and Europe in order to obviate the risk of a bigger crisis. Lamb criticized the existing policy of the Powers which consisted of allowing Austria-Hungary and Italy to reach an understanding regarding the Albanian coast and because of this understanding the Balkan states were to be compensated with territory in the interior part of Albania.[108]

Following the assassination of the Austro-Hungarian Archduke Franz Ferdinand in Sarajevo (28 June 1914), the Powers showed almost no interest in Albania. Albania took a secondary place in the European crisis which led to the outbreak of the First World War in August of that year. The international involvement of the Powers in Albania faded away. The international contingents, commanded by Colonel Phillips, withdrew from Shkodra in early August.[109]

After Great Britain declared war on Germany on 4 August and on Austria-Hungary on 12 August, Harry Lamb left Albania on Foreign Office orders on 17 August. Prince Wied, who was cut off from the Powers' financial and military support, left on 3

September and was soon followed by all the members of the International Control Commission.[110]

International involvement in Albania ended in failure. Albania, with no administrative or state structures, and above all, with no military or police force, was left in a chaotic situation and to the mercy of foreign invaders. In 1923, on his death bed Herbert recalled the situation. His last words about Grey were positive. Although the British government did not see the process through, he felt that the Albanians received their title-deeds at the hands of Edward Grey. Further on this matter, Herbert wrote:

> Sir Edward Grey was always courteous and listened to facts and figures that were not official and did all in his power to mitigate the sufferings of the Albanians. In the face of strong opposition, he recognised publicly that the Albanians had the same right to nationality and autonomy as any other people in the Balkans. The Greeks had been helped by Byron, and the Slav nations had Russia behind them. The Serbs and the Bulgars had the liberal inheritance of Gladstone's speeches and the active support of the Buxtons and the Balkan Committee, and the Albanians, who were the smallest in population and the most ineffectively equipped, received their title-deeds, which their neighbours would have stolen from them, at the hands of Lord Grey.[111]

However, the most important personality in Britain who helped Albania in securing the status of the statehood among the European nations was Aubrey Herbert. Herbert, through the Albanian Committee and with his personal actions, from 1912 to the end of his life, had put in motion all possible mechanisms in Britain to help the Albanian state.

In 1926, three years after Herbert died, an Albanian newspaper published a front-page article on his life and contribution to Albania under the title: 'Albania will never forget his friends and their names in our history will be written in gold.'[112] Yet, after 1945 nobody in Albania knew who Aubrey Herbert was. This was the result of the official ideology of the communist regime which made Herbert, a member of the British aristocratic ruling class and descendant of a family of landowners, politically unwanted and never mentioned.

Conclusion

For a long time Albanians saw the Ottoman Empire as their best option as a protector. As traditional patterns of Ottoman governance started to fail and the question of autonomy came into play, relations between the Ottomans and the Albanians entered into a crisis of modernization in which old and new political elements came into conflict. Albanians desired autonomy while remaining inside the Ottoman Empire, which it was believed would lead to independence after the empire's impending collapse. When this collapse eventually became apparent, Albanian leaders looked for another protector in Britain.

Britain's relationship with the Ottoman Empire from 1876 to 1914 and, subsequently, its approach to the Albanian Question can be best understood through the prism of British interests in the East. During this period the British Empire's main aim was to protect the route to India, their rule in Egypt and to prevent the expansion of Russian and later German power. In this regard, British governments considered Albania an indirect interest and the prevention of Russian expansion into the Balkans thus became a common goal for both the Albanians and the British.

However, this common interest did not manifest itself consistently, with the British showing a higher degree of interest in Albania only on two occasions: the Russo-Turkish Wars (1877–8) and Balkan Wars (1912–13). These conflicts challenged the very existence of the Ottoman Empire and led to two international peace conferences: the Conference of Berlin (1878) and the London Conference of Ambassadors (1912–13). It was only during these wars that the British believed their major interests would be endangered if parts of the Balkans, and specifically Albania, which held a strategic position, were to fall under Russian rule or influence. Therefore, from the nineteenth to the beginning of the twentieth century, British policy took measures to preserve the presence of the Ottoman Empire in the Balkans for as long as possible. If the Ottoman Empire were to collapse, then British policy would seek to ensure that the Balkans would not come under Russian or Austro-Hungarian rule. The fall of Albania to either of these two empires would have endangered British interests in the eastern Mediterranean and the Adriatic.[1]

The existence of a distinct Albanian ethnicity and the desire of the Albanians to live autonomously from the Porte had been noted by British commentators since the beginning of the nineteenth century. Yet, it was not until 1878 that Albanian nationalism came to the surface as an organized political and military force and made a request for autonomy to the Powers at the Congress of Berlin. The Congress was the first international diplomatic event to which the Albanian leaders, through the Albanian League, addressed their request for autonomy.[2] Although this request was ignored, for the first time the question of Albania had been raised as an international problem to be solved by the European Powers. Though the Albanian League failed to achieve its political goal, it succeeded in elevating Albanian nationalism through subsequent developments in language, literature, education and culture. In the late nineteenth century, nationality was considered synonymous with language and ethnicity and so Albanian ideologists aspired to include all Albanian speakers in one independent state. In seeking to apply this idea, Albanian nationalism produced major developments in the Balkans. By 1912 the activities of the Albanian nationalists, by this time directed against Young Turk rule, destabilized the balance of power and strengthened the position of Albania's neighbouring states. The actions of Albanian nationalists therefore became a catalyst for broader changes in the Balkans and across the political spectrum of Albanian leaders.

By taking a stance against the Porte and the neighbouring countries, and without support from a European Power, Albanian efforts for independence would have been doomed to fail from the start. Albanian leaders feared failure would bring catastrophic results, possibly leading to the land being further divided between Albania's neighbours, who never ceased their territorial ambitions in the region. Therefore, staying under the umbrella of the Porte remained the only viable option. Thus, the future of the Albanian national movement, which continued its bid for autonomy as a step towards independence, was closely linked with the fate of the Ottoman Empire.

The image of Albania, which was initially constructed by travel writers and diplomats, had an impact on both public perceptions and politicians. The origins and complexity of this subject demonstrate that images of the Balkans and Albania in British public and political discourse continued to be presented and interpreted predominantly by the Liberals. Such images appeared primarily during times of crisis, when the Balkans was often presented as an imagined place 'marked by a variety of essentially invented caricatures'.[3] The Conservatives viewed the Balkans without religious bias and, to a degree, held a favourable position towards the Albanian Question. Conversely, the religiously framed view, which was built by Gladstone and adopted by many Liberals, ignored the Albanian national cause and gave priority to the liberation of Balkan Christians. This view was also widely adopted by British public opinion.

Differences between the Conservatives and the Liberals were most visible when Gladstone accused Disraeli, on several occasions, of deliberately delaying the implementation of the Treaty of Berlin and encouraging the Albanians to continue their refusal to give up territories that were assigned to Montenegro and Greece. However, the aftermath of the Congress also revealed that both parties had accepted the need to maintain an Ottoman presence in the Balkans.[4]

From 1903, when the Macedonian crisis came to the surface, British policy was, to a degree, influenced by the Balkan Committee. As an organization, dominated by Gladstonian Liberals, the Committee initially showed considerable interest in the Albanian Question but this gradually began to wane. As a result of its adherence to Gladstonian principles, the Committee showed little or no consideration for those nationalities or ethnic groups which did not belong to its preferred religion. For this reason, the Albanian Question in Macedonia did not receive sufficient attention from Committee members, the British government or the Powers, despite becoming increasingly international problem.

Following the Macedonian crisis, British policy became more active in the Balkans. In reality, it was again considerations of their interests in India and Egypt that influenced this move, leading the British government to seek an understanding with Russia and sign the Reval Agreement in 1908. Thus, those Albanian leaders who considered Macedonia, and particularly the western part of it, as one of their major national interests felt themselves ignored by the Powers and the Porte. As a result, Albanian leaders intensified their search for a solution to their national question. The engagement of the Albanian nationalists in the structures of the Young Turk movement produced a new situation, not only in Albania but throughout the Balkans and elsewhere in the Ottoman Empire. The Albanian leaders had hoped that the Young Turk Revolution would create favourable conditions to advance their national cause.

The British also supported the Young Turks hoping to regain the influence they had lost to the Germans. Although the Young Turk Revolution brought back the Ottoman Parliament as an important institution of democracy, it soon became clear that the Albanian Question could not be solved by peaceful political means. The activities of the Young Turks gave rise to Turkism as a new ideology, thereby changing the political landscape of the Ottoman Empire. The tensions between Albanian nationalism and Ottomanism were subsequently transformed into a confrontation with Turkism. The Albanian insurrections against the Porte that started in 1909 and went on until 1912 had severe repercussions throughout the Balkans.

By the time the Balkan Wars of 1912–13 broke out, the British had turned their back on the crumbling Ottoman Empire and supported the advance of the Balkan armies. The result of the Balkan Wars was also supported by public opinion. Liberal opinion did not favour the Albanian national cause, but the emergence of an Albanian state had shifted British interests in favour of the creation of an independent Albania. Albania's strategic position in the Balkans became an interest for the British government and British policy makers considered Albania an instrument through which they could achieve their political objectives. An independent Albania, which came out of the Balkan Wars and the dismemberment of the Ottoman Empire in Europe, prevented the replacement of the Porte's rule by Russia or Austria-Hungary. This was the aim of the British government and their policy towards the new-born state of Albania thus became supportive.

However, such British interests were not so vital as to lead them to provide a king and support an Albania within ethnic borders. For the British government, geopolitical interests were more important than the sentiment of the Albanians regarding their nationality. The British believed that the claims of the Albanians on ethnic settlement were too ambitious or radical. Thus, the claim of Albanian nationalism was not entirely compatible with the interests of the policy being made in London. Support for the Albanian state was stopped once it became obvious that the Russian and Habsburg empires would not extend their rule to the Adriatic and Mediterranean and thereby endanger British interests. The British government believed it had secured its interests and did not continue to support the development of Albanian state institutions, nor did it show interest in the geographical size of Albania.

The British Liberals judged the Balkans from a historical and ideological context and regarded the expulsion of the Ottomans from Europe as long overdue. Those who did not see the liberation of the Christians as a religious duty were in the minority. Some of them even blamed the Christians as generators of the violence in the Balkans. They originated from the ranks of the Conservatives, and as such were anti-Liberal, and were also against Russian pan-Slav policies. Supporters of this policy were Conservatives, mostly heirs of Disraeli, and other non-Liberals, supporters of the principle of nationality or self-determination, including British imperialists, Muslims and Jews. They gathered to support Aubrey Herbert's idea of forming the Albanian Committee. Therefore, the Albanian Committee came as a response to the Balkan Committee.

The work of Edith Durham and the activities of Aubrey Herbert through the Albanian Committee could not undo the effect that the Liberals had created on British public opinion and government. Herbert's work on behalf of the Albanian state could be characterized as an effort to influence the public and the British government to go beyond existing interests. But it became apparent this was not possible and Herbert was therefore willing to accept the actions of Edward Grey. The international effect of Liberalism, seen in the London Conference, did not treat the Albanians according to the principle of nationality. Under these circumstances, unfavourable for the Albanians, Grey, pursuing the line of the British interest, had recognized the right of the Albanians to establish their own state. For that reason, Herbert praised the British government, specifically the foreign policy of Edward Grey. In Herbert's words, a great number of Albanian lives were spared because of the diplomatic and humanitarian work of the British government. Albania became independent but without most of the territories of Kosovo and the Janina *vilayets*. Yet, as Herbert declared on more than one occasion, things could have been worse for Albania if it was not for the British interest which was manifested by Edward Grey at the London Conference. However, the disinterested position of the British government on Albania that followed the London Conference caused Herbert to clash with Grey. The British government did not play its part in the international project of supporting the state building process of Albania. Partly as a result of this disinterested attitude, Albania failed as an international project as envisaged by the Great Powers in the Conference of London.

Appendix

Map of Albania – proposed by Albanian Committee (courtesy of Centre for Albanian Studies).

Notes

Introduction

1. Mark Wheeler, 'Not So Black As It's Painted – The Balkan Political Heritage', in *The Changing Shape of the Balkans*, ed., Francis Carter and Harry Norris (London: UCL Press, 1996), 4.
2. Marcus Tanner, *Albania's Mountain Queen – Edith Durham and the Balkans* (London: I. B. Tauris, 2014).
3. See: Bejtullah Destani, *M. Edith Durham: Albania and the Albanians, Selected Articles and Letters, 1903–1944* (London: Centre for Albanian Studies, 2001); Elsie, Robert and Bejtullah Destani, *The Blaze in the Balkans, M. Edith Durham, Selected Writings 1903–1914* (London: I. B. Tauris, 2014).
4. Noel Malcolm, *Rebels, Believers, Survivors – Studies in the history of the Albanians* (Oxford: Oxford University Press, 2022), ix.
5. James N. Tallon, '*The Failure of Ottomanism:* The Albanian Rebellions of 1909–1912' (PhD diss., University of Chicago, 2012), 1–16.
6. Noel Malcolm, *Kosovo: A Short History* (London: Macmillan, 1998).
7. Stavro Skendi, *The Albanian National Awakening, 1878–1912* (New Jersey: Princeton University Press, 1967).
8. George Gawrych, *The Crescent and the Eagle: Ottoman Rule, Islam and the Albanians, 1874–1913* (London: I. B. Tauris, 2006).
9. Robert William Seton-Watson, *The Rise of Nationality in the Balkans* (New York: Dutton, 1918), 21.
10. William Norton Medlicott, *The Congress of Berlin and After: A Diplomatic History of the Near Eastern Settlement 1878–1880* (London: Franc Cass & Co. Ltd., 1963), 7.

Chapter 1

1. Leslie A. Marchand, *Lord Byron: Selected Letters and Journals* (Cambridge, MA: Harvard University Press, 1982), 33.
2. Ebru Boyar, *Ottoman Turks and the Balkans – Empire Lost, Relations Altered* (London: I.B. Tauris, 2007), 37.
3. Richard Crampton, *Balkans*, accessed 15 March 2022, http://www.britannica.com/EBchecked/topic/50325/Balkans.
4. Maria Todorova, *Imagining the Balkans* (Oxford: Oxford University Press, 2009), 27.
5. John Morritt and G. E. Marindin, *The Letters of John B. S. Morritt of Rokeby: Descriptive of Journeys in Europe and Asia Minor in the Years 1794–1796* (Cambridge: Cambridge University Press, 1914), 65.
6. Robert Walsh, *Narrative of a Journey from Constantinople to England* (Philadelphia: Carey, Lea & Carey, 1828), 154–9.

7   Todorova, *Imagining the Balkans*, 27.
8   Ibid., 11.
9   Noel Malcolm, *Agents of Empire, Knights Corsairs, Jesuits and Spies in the Sixteenth – Century Mediterranean World* (London: Allen Lane & Penguin Books, 2015), 13–14.
10 Arnold Toynbee, *The Western Question in Greece and Turkey* (London: Constable, 1922), 6.
11 Noel Malcolm, *Useful Enemies, Islam and the Ottoman Empire in Western Political Thought 1450–1750* (Oxford: Oxford University Press, 2019), 1–29.
12 Todorova, *Imagining the Balkans*, 11.
13 Dušan I. Bjelić and Obrad Savić, eds., *Balkan as Metaphor – Between Globalization and Fragmentation* (Massachusetts: The MIT Press, 2005), 165.
14 Todorova, *Imagining the Balkans*, 32.
15 Slavoj Žižek, 'You May!' London Review of Books, no. 21 (June 1999), https://www.lrb.co.uk/the-paper/v21/n06/slavoj-zizek/you-may!
16 John Morrit of Rokeby, *A Grande Tour: Letters and Journeys 1794–96* (London: David & Charles, 1985), 245.
17 Thomas Smart Hughes, *Travels in Sicily, Greece and Albania* (London: J. Mawman, 1820), 305.
18 Tatiani G. Rapatzikou, ed., *Anglo-American Perceptions of Hellenism* (Newcastle: Cambridge Scholars Publishing, 2007), 273.
19 Todorova, *Imagining the Balkans*, 20.
20 Ibid., 73.
21 Flora Sandes, *An English Women-Sergeant in the Serbian Army* (London: Hodder and Stoughton, 1916), 120–1.
22 Andrew Hammond, *British Literature and the Balkans: Themes and Contexts* (London: Rodopi, 2010), 9–11.
23 Eugene Michail, *The British and the Balkans – Forming Images of Foreign Lands 1900–1950* (London: Bloomsbury, 2011), 6–11.
24 Hammond, *British Literature*, 30.
25 Vesna Goldsworthy, *Inventing Ruritania – the Imperialism of the Imagination* (London: Hurst, 2013), 1.
26 Michail, *The British and the Balkans*, 11.
27 List of British Consular Officials in the Ottoman Empire and its former territories, from the sixteenth century to about 1860, accessed 28 March 2022, http://levantineheritage.com/pdf/List_of_British_Consular_Officials_Turkey%281581-1860%29-D_Wilson.pdf.
28 His Majesty's Appointment of J. P. Morrier, 30 June 1804. NA, SP, 105/109, Nr. 314; *Papers of the Morier Family*, Balliol College Archives & Manuscripts, accessed 28 March 2022, http://archives.balliol.ox.ac.uk/Modern%20Papers/Morier%20family/morierfambiog.asp.
29 Malcolm, Rebels, Believers, Survivors, 153.
30 See chapters 1, 2, 7 & 8 in William Leake, *Travels in Northern Greece* (London: J. Rodwell, 1835).
31 See: John Cam Hobhouse, *A Journey through Albania, and Other Provinces of Turkey in Europe and Asia, to Constantinople, During the Years 1809 and 1810* (London: James Cawthorn, 1813).

32 Laurie Kain Hart, 'Culture, Civilization, and Demarcation at the Northwest Borders of Greece', *Journal of the American Ethnological Society*, 26, no. 1 (February 1999): 196–220.
33 Friz Greene Halleck, ed., *The Works of Lord Byron in Verse and Prose* (Hartford: Silas Andrus & Son, 1840), 19.
34 Thomas Moore, *Life of Lord Byron*, vol. I. With his Letters and Journals, Letter 40 to Mrs. Byron (London: John Murray, 1854), 110.
35 Alan Wace and Maurice Thompson, *Nomads of the Balkans* (London: Methuen, 1914), 192.
36 Henry Holland, *Travels in the Ionian Isles, Albania, Thessaly, Macedonia, etc. during the Years 1812–1813* (London: Longman, Hurst, Rees, Orme, and Brown, 1815), 99.
37 Ibid., 100.
38 Thomas Robert Jolliffe, *From Corfu to Smyrna through Albania and the North of Greece* (London: Black, Young, and Young, 1827), 57.
39 Edward Lear, *Journals of a Landscape Painter in Albania* (London: Richard Bentley, 1851), 21.
40 Barbara Jelavich, *History of the Balkans – Eighteenth and Nineteenth Centuries* (Cambridge: Cambridge University Press, 1983), 84.
41 Sabine Rutar, ed. *Beyond the Balkans: Towards an Inclusive History of Southeastern Europe* (Wien: Lit Verlag, 2014), 106.
42 Kristo Frashëri, *The History of Albania – A Brief Survey* (Tirana: Naim Frashëri, 1964), 102.
43 Skendi, *The Albanian National Awakening*, 26–7.
44 James Henry Skene, *The Albanians*, accessed 3 March 2022, http://www.albanianhistory.net/1848_Skene/index.html.
45 Hobhouse, *A Journey through Albania*, 9–94.
46 George Gordon Byron, *Letters and Journals of Lord Byron: With Notices of His Life, Vol. 1* (London: John Murray, 1830), 208.
47 C. M. Woodhouse, *The Philhellenes* (London: Hodder and Stoughton, 1969), 46.
48 Byron, *Letters and Journals*, 88.
49 Katarina Gephardt, *The Idea of Europe in British Travel Narratives, 1789–1914* (New York: Routledge, 2016), 62–3.
50 Ibid., 73.
51 Byron, *Letters and Journals*, 346–7; 'Childe Harrold's Pilgrimage', *BBC*, accessed 30 April 2022, http://www.bbc.co.uk/programmes/b00xmx42.
52 Moore, *Life of Lord Byron*, 110.
53 Gephardt, *The Idea of Europe*, 89.
54 Woodhouse, *The Philhellenes*, 36.
55 Ibid., 57.
56 Hobhouse, *A Journey through Albania*, 98.
57 George Gordon Byron, *The Life, Writings, Opinions, and Times of the Right Hon George Gordon Noel Byron, Lord Byron*, vol. 1 of 3 (London: Matthew Iley, 1825), 94.
58 'The London Greek Committee', *Cambridge Library Collection*, accessed 11 December 2021, https://cambridgelibrarycollection.wordpress.com/2014/08/21/the-london-greek-committee/.
59 43. Letter to Byron from the London Greek Committee, *NLS Ms.43530*, accessed 10 December 2021, http://www.kingscollections.org/exhibitions/specialcollections/byron/greece/letter-from-london-greek-committee.

60 Edward Blaquiere, *Narrative of a Second Visit to Greece* (Cambridge: Cambridge Library Collection, 2014), 10.
61 Thomas Moore, *Life, Letters, and Journals of Lord Byron* (London: John Murray, 1839), 596.
62 Charles Cockerell, *Travels in Southern Europe and the Levant, 1810-1817* (London: Longmans, 1903), 244-5.
63 Holland, *Travels in the Ionian Isles*, 133-40.
64 Ibid., 201.
65 Woodhouse, *The Philhellenes*, 31.
66 Malcolm, *Rebels, Believers, Survivors*, 150.
67 Ibid., 180-9.
68 Seton-Watson, *The Rise of Nationality*, 48.
69 Hughes, *Travels in Sicily*, 138.
70 Hammond, *British Literature*, 69-70.
71 Ibid.
72 Peter Cochran, *The Gothic Byron* (Newcastle upon Tyne: Cambridge Scholars Publishing, 2009), 2.
73 Goldsworthy, *Inventing Ruritania*, 23.
74 Hammond, *British Literature*, 71-2.
75 Ibid.
76 William Flawelle Moneypenny, *The Life of Benjamin Disraeli Earl of Beaconsfield* (London: John Murray, 1910), 158.
77 Donald Sultana, *Benjamin Disraeli in Spain, Malta and Albania 1830-32* (London: Tamesis Books, 1976), 43.
78 Frashëri, *The History of Albania*, 115-16.
79 Sarah Inglis, 'Origins of the Albanian National Awakening', *Haemus Journal*, 2 (2013): 80.
80 Benjamin Disraeli, *The Works of Benjamin Disraeli, Earl of Beaconsfield, Volume II* (New York and London: M. Walter Dunne, 1904), 18.
81 Earl of Beaconsfield, *Home Letters* (London: John Murray, 1885), 78.
82 See: Benjamin Disraeli, *The Rise of Iskander* (London: Saunders and Otley, 1833).
83 Sultana, *Benjamin Disraeli*, 52.
84 Beaconsfield, *Home Letters*, 79.
85 Sultana, *Benjamin Disraeli*, 54.
86 Geoffrey Nash, *From Empire to Orient – Travellers to the Middle East 1830-1926* (London: I.B. Tauris, 2005), 7.
87 Katerina Zacharia, ed., *Hellenisms: Culture, Identity, and Ethnicity from Antiquity to Modernity* (Aldershot: Ashgate Publishing, 2008), 190-200.
88 David Urquhart, *The Spirit of the East, Vol. 1* (London: Henry Colburn, 1830), 51.
89 Ibid., 181.
90 Ibid., 182-3.
91 Ibid., 229.
92 See Urquhart: Chapter XIII, XIV & XI in The Spirit of the East.
93 Gladstone to Lytton, December 1858-February 1859, NA, CO 883/1/12.
94 John Morley, *The life of William Ewart Gladstone, Vol. 1: 1809-1859* (Cambridge: Cambridge University Press, 2011), 606.
95 H. C. G. Mathew, *Gladstone 1809-1898* (Oxford: Oxford University Press, 1997), 167.

96 Robert Holland and Diana Markides, *The British and the Hellenes: Struggle for Mastery in the Eastern Mediterranean 1850–1960* (Oxford: Oxford University Press, 2006), 32.
97 David Bebbington, *William Ewart Gladstone: Faith and Politics in Victorian Britain* (Michigan: William B. Publishing Company, 1993), 115.
98 David Bebbington, *The Mind of Gladstone: Religion, Homer, and Politics* (Oxford: Oxford University Press, 2004), 184–6.
99 See: Hahn and Albania or Albanian Language in: William Ewart Gladstone, *Juventus Mundi: The Gods and Men of the Heroic Age* (London: Macmillan and CO., 1869).
100 Bebbington, *The Mind of Gladstone*, 184–6.
101 Keith Robbins, *Politicians, Diplomacy and War in Modern British History* (London: The Hambledon Press, 1994), 48.
102 Ibid.
103 Catherine Hall, Keith McClelland, Nick Draper, Kate Donington and Rachel Lang, *Legacies of British Slave-Ownership: Colonial Slavery and the Formation of Victorian Britain* (Cabridge: Cambridge University Press, 2014), 107.
104 Edmund Fawcett, *Liberalism: The Life of an Idea* (New Jersey: Princeton University Press, 2014), 115.
105 Jim Potts, *The Ionian Islands and Epirus: A Cultural History* (Oxford: Oxford University Press, 2010), 100.
106 Ibid., 101.
107 Parga, HC Deb 29 June 1820 vol 2 cc106-16, accessed 3 June 2022, https://api.parliament.uk/historic-hansard/commons/1820/jun/29/parga.
108 Hammond, *British Literature*, 149–51.
109 Ibid., 169.
110 Georgina Muir Mackenzie and Adeline Paulina Irby, *Travels in the Slavonic Provinces of Turkey in Europe* (London: Daldy, Isbister & Co., 1877), VII–XIV.
111 William Ewart Gladstone, *Bulgarian Horrors and the Question of the East* (New York: Lovell, Adam, Wesson & Company, 1876), 26–7.
112 Cathie Carmichael, *Ethnic Cleansing in the Balkans – Nationalism and the Destruction of Tradition* (London: Routledge, 2002), 22.
113 Heraclides Alexis and Dialla Ada, eds., *Humanitarian Intervention in the Long Nineteenth Century: Setting the Precedent* (Manchester University Press, 2015), 155.
114 Philip Broadhead and Damian Keown, *Can Faith Make Peace?: Holy Wars and the Resolution of Religious Conflict* (London: I. B. Tauris, 2007), 77–8.
115 Arthur Evans, *Ancient Illyria – An Archaeological Exploration* (London: I. B. Tauris, 2006), i–xvii.
116 See: compiled articles in: Bejtullah Destani and Jason Tomes, eds., *Arthur Evans, Albanian Letters: Nationalism, Independence and the Albanian League* (London: I. B. Tauris, 2017).
117 Anna Mazurkiewicz, ed., *East Central Europe in Exile Volume 1* (Newcastle upon Tyne: Cambridge Scholars Publishing, 2013), 11.
118 Ibid.
119 Marija Krivokapić and Neil Diamond, *Images of Montenegro in Anglo-American Creative Writing and Film* (Newcastle upon Tyne: Cambridge Scholars Publishing, 2017), 26.
120 Tim Youngs, ed., *Travel Writing in the Nineteenth Century: Filling the Blank Spaces* (London: Anthem Press, 2006), 28.
121 Alfred Tennyson, 'Montenegro', *The Nineteenth Century Review* 5 (1877): 358–9.

122 Kathryn Ledbetter, *Tennyson and Victorian Periodicals: Commodities in Context* (London: Rutledge, 2016), 130; Antonello Biagini and Giovanna Motta, *Empires and Nations from the Eighteenth to the Twentieth Century, Vol. 2* (Newcastle upon Tyne: Cambridge Scholars Publishing, 2014), 190.
123 'Miscellany: Disraeli Goes Albanian', accessed 16 February 2017, https://0searchproquestcom.wam.leeds.ac.uk/docview/484613998?pqorigsite=summon.

Chapter 2

1 Green to Layard, 12 & 13 January 1878, NA, FO 424/67, Nr. 537 & 538, (Enclosure 1 & 2 in 537).
2 Green to Darby, 13 January 1878, NA, FO 424/67, Nr. 200.
3 Layard to Salisbury, 9 April 1878, NA, FO 424/69, Nr. 399.
4 Cooper to Freeman, 28 February 1878, NA, FO 424/69, Enclosure in Nr. 39.
5 Justin McCarthy, *Death and Exile – the Ethnic Cleansing of Ottoman Muslims 1821–1922* (New Jersey: Princeton, 1995), 90–4.
6 Layard to Salisbury, 18 May 1878, NA, FO 424/70, Nr. 700.
7 Layard to Salisbury, 4 May 1878, NA, FO 424/70 Nr. 382.
8 Green to Salisbury, 12 April 1878, NA, FO 424/70 Nr. 511.
9 Green to Salisbury, 3 May 1878, NA, FO 424/70 Nr. 361.
10 Jovan Hadži-Vasiljević, *Arbanaska Liga* (Beograd: Ratnik, 1909), 39–40.
11 See full text of these documents in: Robert Elsie, *The Resolutions of the League of Prizren*, accessed 10 July 2022, http://www.albanianhistory.net/1878_League-of-Prizren/index.html.
12 Malcolm, *Kosovo*, 221.
13 The Albanian League, 5 October 1878, accessed 13 June 2022, http://archive.spectator.co.uk/article/5th-october-1878/2/the-albanian-league-has-completely-thrown-off-the-.
14 Bernard Stulli, *Albansko Pitanje 1875–1882* (Zagreb: Jugoslavenska Akademija Znanosti i Umjetnosti, 1972), 346.
15 Robert William Seton-Watson, *Disraeli, Gladstone and the Eastern Question* (New York: Norton & Co, 1972), 380.
16 Ibid., 380.
17 Layard Papers (Layard to Salisbury) – Add. MSS 39149 Nr. 505.
18 Edwin Pears, *Forty Years in Constantinople* (London: Herbert Jenkins Ltd., 1916), 82.
19 Medlicott, *The Congress of Berlin*, 44.
20 Malcolm, *Kosovo*, 222.
21 Medlicott, *The Congress of Berlin*, 46.
22 Skendi, *Albanian National Awakening*, 48.
23 Pyrrhus J. Ruches, *Albania's Captives* (Chicago: Argonaut, 1965), 57.
24 Henry Fraser Munro, *The Berlin Congress*, (Washington: Library of Congress, 1918), 30.
25 Ibid., 99–100.
26 Medlicott, *The Congress of Berlin*, 99–100.
27 Stulli, *Albansko Pitanje 1875–1882*, 336–7.
28 Kenneth Morrison and Elizabeth Roberts, *The Sandžak: A History* (London: Hurst, 2013), 61–2.

29 Davide Rodogno, *Against Massacre: Humanitarian Interventions in the Ottoman Empire 1815–1914* (Princeton: Princeton University Press, 2012), 15.
30 Lord Broughton, *Travels in Albania and other Provinces of Turkey in 1809 & 1810, Vol. I* (London: Murray, 1858), 138.
31 George Byron, *The Works of Lord Byron: Including the Suppressed Poems* (Paris: A. and W. Galignani, 1831), 88.
32 See: Eric Hobsbawm, *Nations and Nationalism since 1780* (Cambridge: Cambridge University Press, 1992) – Hobsbawm argues that national awareness develops unevenly among the social groups and parts of regions of a country. In the Albanian case, it first appeared in the south than it was transferred to the north.
33 Stephanie Schwandner and Bernard Fisher, eds., *Invention of Nationalism in Albanian Identities – Myth and History* (London: Hurst, 2002), 33.
34 Sebright to Salisbury, 25 January 1879, NA, FO 424/80, Nr. 7 & Enclosure 1.
35 Memorandum to Lord Beaconsfield, accessed 5 June 2022, http://www.albanianhistory.net/1878_Memorandum/index.html.
36 Ibid.
37 Green to Salisbury, 20 April 1879, NA, FO 424/83 Nr. 70.
38 Salisbury to Layard, 12 May 1879, NA, 424/83 Nr. 298.
39 Ibid.
40 Ibid.
41 Treaty of Berlin – Protocol 13, HC Deb 17 April 1879 vol 245 cc525-71037, accessed 9 June 2022, http://hansard.millbanksystems.com/commons/1879/apr/17/treaty-of-berlin-protocol-13-greece-and.
42 Document communicated to Salisbury by Albanian Delegates, 12 May 1879, NA, FO 424/83 Nr. 286.
43 The Treaty of Berlin – Execution of the Articles, HC Deb 18 June 1880 vol 253 cc297-9299, accessed 10 May 2022, http://hansard.millbanksystems.com/commons/1880/jun/18/the-treaty-of-berlin-execution-of-the.
44 Observations, HC Deb 2 September 1880 vol 256 cc1119-56, accessed 11 August 2022, OBSERVATIONS. (Hansard, 2 September 1880) (parliament.uk).
45 Fitzmaurice to Granville, 27 July 1880, NA, FO 424/101, Nr. 32.
46 Goschen to Granville, 26 July 1880, NA, FO 424/101 Nr. 34.
47 Ibid.
48 Stephen Gwynn and Gertrude Tuckwell, *The Life of the Rt. Hon. Sir Charles W. Dilke* (London: John Murray, 1917), 328.
49 Ibid., 328. – On June 1880, in London, Dilke met the King of Greece. They met several times during the two weeks of the king's visit to Britain and discussed chiefly the Albanian Question but there was no agreement.
50 Skendi, *Albanian National Awakening*, 55.
51 Gwynn and Tuckwell, *The Life*, 328.
52 Treaty of Berlin – Eastern Affairs – The Principle of Nationalities, HC Deb. 4 September 1880 vol 256 cc1298-3281303 – 1305, accessed 11 August 2022, OBSERVATIONS. (Hansard, 4 September 1880) (millbanksystems.com).
53 The Treaty of Berlin, HC Deb 18 June 1880 vol 253 cc297-9, accessed 15 August 2022, THE TREATY OF BERLIN – EXECUTION OF THE ARTICLES. (Hansard, 18 June 1880) (millbanksystems.com).
54 Treaty of Berlin – Eastern Affairs – The Principle of Nationalities, HC Deb. 4 September 1880 vol 256 cc1298-3281303 – 1305, accessed 25 June 2022, OBSERVATIONS. (Hansard, 4 September 1880) (parliament.uk).

55 John Morley, *The Life of William Ewart Gladstone 1878-1898, Vol. II, 1878-1898* (New York: Macmillan, 1907), 183-4.
56 George Earle Buckle, *The Life of Benjamin Disraeli Earl of Beaconsfield, Vol. VI* (New York: Macmillan, 1920), 314-5.
57 Seton-Watson, *Disraeli, Gladstone*, 565.
58 Miloš Ković, *Disraeli and the Eastern Question* (Oxford: Oxford University Press, 2011), 316.
59 William Flavelle Moneypenny, *The Life of Benjamin Disraeli Earl of Beaconsfield, Vol. I* (New York: The Macmillan, 1910), 158-64; Sultana, *Benjamin Disraeli*, 43-51.
60 D. M. Kesley, *Life and Public Services of Hon, W M. E. Gladstone* (Philadelphia: National Publishing Co., 1898), 486.
61 Noel Malcolm, "Diplomacia Britanike dhe Lidhja e Prizrenit 1878-1880," in *Lidhja Shqiptare e Prizrenit dhe Vendi i Saj në Histori*, ed. Jusuf Bajraktari (Prishtinë: Universiteti i Prishtinës, 2008), 41-55.
62 Layard was a well-known archaeologist and art historian, turned politician and diplomat. In 1852 he was elected as a Liberal Member of Parliament and also served as undersecretary for foreign affairs. Liberals disliked him for joining the Conservatives and regarded him as anti-Russian.
63 Henry Layard, *Memoirs*, Add. 38,934, Section I.
64 William Miller, *The Ottoman Empire 1801-1913* (Cambridge: Cabridge University Press, 1913), 403-4.
65 Daut Dauti, *Çështja Shqiptare në Diplomacinë Britanike 1877-1880* (Shkup: Logos A, 2012), 47-8.
66 Malcolm, *Kosovo*, 222.
67 Skënder Anamali and Kristaq Prifti, eds., *Historia e Popullit Shqiptar, vol. II* (Tirana: Botimet Toena, 2002), 169.
68 Ibid.
69 The news of the week, *The Spectator*, accessed 6 July 2022, http://archive.spectator.co.uk/article/14th-september-1878/1/news-of-the-week.
70 Malcolm, *Kosovo*, 223 – These demands were: The four Albanian *vilayets* to be included in a single unit, with elected members to a single Assembly, the appointment of Albanian-speaking functionaries in the state administration, Albanian language schools, and elected local councils of both Muslim and Christian faith.
71 Green to Salisbury, 9 September 1878, NA, FO 424/74, Nr. 400.
72 Ibid.
73 Layard to Salisbury, 23 September 1878, NA, FO 424/75, Nr. 81.
74 HR. SFR (3) 270/ 1 / 70.
75 Sebright to Salisbury, 25 January 1879, NA, FO 424/80, Nr. 7 & Inclosure 1.
76 Medlicott, *The Congress of Berlin*, 135.
77 Lyons to Salisbury, 24 February 1879, NA, FO 424/80, Nr. 516.
78 Mémoire, le Décembre 1879, HR. SFR (3) 270 /1/ 53.
79 Treaty of Berlin – Protocol 13 – Greece and Turkey – Rectification of Frontier. – Resolution, HC Deb 17 April 1879 vol. 245 cc525-70528, accessed 9 June 2022, http://hansard.millbanksystems.com/commons/1879/apr/17/treaty-of-berlin-protocol-13-greece-and.
80 Buckle, *The Life of Benjamin Disraeli*, 341.

81 Congress of Berlin – Motion for an address, HC Deb 22 July 1879 vol 248 cc1027-90, accessed 20 July 2022, http://hansard.millbanksystems.com/commons/1879/jul/22/motion-for-an-address#S3V0248P0_18790722_HOC_126.
82 Medlicott, *The Congress of Berlin*, 353.
83 Granville to Goschen, 18 May 1880, NA, FO 78/3074, Nr. 1.
84 Anamali and Prifti, *Historia e Popullit*, 195.
85 Erich Eyck and Bernard Miall, *Gladstone* (London: Routledge, 1966), 290.
86 Ibid., 291.
87 Seton-Watson, *Disraeli, Gladstone*, 519.
88 Malcolm, *Kosovo*, 227.
89 'Sketches in Albania, A Meeting of the Albanian League', *The Illustrated London News*, 10 April 1880, 346; See also: Bejtullah Destani and Jason Tomes, *Arthur Evans, Albanian Letters: Nationalism, Independence and the Albanian League* (London: I. B. Tauris, 2017), 91–6.
90 'The Albanian Question', *The Manchester Guardian*, 15 May 1880, pp. 7–8, accessed 11 April 2018, http://0-search.proquest.com.wam.leeds.ac.uk/docview/478840433/pageview/FA92C44923D64587PQ/1?accountid=14664.
91 'The Declaration of Albanian Independence', *The Manchester Guardian*, 23 August 1880, 5, accessed 15 April 2018, <http://0-search.proquest.com.wam.leeds.ac.uk/docview/478835786?pq-origsite=summon.
92 Malcolm, *Kosovo*, 227.
93 Robert Elsie, *Historical Dictionary of Albania* (Plymouth: Scarecrow Press, 2010), VII.
94 Medlicott, *The Congress of Berlin*, 7.
95 Gordon Martel, 'Liberalism and Nationalism in the Middle East: Britain and the Balkan Crisis of 1886', *Middle Eastern Studies* 21, no. 2 (1985): 172–91.
96 Ibid.
97 Ibid.
98 MS 405/203 – Edith Durham, *Albania – Special Afternoon Lecture at Royal Institution of Great Britain, 4 February 1941*.
99 Fredrik Edward Knight, *Albania: A Narrative of Recent Travel* (London: Simpson Low, Marston, Searle & Rivington, 1880), 115.
100 Green to Granville, 3 May 1881, NA, FO 424/136, Nr. 24.
101 Goschen to Granville, 14 May 1881, NA, FO 424/136, Nr. 28.
102 Fitzmaurice to Granville, 22 July 1880, NA, FO 424/101, Nr. 28.

Chapter 3

1 Green to Granville, 11 June 1883, NA 424/129, Nr. 100.
2 HR SFR 3 – 315, 3. 5., Anexe Au Nr. 851, 683.
3 Skendi, *Albanian National Awakening*, 306.
4 HR. SFR 3, 315, 3, 6 - 7; HR. SFR 3 – 315, 3, 7.
5 Green to Granville, 23 December 1882, NA, FO 424/128, Nr. 8 and 9.
6 HR. SFR 3 – 315, 3, 10–11.
7 Dimitris Livanios, *The Macedonian Question – Britain and the Southern Balkans 1939–1949* (Oxford: Oxford University Press, 2008), 16.
8 Goschen to Grey, 1 March 1908, NA, FO 195/2304, Nr. 26.
9 Michail, *The British and the Balkans*, 13–17.

10 Livanios, *The Macedonian Question*, 43.
11 Martel, *Liberalism and Nationalism*, 181.
12 Bejtullah Destani, ed., *Faik Konitza – Selected Correspondence* (London: The Centre for Albanian Studies, 2000), 144–66.
13 Ibid., 10.
14 Korrespondenca e personaliteteve shqiptare, AQSH F19: D. 32/4, F. 149.
15 Michail, *The British and the Balkans*, 5.
16 James Evans, *Great Britain and the Creation of Yugoslavia: Negotiating Balkan Nationality and Identity* (London: I.B. Tauris, 2008), 88.
17 Anamali dhe Prifti, *Historia e Popullit*, 311–12.
18 Rodogno, *Against Massacre*, 238.
19 Robbins, *Politicians, Diplomacy and War*, 216.
20 James Andrew Perkins, 'British Liberalism and the Balkans, c. 1875–1925' (PhD diss., Birkbeck University, 2014), 11.
21 Ibid. 13.
22 Montserrat Guibernau, *The Ethnicity Reader: Nationalism, Multiculturalism and Migration* (Cambridge: Polity Press, 2010), 256.
23 Ibid.
24 The Balkan Committee, *Macedonia 1903* (London: Adelphi, 1903), 3.
25 James Perkins, 'The Congo of Europe: The Balkans and Empire in Early Twentieth Century British Political Culture', *The Historical Journal*, 58, no. 2 (2015): 565–87, http://journals.cambridge.org/abstract_S0018246X14000260.
26 The Balkan Committee, *Macedonia 1903*, 7.
27 Ibid., 31.
28 Rodogno, *Against Massacre*, 236.
29 Robbins, *Politicians, Diplomacy and War*, 216–17.
30 Michail, *The British and the Balkans*, 29–46.
31 Ibid., 58–9.
32 See: Henry N. Brailsford, *Macedonia, Its Races and Their Future* (London: Methuen & Co., 1906).
33 Michail, *The British and the Balkans*, 41.
34 A. J. P. Taylor, *The Trouble Makers: Dissent over Foreign Policy 1792–1939* (London: H. Hamilton, 1957), 96.
35 Michail, *The British and the Balkans*, 12.
36 Noel Buxton, *Europe and the Turks* (London: John Murray, 1907), 28.
37 Ibid., 128.
38 Brailsford, *Macedonia*, 111.
39 Edith Durham, *The Burden of the Balkans* (London: Thomas Nelson & Sons, 1905), 205–6.
40 Edith Durham, *Twenty Years of Balkan Tangle* (London: George Allen & Unwin ltd., 1920), 87.
41 Rodogno, *Against Massacre*. 239.
42 David Gillard, ed., *British Documents on Foreign Affairs – Reports and Papers from the Foreign Office Confidential Print, Part 1, Series B, Vol. 19, The Ottoman Empire: Nationalism and Revolution 1885–1908* (Balkan Wars: University Publications of America, 1985), 176.
43 Ibid., Doc. 51, 196; Doc. 52, 226–7, Memorandum on Macedonia – Foreign Office Memorandum Nr. 8294, 8 December 1904.
44 O'Conor to Grey, 4 April 1906, NA, FO 371/149, Nr. 232.

45 Rodogno, *Against Massacre*, 244.
46 Francis Harry Hinsley, ed., *British Foreign Policy under Sir Edward Grey* (Fredrick: University of Cambridge, 1977), 167.
47 *Gillard, British Documents, Vol. 19,* Lansdowne to Bertie, Doc. 59, Enclosure in Doc. 55.
48 Ismet Dërmaku, *Lidhjet Shqiptaro-Maqedone dhe Çështja e Reformave në Turqinë Evropiane në fund të shek. XIX dhe në fillim të shek XX* (Prishtinë: Vjetari i Arkivit të Kosovës, X-XI, 1979), 75.
49 O'Conor to Grey, 29 May 1906, NA, FO 371/151, Nr. 370.
50 Lillian Parker Wallace and William C. Askew, eds., *Power, Public Opinion, and Diplomacy* (Cambridge: Duke University Press, 1959), 198–9.
51 Lucian M. Ashworth, 'David Mitrany and South-East Europe: The Balkan Key to World Peace', *The Historical Review/La Revue Historique* 2 (January 2006): 203–24, https://doi.org/10.12681/hr.190.
52 Michail. *The British and the Balkans*, 81.
53 Durham, *The Burden of the Balkans*, 81.
54 Skendi, *Albanian National Awakening*, 200–1.
55 Perkins, *British Liberalism*, 174–5.
56 Brailsford, *Macedonia*, 241.
57 Ibid., 235.
58 Ibid., 287–8.
59 Ibid., 289.
60 Robbins, *Political Diplomacy,* 196.
61 Balkan Committee to Foreign Office, 1 August 1913, NA, FO 371/1893, Nr. 36157, 2.
62 Balkan Committee to Foreign Office, 5 August 1913, NA, FO 371/1893, Nr. 36157, 70.
63 Frances Radovich, 'The British Court and Relations with Serbia, 1903–1906', *East European Quarterly*, 14, no. 4 (Winter 1980): 461–8.
64 Evans, *Great Britain*, 98–9.
65 Ibid., 84.
66 Michail, *The British and the Balkans*, 17.
67 Tim Judah, *The Serbs, Myth and the Destruction of Yugoslavia* (New Haven: Yale University Press, 1997), 90.
68 WORK 12/290.
69 Todorova, *Imagining the Balkans*, 118.

Chapter 4

1 Lowther to Grey, 13 November 1908, NA, FO 40852/39815/08/44, Nr. 773.
2 Stanford J. Shaw and Ezel Kural Shaw, *History of the Ottoman Empire and Modern Turkey: Volume 2, Reform, Revolution, and Republic: The Rise of Modern Turkey 1808–1975* (Cambridge: Cambridge University Press, 1977), 211.
3 Robert Elsie and Bejtullah Destani, eds., *The Macedonian Question in the Eyes of British Journalists 1899–1919* (London: Centre for Albanian Studies, 2015), 92; William Miller, *The Macedonian Claimants* (London: The Contemporary Review, 1903), 468–84.
4 Bejtullah Destani and Jason Tomes, eds., *Albania's Greatest Friend: Aubrey Herbert and the Making of Modern Albania - Diaries and Papers 1904–1923* (London: I. B. Tauris, 2011), 11.

5   Elsie and Destani, *The Macedonian Question*, 91.
6   Vesna Lopičić and Biljana Mišić Ilić, eds., *Values across Cultures and Times* (Newcastle upon Tyne: Cambridge Scholars Publishing, 2014), 88.
7   Срђан Рудић, *Велика Британија и македонско питање 1903-1908* (Београд: Историјски институт, 2011), 133-5.
8   Bejtullah Destani, ed., M. Edith Durham, *Albania and the Albanians - Selected Articles and Letters 1903-1944* (London: Centre for Albanian Studies, 2001), 3-4.
9   Destani and Tomes, *Albania's Greatest Friend*, 4.
10 Justin McCarthy, *The Ottoman Peoples and the End of Empire* (London: Arnold, 2003), 35.
11 Elsie and Destani, *Macedonian Question*, 238-9.
12 Мариглен Демири and Здравко Савески, *Национализмот во (н) контекст: соработка на Албанците и Македонците од Илинденското востание до Народноослободителната војна* (Скопје: Левичарско Движење Солидарност, 2014), 5-13.
13 Ismet Dermaku, *Lidhjet shqiptaro-maqedone dhe çështja e reformave në Turqinë evropiane në fund të shek. XIX dhe në fillim të Shek. XX* (Prishtinë: Vjetari i Arkivit të Kosovës X-XI 1974-1975, 1978), 63-9; Hristo Andonov-Polanski, *Kontributi për lidhjet maqedono-shqiptare në të kaluarën* (Shkup: Jehona, 1967), 15-20.
14 Ahsene Gül Tokay, 'The Macedonian Question and the Origins of the Young Turk Revolution, 1903-1908' (PhD diss., SOAS - University of London), 89-90.
15 Letra e Ismail Qemalit dërguar Edward Grey-it, AQSH F. 19. D. 32/3, f. 432.
16 Noel Buxton, 'Balkan Geography and Balkan Railways', *The Geographical Journal*, 32, no. 3 (1908): 225-32.
17 Grey to Lascalles, 24 February 1908, NA, FO 371/581.
18 NA, FO 371/581, Section 2, Nr. 6758.
19 Ibid.
20 Ernest Jackh, *The Rising Crescent - Turkey Yesterday Today and Tomorrow* (New York: Farrar & Reinhart, 1944), 90.
21 Livanios, *The Macedonian Question*, 47.
22 McCarthy, *The Ottoman People*, 42.
23 Noel Malcolm, 'Myths of Albanian National Identity: Some Key Elements as Expressed in the Works of Albanian Writers in America in the Early Twentieth Century', in *Albanian Identities - Myth and History*, ed. Stephanie Schwandner-Sievers and Bernard Fischer (London: Hurst, 2002), 72-3.
24 Gawrych, *The Crescent*, 11.
25 Wassa Effendi, *The Truth on Albania and the Albanians* (London: National Press Agency, 1879).
26 Ibid., 39-40.
27 Sami Frashëri, *Shqipëria - Ç'ka Qënë, çështë E ç'do Të Bëhetë* (Tiranë: Mësonjëtorja e Parë, 1999), 5-20.
28 Bülent Bilmez, 'Shemseddin Sami Frashëri (1850-1904): Contributing to the Construction of Albanian and Turkish Identities', in *We, the People: Politics of National Peculiarity in South-Eastern Europe*, ed. Diana Mishkova (Budapest: Central European University Press, 2009), 341-71.
29 Gawrych, *The Crescent*, 129.
30 Sami Bey Frashëri, *What Will Become of Albania*, as of 9 August 2022, http://www.albanianhistory.net/texts19_2/AH1899_1.html.
31 Gawrych, *The Crescent*, 130-1.

32 Anamali dhe Prifti, *Historia e Popullit*, 274.
33 Ibid.
34 Yusuf Sarınay, Yıldırım Ağanoğlu, Sebahattin Bayram and Mümin Yıldıztaş, *Osmanli Arsiv Belgelerinde Arnavutluk – Shqipëria në Dokumentet Arkivale Otomane* (Istanbul: T.C. Basbakanlik Devlet Arsivleri Genel Müdürlügü, 2008), 43–5.
35 Frashëri, *The History of Albania*, 128–9.
36 Ismail Kemal, *The Memoirs* (London: Constable, 1920), 214–16.
37 Ibid., 217.
38 Ibid., 219.
39 Sulltan Abdylhamiti, *Kujtime e mia nga politika* (Shkup: Logos A, 2010), 121–35.
40 Chermside to Ford, 22 March 1892, NA, FO 78/4791, Nr. 1; Lane to Rosebery, 23 October 1893, NA, FO 78/4791, Nr. 498.
41 Kemal, *The Memoirs*, 187–8.
42 Anamali dhe Prifti, *Historia e Popullit*, 295.
43 Renzo Falaschi, *The Memoirs of Ismail Kemal Vlora and His Work for the Independence of Albania* (Tirana: Toena, 1997), 451.
44 Albanian dynasty in Egypt established by Mehmet Ali Pasha.
45 Ismail Kemal Bey'in Arnavutluk ve Avrupa'daki, Y. EE. 15, 21, 1318 R, 13, 1.
46 Djemil Pasha to Tevfik Pasha, 19 November 1902, HR. SYS. 00118/28, 17.
47 Ahsene Gül Tokay, 'Macedonian Reforms and Muslim Opposition during the Hamidian Era: 1878–1908', *Islam and Christian–Muslim Relations*, 14:1, no. 51 (Spring 2010): 51–65, http://dx.doi.org/10.1080/09596410305258.
48 See chapter XXX, The Sultan and his executives, in: G. P. Gooch and Harold Temperly, eds., *British Documents on the Origins of the War 1898–1909, V. 5* (London: His Majesty's Stationary Office, 1928).
49 Anamali dhe Prifti, *Historia e Popullit*, 307.
50 Jusuf Osmani, *Vrasja e konsullit rus Shqerbinit më 1903 në Mitrovicë sipas burimeve arkivore* (Prishtinë: Arkivi Kombëtar i Kosovës, Vjetari XXVII – XXVIII, 2002), 177–8.
51 *Koleksioni i Aleksandar Bukvičit*, viti 1902, Nr. 20, Arkivi i Kosovës.
52 Osmani, *Vrasja e Konsullit*, 185.
53 Shahin Kolonja, 'Një puhi e re në Maqedoni', *Gazeta Drita*, 23 Shkurt 1904, Nr. 39, 3.
54 David Gillard, ed. *Part 1, Series B, Vol. 19, The Ottoman Empire: Nationalism and Revolution 1885–1908*, 145 – Currie to Salisbury, 2 April 1986, Nr. 259.
55 Christopher Psilos, *'The Young Turk Revolution and the Macedonian Question 1908–1912'* PhD diss, University of Leeds, 2000.
56 Bilgin Çelik, 'Romanya'da Bir Jön Türk: Ibrahim (Ethem) Temo ve Romanya'daki Faaliyetleri', *International Journal of History, History Studies*, 2, no. 2 (2010): 257–367, http://www.historystudies.net/english/DergiTamDetay.aspx?ID=103&Detay=Ozet.
57 Malcolm, *Kosovo*, 236.
58 Ibid., 237.
59 Prince Sabahudin was a nephew of the Sultan who had joined the movement in 1899 along with his brother Lûtfullah Bey and his father Damad Mahmud Pasha. They all became engaged in organizing the congress in Paris in order to unite the Young Turk factions.
60 Şükrü Hanioğlu, *The Young Turks in Opposition* (Oxford: Oxford University Press, 1995), 187–8.
61 Şükrü Hanioğlu, *Preparation for a Revolution: The Young Turks, 1902–1908* (Oxford: Oxford University Press, 2001), 15.
62 Ibid., 15–16.

63 Ibid., 17.
64 See further details about the coup d'état attempt in: Hanioğlu, *Preparation for a Revolution*, 20–4.
65 Alexander Lyon Macfie, *The End of the Ottoman Empire, 1908–1923* (London: Routledge, 2013), 18.
66 Courtney Penwith, *Nationalism and War in the Near East* (Oxford: Clarendon Press, 1915), 111–12.
67 Mark Mazower, *Salonica, City of Ghosts*, (London: Harper Perennial, 2005), 272.
68 Andrew Mango, *Atatürk – the Biography of the Founder of Modern Turkey* (New York: The Overlook Press, 2002); Ian Brundskill, ed., *Great Military Lives – A Century in Obituaries: Atatürk* (London: Times books, 2005), 175–86.
69 Tokay, *Macedonian Question*, 207.
70 Ibid., 159–60.
71 Ibid., 234–9.
72 Skendi, *Albanian National Awakening*, 206–9.
73 Gooch and Temperley, *British Documents, Vol. V*, 290.
74 Tokay, *Macedonian Reforms*, 61.
75 Nathalie Clayer, *Në Fillimet e Nacionalizmit Shqiptar – Lindja e Një Kombi me Shumicë Myslimane në Evropë* (Tiranë: Përpjekja, 2012), 547–8.
76 Gillard, *British Documents, Vol. 19*, 490 – Heathcote to Barclay, 5 July 1908, Nr. 36.
77 Ibid., 491.
78 Joseph Heller, *British Policy towards the Ottoman Empire 1908–1914* (Routledge: London, 2014), 9.
79 Gawrych, *The Crescent*, 151.
80 Gillard, *British Documents, Vol. 19*, 492–3.
81 Ibid., 491.
82 Ibid., 492.
83 Malcolm, *Kosovo*, 237.
84 Gillard, *British Documents, Vol. XIX*, 497–8.
85 Ibid., 497.
86 Isa Boletinaz, HR.SYS. 00118/28.
87 Pears, *Forty Years*, 255.
88 Ramiz Abdyli, *Lëvizja Kombëtare Shqiptare, 1908–1910, Vol.1* (Prishtinë: Instituti i Historisë, 2004), 30.
89 Ibid., 33.
90 Malcolm, *Kosovo*, 237–8.
91 Abdulhamit Kirmizi, *Ferid Pashë Vlora – Një jetë shtet*, (Shkup: Logos A, 2018), 351–3.
92 Pears, *Forty Years*, 235.
93 Tokay, *The Macedonian Question*, 251.
94 Barcley to Grey, 28 July 1908, Nr. 1, CAB 37/95.
95 Abdyli, *Lëvizja Kombëtare*, 35.
96 Mazower, *Salonica*, 275.

Chapter 5

1 Gerald Fitzmaurice (1865–1939) was the Chief Dragoman of the British Embassy in Constantinople. He had enormous influence over the Foreign Office and also within the Ottoman Empire.

2. William Tyrell (1866–1947) was a private secretary to Sir Edward Grey from 1907 to 1915.
3. G. P. Gooch and Harold Temperley, eds., *British Documents on the Origins of the War, 1898-1914, Young Turk Revolution, Vol. V*, (London: His Majesty's Stationary Office, 1928), 247.
4. Ibid., 250.
5. Ibid., 254.
6. Memorandum respecting the Turkish revolution and its consequences – Foreign Office, 1 March 1909, NA, FO 371/581, Nr. 1, 1 March 1909.
7. Gooch and Temperley, *British Documents, Vol. V*, 309.
8. Ibid., 310.
9. Ibid., 266–7.
10. Hasan Ünal, 'Ottoman Policy during the Bulgarian Independence Crisis, 1908-9: Ottoman Empire and Bulgaria at the Outset of the Young Turk Revolution', *Middle Eastern Studies*, 34, no. 4 (Spring, 1998): 135–76.
11. Lonnie Johnson, *Central Europe: Enemies, Neighbours, Friends* (Oxford: Oxford University Press, 1996), 173; Christopher Clark, *The Sleepwalkers, How Europe Went to War in 1914* (London: Penguin Books, 2013), 34–7.
12. Richard C. Hall, ed., *War in the Balkans: An Encyclopaedic History from the Fall of the Ottoman Empire to the Breakup of Yugoslavia* (Santa Barbara, Denver, Oxford: ABC-CLIO, 2014), 41.
13. Whitehead to Grey, 13 October 1908, NA, FO 36207/31738/08/44A, Nr. 72.
14. Carl Cavanagh Hodge, ed., *Encyclopaedia of the Age of Imperialism 1800-1914, Vol. 1* (London: Greenwood Press, 2008), 38.
15. Gooch and Temperley, *British Documents, Vol. V.* 461–2; Foreign Office Memorandum, 21 October 1908, NA, FO 36795/31738/08/44.
16. Ibid., 463.
17. Durham, *Twenty Years*, 173.
18. Feroz Ahmad, 'Great Britain's Relations with the Young Turks, 1908-14', *Middle Eastern Studies*, 2 (1965–6): 309–15.
19. Hasan Ünal, 'Britain and Ottoman Domestic Politics: From the Young Turk Revolution to the Counter-Revolution, 1908-9', *Middle Eastern Studies*, 37, no. 2 (2001): 1–22.
20. Bruce Clark, 'Shifting Western Views on Turkey', *Asian Affairs*, 43 (May 2012): 195, http://dx.doi.org/10.1080/03068374.2012.682365.
21. Aubrey Herbert, *Ben Kendim: A Record of Eastern Travel* (London: Hutchinson, 1924), 313.
22. Ünal, *Britain and Ottoman Domestic Politics*, 1–22.
23. Heller, *British Policy*, 32.
24. The Communication of the Ottoman Embassy, *The Times*, 7 April 1910, HR.SYS.00135/5.
25. George Frederick Abbott (1874–1947) was a British author and journalist (war correspondent). In 1900 he was sent to Macedonia by Cambridge University to study the folklore of the Balkan people. He is the author of *The Tale of a Tour in Macedonia* and was considered a Balkan expert.
26. George Frederick Abbott, 'Young Turks in Albania', *The Saturday Review of Politics, Art and Science, (1910)*: 659, http://0-search.proquest.com.wam.leeds.ac.uk/docview/876924107?pq-origsite=summon.
27. Heller, *British Policy*, 24.

28 Ibid., 40.
29 Edith Durham, *Of the Turkish Constitution*, RAI, MS 51:4.
30 Anamali dhe Prifti, *Historia e Popullit, Vol. II*, 380–1.
31 Feroz Ahmad, *The Young Turks and the Ottoman Nationalities – Armenians, Greeks, Albanians, Jews, and Arabs 1908–1918* (Salt Lake City: The University of Utah Press, 2014), 57.
32 Lowther to Gray, 17 February 1909, NA, FO 371/581, Nr. 105.
33 Robert Elsie, *Albanian Literature – A Short History* (London: I. B. Tauris, 2005), 66.
34 Rexhep Ismajli, *Tekste të vjetra* (Pejë: Dukagjini, 2000), 29.
35 Frok Zefi, *Mikel Summa – Arqipeshkëvi i Shkupit 1695–1777* (Zagreb: Unija Zajednica Albanaca u Republici Hrvatskoj, 2003), 99.
36 Elsie, *Albanian Literature*, 12.
37 Robert Elsie, *A Biographical Dictionary of Albanian History* (London: I. B. Tauris, 2012), 44–5.
38 Skendi, *Albanian National Awakening*, 366.
39 Elsie, *Albanian Literature*, 31–7.
40 Abdullah Hamiti, *Nezim Frakulla Dhe Divani i Tij Shqip* (Shkup: Logos A, 2008), 21–5.
41 Elsie, *Albanian Literature*, 38–9.
42 Ibid., 42–3.
43 Skendi, *Albanian National Awakening*, 368.
44 Peter Mackridge, *Language and National Identity in Greece, 1766–1976* (Oxford: Oxford University Press, 2009), 95–100.
45 Anthony D. Smith, *Ethno-Symbolism and Nationalism: A Cultural Approach* (London: Routledge, 2009), 3; Stephen Tierney, ed., *Accommodating National Identity: New Approaches in International and Domestic Law* (The Hague: Kluwer Law International, 2000), 2–3.
46 Nicola Guy, *The Birth of Albania – Ethnic Nationalism, the Great Powers of World War I and the Emergence of Albanian Independence* (London: I. B. Tauris, 2012), 6–7.
47 Ibid., 8.
48 Mackridge, *Language and National Identity*, 102.
49 Hobsbawm, *Nations and Nationalism*, 51.
50 Mackridge, *Language and National Identity*, 108.
51 Stavro Skendi, 'Language as a Factor of National Identity in the Balkans of the Nineteenth Century', *Proceedings of the American Philosophical Society*, 119, no. 2 (1975): 186, http://www.jstor.org/stable/986634.
52 Mackridge, *Language and National Identity*, 108.
53 Skendi, *Language as a Factor*, 189.
54 Stark Draper, 'The Conceptualization of an Albanian Nation', *Ethnic and Racial Studies*, 20, no. 1 (1997): 143.
55 Zhan Klod Faveirail, *Historia e Shqipërisë* (Tirana: Plejad, 2007), 485.
56 Prince Louis-Lucien Bonaparte, *Albanian Dialects* (London: The Centre for Albanian Studies, 2014), 15.
57 Xhevat Lloshi, *Përkthimi i V. Meksit dhe Redaktimi i G. Gjirokastritit 1819–1827* (Tirana: Onufri, 2012), 23–4.
58 David Hosaflook, ed., *Albania and the Albanians in Annual Reports of the British and Foreign Bible Society 1805–1955* (Tirana: Institute for Albanian and Protestant Studies, 2017), 14.

59 The Thirteenth Report of the British and Foreign Bible Society (London: Forgotten Books, 1817), 93.
60 Lloshi, *Përkthimi i V. Meksit*. 89.
61 Tanner, *Albania's Mountain Queen*, 78.
62 Elsie, *A Biographical Dictionary of Albanian History*, 257.
63 David Hosaflook, *Lëvizja Protestante te Shqiptarët 1816–1908* (Shkup: ITSHKSH, 2019), 194.
64 John Quanrud, *Gerasim Kyrias and the Albanian National Awakening 1858–1894* (Tirana: Institute for Albanian and Protestant Studies, 2016), 217–19.
65 Durham, *Twenty Years*, 89.
66 Ibid., 90.
67 Leake, *Travels in Northern Greece*, 237–92.
68 Jelavich, *History of the Balkans*, 225.
69 Skendi, *Albanian National Awakening*, 114–15.
70 Miroslav Hroch, *European Nations: Explaining Their Formation* (London: Verso, 2015), 105.
71 Hysni Myzyri, *National Education During Albanian Renaissance* (Tirana: Mileniumi i Ri, 2007), 31–2.
72 Muharrem Fetiu, *Komiteti i Stambollit* (Prishtinë: SAS, 2017), 72–5.
73 Charles and Barbara Jelavich, *The Establishment of the Balkan National States: 1804–1920* (Seattle: University of Washington Press, 2000), 225.
74 Myzyri, *National Education*, 72.
75 Anamali dhe Prifti, *Historia e Popullit*, 146.
76 Myzyri, *National Education*, 87.
77 Elsie, *Albanian Litarature*, 71.
78 Ipen to Zweidinek von Südenhorst, Nr. 110/2, Shkodër, 31 January 1898 – as registered in *Vjetari i Arkivit të Kosovës X-XI, 1974–1975*, 452–3.
79 Ibid., 446–65.
80 Sevasti Qiriazi-Dako, *Jeta Ime* (Shkup: ITSHSH, 2016), 13.
81 See: Parashkevi D. Kyrias, *The School for Girls in Kortcha* (Chicago: Women's Board of Missions of the Interior, 1913); Charles H. Woods, *The Danger Zone of Europe: Changes and Problems in the Near East* (London: Forgotten Books, 2013), 137–8.
82 Robert Pichler, ed., *Legacy and Change: Albanian Transformation from Multidisciplinary Perspectives* (Hamburg: LIT Verlag Münster, 2014), 14.
83 Denisa Kostovicova, *Kosovo: The Politics of Identity and Space* (London: Routledge, 2005), 32.
84 Elsie, *Albanian Literature*, 117.
85 Myzyri, *National Education*, 231–2.
86 Lowther to Grey, 17 February 1909, NA, FO 371/581, Nr. 105.
87 Elsie, *A Biographical Dictionary of Albanian History*, 248.
88 Hanioglu, *Preparation for a Revolution*, 317.
89 Sami Frashëri, *Personalitetet Shqiptare në Kâmûs Al-a`lâm* (Shkup: Logos – A, 2002), 75.
90 Nader Sohrabi, 'Reluctant Nationalists, Imperial Nation-State, and Neo-Ottomanism: Turks, Albanians, and the Antinomies of the End of Empire', *Social Science History* 42, no. 4 (Winter 2018): 835–70, https://www.cambridge.org/core/journals/social-science-history/article/reluctant-nationalists-imperial-nationstate-and-neoottomanism-turks-albanians-and-the-antinomies-of-the-end-of-empire/4E998833CC1E39FD117672FA77E21EB0.

91 Emiddio Pietro Licursi, '*Empire of Nations:* The Consolidation of Albanian and Turkish National Identities in the Late Ottoman Empire, 1878–1913' (PhD Thesis, Columbia University, 2011), 85.
92 Ibid., 87.
93 Hans Lukas Kieser, *Turkey beyond Nationalism: Towards Post-Nationalist Identities* (London: I. B. Tauris, 2006), 70.
94 Hanioğlu, Prep*aration for a Revolution,* 315.
95 Lowther to Grey, 17 February 1909, NA, FO 371/581 Nr. 105.
96 Ibid.
97 Bejtullah Destani, ed., *M. Edith Durham, Albanian and the Albanians – Selected Articles and Letters 1903–1944* (London: Centre for Albanian Studies, 2001), 127.
98 Ibid., 9.
99 Gawrych, *The Crescent,* 155.
100 Lowther to Grey, 12 October 1908, NA, CAB 37/95, Nr. 1.
101 Heathcote to Lowther, 16 September 1908, NA, CAB 37/95, Nr. 1, Enclosure 2 in Nr. 1.
102 Keneth Bourne and Cameron Watt, eds., *British Documents on Foreign Affairs, Vol. XX, The Ottoman Empire under the Young Turks 1908–1914* (Washington: University Publications of America Inc., 1985), 9.
103 Gawrych, *The Crescent,* 156.
104 Emre Sencer, 'Balkan Nationalisms in the Ottoman Parliament 1909', *East European Quarterly* 38, no. 1 (Spring 2004): 52.
105 Joseph Swire, *Albania: The Rise of a Kingdom* (London: William & Notgate, 1929), 92.
106 Constantin Chekrezi, *Albania Past and Present* (New York: The Macmillan company, 1919), 67.
107 Lowther to Grey, 26 February 1909, NA, FO 371/581, Nr. 130; Lamb to Lowther, 30 March 1909, NA, FO 371/581, Nr. 40.
108 Christophoros Psilos, 'Albanian Nationalism and Unionist Ottomanization, 1908 to 1912', *Mediterranean Quarterly* 17, no. 3 (September, 2006): 26–42.
109 Lowther to Grey, 14 April 1909, NA, FO 371/ 581, Nr. 14544.
110 George Frederick Abbot, *Turkey in Transition* (London: Edward Arnold, 1909), 200.
111 Lowther to Grey, 14 April 1909, NA, FO 371/ 581, Nr. 14544.
112 Lowther to Grey, 14 April 1909, NA, FO 371/581, Nr. 14544; CAB 37/99, Nr. 62.
113 Bourne and Watt, 117.
114 Lamb to Lowther, 25 April 1909, NA, FO 195/2328, Nr. 53.
115 Lamb to Lowther, 26 April 1909, NA, FO 195/2328, Nr. 54.
116 Gawrych, *The Crescent,* 167.
117 Durham, *Twenty Years,* 174.
118 Gawrych, *The Crescent,* 167.
119 Lowther to Grey, 5 May 1909, NA, FO 371/770; CAB 37/99, Nr. 74.
120 Fred A. Reed, *Salonica Terminus* (Burnaby: Talonbooks, 1996), 16.
121 Skendi, *Albanian National Awakening,* 405.
122 Malcolm, *Kosovo,* 240.
123 Cartwright to Grey, 12 May 1909, NA, FO 371/758, Nr. 82.
124 Ibid.
125 Malcolm, *Kosovo,* 240.
126 Prohaska's Report: *Izveštaji austrougarskih konzula iz Prizrena, Mitrovice i Skoplja o prilikama na Kosovu u prvim mesecima ustavnosti u Turskoj, Avgust–Decembar 1908,* ed., by Đorđe Mikić (Prishtinë: Vjetari i Arkivit të Kosovës, 1975), 238.

127 Ibid., 242–3.
128 Malcolm, *Kosovo*, 241.
129 Abdyli, *Lëvizja Kombëtare*, 383–90.
130 Ahmad, *The Young Turks*, 59.

Chapter 6

1 Anamali dhe Prifti, *Historia e Popullit*, 442–3.
2 Maringlen Verli, *Shqiptarët në Optikën e Diplomacisë Austro-Hungareze 1877–1918* (Tiranë: KLEAN, 2014), 199–201.
3 Arnavutluk İhtilali Komitesi Katibi ünvani verilen Nikola İvanay, HR. SYS. 140 9 1911 06 06 5.
4 Korrespondenca e personaliteteve shqiptare, AQSH, F.2, V.1911, D.73, N. 13.
5 Basil Kondis, *Greece and Albania 1908–1914* (Thessaloniki: Institute for Balkan Studies, 1976), 51.
6 Petrit Imami, *Srbi i Albanci kroz vekove* (Beograd: Samizdat B92, 1999), 186–93.
7 Anamali dhe Prifti, *Historia e Popullit*, Vol. II, 446.
8 Richard C. Hall, *The Balkan Wars 1912–1913: Prelude to the First World War* (London: Routledge 2002), 9.
9 Ibid. 10.
10 Erik J. Zürcher, *The Young Turk Legacy and Nation Building: From the Ottoman Empire to Atatürk's Turkey* (London: I. B. Tauris, 2012), 89.
11 David Gillard, ed., *British Documents in Foreign Affairs, Vol. XX – The Ottoman Empire Under the Young Turks 1908–1914* (Washington: University Publications of America, 1985), 302.
12 Hall, *The Balkan Wars*, 11.
13 Gillard, *British Documents, Vol. XX*, 296–7.
14 Anamali dhe Prifti, *Historia e Popullit*, 450.
15 Sinan Kuneralp and Gül Tokay, eds., *Ottoman Diplomatic Documents on the Origins of World War One – Macedonian Issue 1879–1912 Vol. II* (Istanbul: Isis Press, 2011), 445–6.
16 Ibid., 447.
17 Lord Crew ile Lord Lansdowne'nin Bağdat demiryolu, HR.SYS. 109. 22. 1911. 02. 11 4.
18 Marilyn Lake and Henry Reynolds, *Critical Perspectives on Empire: Drawing the Global Colour Line* (Cambridge: Cambridge University Press, 2008), 251.
19 'Ottoman Reform: Progress made by the by the Young Turks a Steady Revival', *The Manchester Guardian*, 26 July 1911, 4.
20 Ibid.
21 Gillard, *British Documents, Vol. XX*. 280.
22 Heller, *British Policy*, 40–1.
23 See: Memorandum, RAI, MS 55.
24 Douglas to Grey, 19 June 1911, NA, FO. 289G8/14/12/44, Nr. 21.
25 Grey to de Salis, 24 June 1911, NA, FO 24187/14/11/44, Nr. 114.
26 Grey to de Salis, 26 June 1911, NA, FO. 24519/14/11/44, No. 115.
27 Ibid.
28 O'Beirne to Grey, 28 June 1911, NA, FO. 25702/14/11/44, No. 183.

29 De Salis to Grey, 28 June 1911. NA, FO, 25261/14/11/44, No. 501.
30 Lowther to Grey, 2 July 1911, NA FO, 25647/14/11/44, No. 151.
31 Shefqet Zekolli, ed., *Veprimtaria e Hasan Prishtinës – Dokumente* (Shkup: ITSHKSH, 2012), 47–8; Hugh to Lowther, September 1911, NA, FO, 371/123, Nr. 41; Архив на Македонија, МФ 1580.
32 Lowther to Grey, 28 September 1911, NA, FO 371/12/123, Nr. 659; Архив на Македонија, МФ 1580.
33 'The Distress in Albania', *The Manchester Guardian*, 10 October 1911, 10.
34 Jön Türklerin Katolik Arnavutlara ve Malisörlere, HR. SYS, 148 37 1911 07 19 3.
35 Heller, *British Policy*, 41.
36 Cartwright to Grey, 17 August 1909, NA, FO. 371/779, Nr. 134.
37 Gooch and Temperley, eds., *British Documents and the Origin of War 1898–1914, Vol. IX, The Balkan Wars* (London: His Majesty's Stationary Office, 1933), 297–8, See minutes: Cartwright to Grey, 12 August 1910, NA. FO, 371/1013. Nr. 137.
38 As cited in Heller, *British Policy*, 42.
39 Gooch and Temperley, *British Documents Vol. IX*, 297–8.
40 Ibid.
41 Gillard, *British Documents, Vol. XX*, 305.
42 Goschen to Grey, 8 September 1911, NA, FO, 35611/14, Nr. 262.
43 Paget to Grey, 9 May 1912, NA, FO, 195/2406, Nr. 75.
44 Durham to Foreign Office, 28 December 1911, NA, FO, 195/2406.
45 Durham's letter to Nevinson, NA, FO, 195/2406, Nr. 15231.
46 Lamb to Lowther, 21 January 1912, NA, FO, 195/2406, Nr. 11.
47 Lamb to Lowther, 23 February 1912, NA, FO, 195/2406, Nr. 28.
48 Kondis, *Greece and Albania*, 31.
49 Bertie to Grey, 24 February 1910, NA, FO 371/1003.6492/5019/10/44A, Nr. 13.
50 Kondis, *Greece and Albania*, 31.
51 Anamali dhe Prifti, *Historia e Popullit, Vol. II*, 461.
52 Hasan Prishtina, *Nji shkurtim kujtimesh mbi kryengritjen shqyptare të vjetit 1912* (Prishtinë: Rrokullia, 2010), 10–12.
53 Crackanthorpe to Grey, 2 October 1913, NA, FO 421/287, Nr. 1, enclosure Nr. 20.
54 Peckham to Lamb, 22 March 1912, NA, FO 195/2406, Nr. 20.
55 Peckham to Lamb, 28 April 1912, NA, FO 195/2406, Nr. 31.
56 Ibid.
57 Hasan Prishtina, *A Brief Memoir of the Albanian Rebellion of 1912* (Prishtinë: Rrokullia, 2010), 17.
58 Heller, *British Policy*, 57.
59 Peckhan to Lamb, 24 May 1912, NA, FO, 195/2406, Nr. 36.
60 Heller, *British Policy*, 58–9.
61 Elsie and Destani, *Macedonian Question*, 263–6.
62 Enclosure in Vice Consul's Report, 28 June 1912, NA, FO 195/2406, Nr. 43.
63 Ramiz Abdyli, *Kryengritja e përgjithshme e vitit 1912 dhe lëvizja e oficerëve* (Prishtinë: Arkivi Kombëtar i Kosovës –Vjetari XXVII-XXVIII, 2002), 199.
64 Gillard, *British Documents, Vol. XX*, 393–4.
65 Grey to Paget, 15 July 1912, NA, FO 29599/2031/12/44, Nr. 10.
66 Inclosure in Consul-General Lamb's Dispatch, NA, FO 195/2407, Nr. 97; Peckham to Lamb, 5 August 1912, NA, FO 195/2407, Nr. 62.
67 Gillard, *British Documents, Vol. XX*, 390–1.
68 Heller, *British Policy*, 67.

69 Frashëri, *History of Albania*, 491.
70 Prishtina, *Nji shkurtim kujtimesh*, 32-3.
71 Ibid.
72 Grey to Buchanan, 2 September 1912, NA, FO 37163/33672/12/44, Nr. 307.
73 Grey to Cartwright, 10 September 1912, NA, FO 38109/31661/12/44, No. 59.
74 Ernst Christian Helmreich, *The Diplomacy of the Balkan Wars 1912-1913* (New York: Russell & Russell, 1969), 98-9.
75 Anamali dhe Prifti, *Historia e Popullit*, 501-3.
76 Barclay to Grey, 14 August 1912, NA, FO, 34876/33672, Nr. 79.
77 Barclay to Grey, 26 August 1912, NA, FO, 36789/34661, Nr. 82.
78 Ramiz Abdyli, *Lëvizja kombëtare shqiptare 1911-1912, Libri 2* (Prishtinë: Instituti i Historisë, 2004), 380-2.
79 Edith Pierpont Stickney, *Southern Albania or Northern Epirus in European International Affairs 1912-1923* (Redwood City: Stanford University Press, 1926), 19.
80 Guy, *The Birth of Albania*, 37.
81 Mark Mazower, *The Balkans – From the End of Byzantium to the Present Day* (London: Phoenix, 2001), 109.
82 Helmreich, *The Diplomacy*, 99.
83 Peckham to Lamb, 24 September 1912, NA, FO 195/2407, Nr. 76.
84 Peckham to Lamb, 17 September 1912, NA, FO 195/2407, Nr. 74.
85 Alexander J. Motyl, *Encyclopaedia of Nationalism – Leaders, Movements, and Concepts, Vol. 2* (London: Academic Press, 2001), 422.
86 Rodney P. Carlisle, *Eyewitness History, World War I* (New York: Facts on File, 2007), 17.
87 Vladimir Dedijer, 'Sarajevo Fifty Years After', *Foreign Affairs*, 42, no. 4 (July, 1964): 569.
88 Leo Freundlich, 'Albania's Golgotha: Indictment of the Exterminators of the Albanian People', last modified 10 May 2022, http://www.albanianhistory.net/1913_Freundlich_Golgotha/index.html.
89 Anamali dhe Prifti, *Historia e Popullit*, 505-6.
90 Clayer, *Në Fillimet e Nacionalizmit*, 634.
91 Skendi, *The Albanian National Awakening*, 452.
92 Ibid.
93 Hall, *The Balkan Wars*, 48.
94 Skendi, *The Albanian National Awakening*, 453.
95 Clark, *The Sleepwalkers*, 281-2.
96 Falaschi, *The Memoirs*, 370.
97 Ibid.
98 Anamali dhe Prifti, *Historia e Popullit*, 509.
99 Kemal, *The Memoirs*, 371.
100 Frasheri, *History of Albanian*, 178.
101 Dokumente të pavarësisë, AQSH, F. 2, 1912, D. 74/1; 73/3; AQSH, F. 12, 1912, D. 12; AQSH. F. 56, V. 1912, D. 26, 61, 65, 96.
102 Owen Pearson, *Albania and King Zog – Independence, Republic and Monarchy 1908-1939* (London: The Centre for Albanian Studies & I. B. Tauris, 2004), 33-4.
103 Destani and Tomes, *Albania's Greatest Friend*, 64.
104 Kemal, *The Memoirs*, 372-3.
105 Herbert, *Ben Kendim – A Record of Eastern Travel*, 307.
106 Ibid., 313.
107 Herbert, *Ben Kendim – A Record of Eastern Travel*, xiv.

108 C. J. Lowe and M. L. Dockrill, *Mirage of Power – the British Foreign Policy 1902–1914, Part 1* (London: Routledge, 2002), 107–8.
109 Heller, *British Policy*, 74.
110 Gillard, *British Documents, Vol. XX*, 371.
111 Edward Grey, *Twenty Five Years 1892–1916, Vol. 1* (New York: Frederik A. Stokes Co., 1925), 259–60.

Chapter 7

1 Edith Durham, *Albania- Special Afternoon Lecture at Royal Institution of Great Britain*, 4 February 1941, MS 405/203.
2 Destani, ed., *M. Edith Durham, Albania and the Albanians*, I–XX.
3 John B. Allcock and Antonia Young, eds., *Black Lambs and Grey Falcons – Women Travelling in the Balkans* (New York: Bergham Books, 2000), 9–10.
4 Durham to her mother, 10 September 1900, RAI, MS 43.
5 Edith Durham, International Episode, RAI, MS 45:16.
6 Ibid.
7 Robert Nash, *The Great Pictorial History of World Crime, Vol. 2* (London: Rowman & Littlefield, 2014), 314.
8 Edith Durham, *Jugoslavia*, RAI, MS 51:1–2.
9 Gary Shanfelt, 'An English Lady in High Albania: Edith Durham and the Balkans', *East European Quarterly* 25, no. 3 (Fall, 1999): 230.
10 Edith Durham, Because of the Berlin Congress – as told by an Austria-Hungarian officer, RAI, MS 54:29.
11 Ibid.
12 Tanner, *Albania's Mountain Queen*, 54.
13 Shanfelt, 'An English Lady', 287.
14 Allcock and Young, *Black Lambs*, 16–17.
15 Elsie and Destani, *The Blaze in the Balkans*, 23; Edith Durham, 'My Golden Sisters: A Macedonian Picture', *The Monthly Review* 44, no. 15 (Spring, 1904): 75.
16 Daut Dauti, 'Gjergj Fishta, the "Albanian Homer," and Edith Durham, the "Albanian Mountain Queen"', in *The Balkan Wars from Contemporary Perception to Historic Memory*, ed. Katrin Boeckh and Sabine Rutar (London: Palgrave Macmillan, 2017), 91–2.
17 Durham, *The Burden of the Balkans*, 64.
18 RAI MS 53, Sunday Morning Herald, 29 April 1905; *The Irish Times*, 23 June 1905 and Tablet 26 August 1905.
19 Tanner, *Albania's Mountain Queen*, 96.
20 Taylor, *The Trouble Makers*, 96.
21 Tanner, *Albania's Mountain Queen*, 119.
22 RAI, MS 53, 'A Troublesome People,' *Pall Mall Gazette*, 1 March 1910.
23 Ibid.
24 Tanner, *Albania's Mountain Queen*, 150–1.
25 Durham, Vol. 1, Case M-10 DUR, 62–3; Durham to Spence, 30 August 1911, NA, FO 371/1231, Nr. 1.
26 Durham's Letter Communicated to Foreign Office, 16 March 1911, NA, FO 371/1228, Nr. 1.

27 Ibid.
28 Durham to Spence, 30 August 1911, NA, FO 371/1231, Enclosure in Nr. 1.
29 Ibid.
30 Destani, *M. Edith Durham*, vii.
31 Durham, Vol. I, M-10 DUR; Durham to Nevinson, 1 March 1912, NA, FO 371/1481, Nr. 19.
32 Robert Elsie and Bejtullah Destani, eds., *The Cham Albanians of Greece: A Documentary History* (London: I. B. Tauris, 2013), 23; Lamb to Grey, 16 July 1914, NA FO 371/1895.
33 Ibid.
34 Edward Boyle (1878–1945) was also a Treasurer of the Serbian Relief Fund in 1914 and served as Acting British Commissioner for Serbia in 1915. After the First World War, Durham and Boyle became close friends. Boyle, who was a Serbophile, changed his mind and continued to view Serbia with some reservations. Most probably because of Durham, Boyle sympathized with the Albanian cause and even became a Secretary of the Anglo-Albanian Association, an organization that derived from the Albanian Committee.
35 Durham to Boyle, 16 September 1943, MS 405/24, Nr. 122.
36 Richard Bassett, *For God and Kaiser: The Imperial Austrian Army, 1619–1918* (New Haven: Yale University Press, 2015), 446.
37 Clark, *The Sleepwalkers*, 45.
38 Lamb to Onslow, 30 April 1913, G173/21.
39 Durham to Boyle, 18 January 1939, MS 405/24, Nr. 26.
40 *Montenegro: Annual Report 1913* (Count de Salis), 10 March 1914, NA, FO 881/10422.
41 In 1909 Lord Onslow became Assistant Private Secretary to Edward Grey and from 1911 to 1913 served as a Private Secretary to the Undersecretary of State for Foreign Affairs.
42 De Salis to Onslow, 13 December 1912, G 173/21.
43 De Salis to Durham, 21 December 1924, RAI, MS 57: 5.
44 Durham to Boyle, 11 May 1939, RAI, MS 57: 5.
45 Ibid.
46 Durham to Herbert, 20 March 1918, DD/DRU 47.
47 Tanner, *Albania's Mountain Queen*, 167.
48 Durham to Spence, 30 August 1911, NA, FO 371/1231, Enclosure 1 in 1.
49 Tanner, *Albania's Mountain Queen*, 167.
50 Michail, *The British and the Balkans*, 82.
51 Edith Durham, 'How Tuzi Fell', *The Daily Chronicle*, 15 October 1912, RAI, MS 42:9.
52 Ibid.
53 Edith Durham, 'Miseria', *The Nation*, 21 December 1912, RAI, MS 54.
54 Edith Durham, Relief Work in Albania and Montenegro between April 1911 and October 1913, RAI, MS 51:3.
55 Durham, *Twenty Years*, 202.
56 Edith Durham, 'Frontiers and Fanaticism', *The Nation*, 26 July 1913, RAI, MS 54.
57 Durham to Boyle, 11 May 1939, MS 405/30.
58 Ibid.
59 Durham to Boyle, 8 September 1943, MS 405/120.

60   Frank Maloy Anderson and Amos Shartle Hershey, *Handbook for the Diplomatic History of Europe, Asia, and Africa 1870–1914* (Washington: Government Printing Office, 1918), 333–4.
61   Clark, *The Sleepwalkers*, 282.
62   Larry Wolff, 'The Western Representation of Eastern Europe on the Eve of World War I: Mediated Encounters and Intellectual Expertise in Dalmatia, Albania, and Macedonia', *The Journal of Modern History* 86, no. 2 (2014): 391, https://www.journals.uchicago.edu/doi/abs/10.1086/675696.
63   Ibid., 392.
64   Александар Растовић, *Велика Британија и Србија 1903–1914* (Београд: Историјски Институт, 2005), 394.
65   James Perkins, 'The Congo of Europe: The Balkans and Empire in Early Twentieth – Century British Political Culture', *The Historical Journal* 58, no. 2 (June, 2015): 566–7, http://journals.cambridge.org/abstract_S0018246X14000260.
66   Durham, *Twenty Years*, 215.
67   Report of the International Commission to Inquiry into the Causes and Conduct of the Balkan Wars (Washington: Carnegie Endowment, 1914), 149. See: Chapter IV.
68   Edith Durham, *Struggle for Scutari* (London: Edward Arnold, 1914), 239.
69   Govor Kralja Nikole: *Harbri moji vojnici*, XXIV/K.1-1-1913.
70   Elsie, *A Biographical Dictionary of Albanian History*, 59.
71   Durham, *Twenty Years*, 205.
72   Edith Durham, 'Miseria', *The Nation*, 21 December 1912, RAI, MS 54.
73   Miller, *The Ottoman Empire*, 508; Erwin A. Schmidl, ed., *Peace Operations between War and Peace* (London: Frank Cass, 2000), 8.
74   Durham to Herbert, DD/DRU 47.
75   Ibid.
76   Barret to Durham, 23 May 1919, MS. 57/7.
77   Lamb to Onslow, 23 October 1913, G 173/22.
78   Durham, *Twenty Years*, 234.
79   Ibid., 239.
80   Durham to Boyle, 11 January 1943, MS 405/94.
81   Tanner, *Albania's Mountain Queen*, 215.
82   Robert William Seton-Watson was also the founder of the School of Slavonic and East European Studies in London and editor of the influential journal the *New Europe*.
83   Tanner, *Albania's Mountain Queen*, 223.
84   Durham to Boyle, 20 May 1943, MS 405/105.
85   Durham to Boyle, 24 August 1943, MS 405/116.
86   Durham, determined to prove that the Serbian government was the 'organizing force' behind the murder of Franz Ferdinand, published the book '*The Sarajevo Crime*' in 1925. R. W. Seton-Watson called *The Sarajevo Crime* a 'poisonous book' and not only anti-Serb but definitely possessing 'anti-British background' and 'treacherously anti-English' in character. As an answer to *The Sarajevo Crime*, R. W. Seton-Watson published *A Study in the Origins of the Great War*.
87   Allcock and Young, *Black Lambs*, 9–10.

Chapter 8

1. Wolff, 'The Western Representation', 390.
2. Margaret Fitzherbert, *The Man Who Was Greenmantle – A Biography of Aubrey Herbert* (Oxford: Oxford University Press, 1985), 7.
3. L. E. Jones, *An Edwardian Youth* (London: Macmillan, 1956), 49.
4. John Buchan, *Greenmantle* (Oxford: Oxford University Press, 1993), xii.
5. Aubrey Herbert, *Mons, Anzac and Kut – A British Intelligence Officer in Three Theatres of the First World War, 1914–18* (London: Leonaur, 2010), 3.
6. Elsie, *A Biographical Dictionary*, 200–1.
7. Fitzherbert, *The Man*, 44–7.
8. Ibid.
9. Destani and Tomes, *Albania's Greatest Friend*, 3–4.
10. Ibid., 7.
11. Ben Kendim, Southern Albania and Epirus, DD/DRU 35.
12. Ibid.
13. Mr. Herbert Speeches, *Parliamentary Debates, House of Commons* (Published by His Majesty's Stationary Office, London, 1911 to 1914), 2565–71; DD/DRU 41.
14. Ibid., 2571–4.
15. Ben Kendim, 'From Novi Bazar to Uskub – in the Albanian Borderland', *Morning Post*, Thursday, 19 September 1912; DD/DRU 43.
16. Fitzherbert, *The Man*, 107.
17. Ottoman Legation in Belgrade to Ottoman Foreign Ministry, HR.SYS. 151 60 2 1912 07 06.
18. Ben Kendim, *A Near Eastern Journey*, The Morning Post, 17 September 1912; DD/DRU 41.
19. 'The Turk out of Europe: Balkan Committee Meeting at Westminster', *The Manchester Guardian*, 28 July 1913; ProQuest Historical Newspapers: The Guardian and The Observer pg. 5. http://0-search.proquest.com.wam.leeds.ac.uk/docview/475670700?pq-origsite=summon.
20. The Balkan Committee to Foreign Office, 1 August 1913, NA, FO 371/1893, Nr. 35809.
21. Arthur Symonds to the editors of the Times: *Balkan Atrocities and Balkan Distress*, 29 August 1913, DD/DRU 4/4.
22. The Balkan Committee, 'Mr. A. Herbert's Retirement', *The Press*, XLIX. 14562 (1913), https://paperspast.natlib.govt.nz/newspapers/CHP19130113.2.82.2.
23. The Albanian Committee, 1912, DD/DRU 31.
24. Destani and Tomes, *Albania's Greatest Friend*, 65.
25. Ben Kendim, *A Record of Eastern Travel*, 210.
26. Michael Berkowitz, 'Moses Gaster', *UCL Library*, https://www.ucl.ac.uk/library/special-collections/moses-gaster.
27. Destani and Jones, *Albania's Greatest Friend*, 87.
28. The Albanian Committee, *Report of First Meeting*, 2–3, DD/DRU 31.
29. Ibid., 3.
30. Ibid., 9.
31. Destani and Tomes, *Albania's Greatest Friend*, 72.
32. Ibid., 74.
33. See Appendix.

34 The Albanian Committee Meeting, DD/DRU 31.
35 Foreign Office to Kemal Bey, May 1913, 5537/7/78.
36 The Albanian Committee Report of 5 February 1913, DD/DRU 31.
37 Ibid.
38 Albanian Committee Publications 1912– 1913: The most important publications were: the report of the first meeting which was held at the Whitehall in 17 December 1912; the new crusader 1912, written by C. F. Ryder; The Albanian congress at Trieste, March 1913; The plea of Albania, with maps and statistical information about the population of Albania and The future of Albania – Reply of the Albanian delegates to the Greek claims; DD/DRU 31.
39 Charles Woods, *Albania and the Albanians*, The Geographical Review, vol. V. Nr. 4, 257–73 (New York: American Geographical Society, 1918), 262.
40 'Albanian Committee', *The Future of Albania, Reply of the Albanian Delegates to the Greek Claims*, DD/DRU 31.
41 Albanian Committee Publications 1912–1913, DD/DRU 31.
42 'Albanian Committee', *Albania for Albanians*, W.T. M65 – 2360, folios 1–5, 7, May 1913, DD/DRU 31.
43 Ibid.
44 Ibid.
45 Destani and Tomes, *Albania's Greatest Friend*, 83.
46 Fitzherbert, *The Man*, 115–16.
47 Bejtullah Destani and Robert Elsie, eds., *The London Conference and the Albanian Question 1912–1914 – The Dispatches of Sir Edward Grey* (London: Centre for Albanian Studies, 2016), 21.
48 Ibid.
49 Heller, *British Policy*, 72.
50 Ibid., 74.
51 Clark, *The Sleepwalkers*, 354.
52 Grey, *Twenty Five*, 263–4.
53 Prince Lichnowsky, *My Mission to London 1912–1914* (New York: George H. Doran, 1918), 10.
54 Helmreich, *The Diplomacy*, 252.
55 Guy, *The Birth of Albania*, 245–6.
56 Grey, *Twenty Five*, 261.
57 Lichnowsky, *My Mission*, 11.
58 Grey to Goschen, 28 October 1912, NA, FO 45926/33672/12, Nr. 44.
59 Destani and Elsie, *The London Conference*, 21.
60 Grey to Paget, 6 November 1912, NA, FO 47559/42842/12, Nr. 44.
61 Hinsley, *British Foreign Policy*, 59.
62 Pearson, *Albania and King Zog*, 40.
63 Ibid., 41.
64 Aubrey Herbert's Speeches, Parliamentary Debates: Albania and Montenegro, 8 May 1913, DD/DRU 41.
65 Ibid., 2305–10.
66 Ibid.
67 Lloyd to Herbert, 16 June 1913, DD/DRU 47.
68 Appeal in Support of a Fund to Relieve the Destitute and Starving in and around Scutari – 8 July 1913, DD/DRU 47.
69 Destani and Tomes, *Albania's Greatest Friend*, 98.

70 Clark, *The Sleepwalkers*, 357.
71 Ibid.
72 Robert William Seton-Watson, *Britain in Europe 1789–1914 – A Survey of Foreign Policy* (Oxford: Oxford University Press, 1945), 641.
73 Kendim, *A Record of Eastern Travel*, 214.
74 Aubrey Herbert's Speech, House of Commons, War in the Balkans, 12 August 1913, 2315 – 2318, DD/DRU 41.
75 See the full text of the London Conference on the Independence of Albania in: Destani and Elsie, *The London Conference*, 349–50.
76 Destani and Tomes, *Albania's Greatest Friend*, 93 & 98.
77 Ibid., 94.
78 Ibid., 98.
79 Ben Kendim, *A Record of Eastern Travel*, 222.
80 The International Force numbered 1,800 soldiers. The strongest contingents came from Austria-Hungary 581 soldiers and Italy 524. The British had 382 soldiers, the French 203, while the Germans sent 112 marines.
81 Ethem Çeku and Bejtullah Destani, *Gjeneral G. F. Phillips: Komiteti 'Mbrojtja Kombëtare e Kosovës' – Dokumente historike nga arkivat britanike 1913–1921*, (Tiranë: Instituti i Çështjeve Kombëtare & Centre for Albanian Studies, 2015), 22.
82 Destani, M. *Edith Durham*, 88.
83 Bejtullah Destani and Jason Tomes, eds., *Albania's Greatest Friend: Aubrey Herbert and the Making of Modern Albania – Diaries and Papers 1904–1923* (London: I. B. Tauris, 2011), 93.
84 Duncan Heaton-Armstrong, *The Six Month Kingdom – Albania 1914* (London: I. B. Tauris & Centre for Albanian Studies, 2005), xi–xiii.
85 Ibid.
86 Destani and Tomes, *Albania's Greatest Friend*, 168.
87 Rroftë Wilhelmi I – Mbreti i Shqipëtarëvet, Perlindja e Shqipëniës, Vjet' i II, 22/27 Mars 1914, 1.
88 Armstrong, *The Six Month Kingdom*, XV.
89 Ibid., 26–7.
90 Guy, *The Birth of Albania*, 83.
91 Lamb to Grey, 19 May 1914, NA, FO 170/802, Nr. 104; Lamb to Grey 4 June 1914, NA, FO 170/802, Nr. 167.
92 Grey to Lamb, 18 June 1914, NA, FO 170/802, Nr. 185.
93 Grey to Rod, 24 June 1914, NA, FO 170/802, Nr. 2897/14.
94 Foreign Office, 7 January 1914, NA, FO 170/802, Nr. 5.
95 Aubrey Herbert, 'Albanian Independence', *Morning Post*, 13 March 1914: DD/DRU 4/6, part 1.
96 Ben Kendim, *A Record of Eastern Travel*, 218.
97 Burney to Admiralty, 4 August 1913, NA, FO 371/1893 Nr. 1; Burney to Admiralty, 10 August 1913, Nr. 1, Enclosure 1.
98 Jonas to George, 17 November 1913, DD/DRU 47.
99 Lamb to Grey, 13 January 1914, NA, FO 371/1887, Nr. 352; Lamb to Grey, 21 January 1914, NA, FO 371/1887, Nr. 19; Lamb to Grey, 27 January 1914, NA, FO 371/1887, Nr. 23; Lamb to Grey, 2 February 1914, FO 371/1887, Nr. 29.
100 Lamb to Grey, 21 February 1914, NA, FO, 371/1887, Nr. 40.
101 Albania, Parliamentary Question, 4 March 1914, NA, FO 371/1887, Nr. 10016.

102 Aubrey Herbert's Speech: Mediterranean Strategic Position, House of Commons, 18 March 1914, 2149–54, DD/DRU 41.
103 Grey, *Twenty Five,* 258.
104 Ibid.
105 Aubrey Herbert Speeches, Parliamentary Debates, 29 June 1914, 97–120, DD/DRU 43.
106 Armstrong, *The Six Month Kingdom,* 134.
107 Lamb to Grey, 21 June 1914, NA, FO 421/293, Nr. 138.
108 Ibid.
109 Schmidl, *Peace Operations,* 8.
110 Pearson, *Albania and King Zog,* 78–9.
111 Ben Kendim, *A Record of Eastern Travel,* 215.
112 'Shqipnia miqt e vet s'i harron kurr', *Afrimi,* 3 Korrik 1926, DD/DRU 31.

Conclusion

1 Guy, *The Birth of Albania,* 246.
2 Stavro Skendi, 'Beginnings of Albanian Nationalist and Autonomous Trends: The Albanian League, 1878–1881', *The American Slavic and East European Review,* 12, no. 2 (April, 1953): 219–32.
3 James Perkins, 'Peasants and Politics: Re-thinking the British Imaginative Geography of the Balkans at the Time of the First World War', *European History Quarterly,* 47, no. 1 (December, 2016): 55–77.
4 Medlicott, *The Congress of Berlin,* 7.

Selected Bibliography

Primary sources

The National Archives: Public Record Office (PRO), Kew, London

Cabinet Papers

CAB, 37/95 – Cabinet Prints, South-Eastern Europe, September to October 1908, Nr. 118
CAB, 37/99 – Cabinet Prints, South-Eastern Europe, March to May 1909, Nr. 62, 68, 71, 72, 73 and 74

Foreign Office Correspondence

FO, 78/3074–78/3074 – Layard and Goschen Drafts, General Correspondence before 1906, Ottoman Empire, Constantinople May to June 1880
FO, 78/4791 – Railways, Constantinople Correspondence 1892–1896
FO, 170/802 – Albania, Commission of Control, Valona 1914
FO, 195/2328 – Salonica 1909, His Britannic Majesty's Consulate Correspondence
FO, 195/2304 – Constantinople 1909, Military Attaché Correspondence
FO, 195/2406 – Embassy and Consulates Correspondence, Albania 1912
FO, 195/2407 – Embassy and Consulates Correspondence, Albania 1912
FO, 371/123 – Political, General Correspondence, Turkey 1906
FO, 371/149 – Political, General Correspondence, Turkey 1906
FO, 371/151 – Political, General Correspondence, Turkey 1906
FO, 421/287 – Correspondence, Affairs of Albania, October to December 1913
FO, 421/293 – Further Correspondence Part III, Affairs of Albania, April to June 1914
FO, 371/581 – Bands in Macedonia 1908, Case 6, Papers 106–8071
FO, 371/758 – Political, General Correspondence, Turkey 1909
FO, 371/770 – Political, General Correspondence, Turkey 1909
FO, 371/779 – Political, General Correspondence, Turkey 1909
FO, 371/1003 – Political, General Correspondence, Turkey 1910
FO, 371/1013 – Political, General Correspondence, Turkey 1910
FO, 371/1231 – Political, General Correspondence, Turkey 1911
FO, 371/1887 – Political 1914, Albania File 352
FO, 371/1893 – Albania, Balkan Committee, General Correspondence 1914
FO, 371/1895 – Albania, General Correspondence 1914
FO, 424/67 – Confidential Print, Affairs of Turkey, Part XXII, 1878
FO, 424/69 – Confidential Print, Affairs of Turkey, Part XXIV, 1878
FO, 424/70 – Confidential Print, Affairs of Turkey, Part XXV, 1878
FO, 424/74 – Confidential Print, Affairs of Turkey, Part XXIX, September 1878

Selected Bibliography 191

FO, 424/75 – Confidential Print, Affairs of Turkey, Part XXX, October 1878
FO, 424/80 – Confidential Print, Affairs of Turkey, Part XXXIV, February 1879
FO, 424/83 – Confidential Print, Affairs of Turkey, Part XXXVII, May 1879
FO, 424/101 – Confidential Print, Affairs of Turkey, Part LII, August 1880
FO, 424/128 – Affairs of Turkey, Kirby Green Correspondence, Part LXXII, Scutari 1883
FO, 424/129 – Confidential Print, Affairs of Turkey, Part LXXIV, 1883
FO, 424/136 – Confidential Print, Macedonia Correspondence, 1881–84
FO, 881/10422 – Confidential Print, Montenegro: Annual Report (Count de Salis), 1913
FO, 35611/14/11/44 – Gooch and Temperley, Vol. IX, the Balkan Wars
WORK 12/290 – Mural Decorations: Goetze Frescoes

British Library:

Henry Layard, Memoirs, Add. 38,934, Section I
Layard Papers, Add. MSS 39149 Nr. 505
Royal Anthropological Institute Archives, London
RAI, MS 42:9 – Diaries of journeys, mainly to the Balkans 1900–36, note-books
RAI, MS 43/1900-08 – Letters to the family, mainly to her mother and her sister Nelly – Letters to W.H. Nevinson. 1900–12
RAI, MS 46:16 – Some tribal origins, laws and customs in the Balkans, [1928], handwritten notes
RAI, MS 51:3 – Political manuscripts
RAI, MS 51:4 – Political manuscripts
RAI, MS 53 – Newspaper cuttings: reviews of M.E. Durham's works, 1905–1909
RAI, MS 54:29 – Newspaper articles and notes from The Nation, etc. on different subjects, mainly by W.H. Nevinson – Letters to the editor of The Nation, etc.
RAI, MS 55 – Balkan politics: articles by various people, memoranda, abstracts, newspapers, letters
RAI, MS 57: 5 – Political correspondence. Various papers, 'Sundry correspondence Albania, 1920'
Başbakanlık Osmanlı Arşivi (The Ottoman Archives of the Prime Minister's Office) Istanbul
HR. SFR 3 – 270 /1/ 53 – Mémoire
HR. SFR 3 – 315/ 3/ 5 – The letter sent by G. W. Leybourn
HR. SFR 3 – 315/ 3/ 6 – 7 – Communication between the Ottoman Foreign Ministry and Lord Salisbury, the British Foreign Secretary
HR. SFR 3 – 315/ 3/ 7 – Communication between Lord Salisbury and the Ottoman Foreign Ministry
HR. SFR 3 – 315/ 3/ 10-1 – Lord Salisbury's letter to the Ottoman ambassador, Musurush Pasha
HR. SYS. 00118/ 28 – Isa Boletinaz (Report)
HR. SYS. 00135/5 – The Communication of the Ottoman Embassy
HR. SFR 3 – 315, 3. 5 – Arnautluk, Annexe Au Nr. 851, 683
HR. SYS. 140/ 9/ 1911/ 06/ 06/5 – Arnavutluk İhtilali Komitesi Katibi ünvanı verilen Dede İvanay (veya Nikola İvanay)
HR. SYS. 151/ 60 /2 /1912/ 07 /06 – İsa Bolatin'in Çetesine yeni iltihaklar olduğu ve Sırp halkını kendisine celbetmeye çalıştığı – Communication between the Ottoman Legation in Belgrade with Ottoman Foreign Ministry

HR. SYS.00119/20 – Ottoman Diplomatic Communication
HR. SYS. 37 /1911/ 07 /19 /3/ 148 – Jön Türklerin Katolik Arnavutlara ve Malisörlere
YEE. 15/ 21/ 1318 /R/ 13/ 1 – İsmail Kemal Bey'in Arnavutluk ve Avrupa'daki
Arkivi i Shtetit Shqiptar (The Albanian State Archive) Tirana
AQSH F19: D. 32/4, F. 149 – Letër e Faik Konicës dërguar Ibrahim Temos
AQSH F. 19. D. 32/3, F. 432 – Letër e Ismail Qemalit dërguar Eduard Grejit
AQSH, F.2, V.1911, D.73, N. 13 – Letërkëmbim i personaliteteve shqiptare me autoritetet britanike
AQSH, F. 2, 1912, D. 74/1; 73/3 – Dokumente të Pavarësisë
AQSH, F. 12, 1912, D. 12 – Letërkëmbim i personaliteteve shqiptare
AQSH. F. 56, V. 1912, D. 26, 61, 65, 96 – Dokumente të Pavarësisë
Edward Boyle Collection, Leeds University Library, Brotherton Library – Special Collections
MS 405/24 – Edward Boyle and Edith Durham Correspondence
MS. 57/7 – Edward Boyle and Edith Durham Correspondence
MS 57: 5 – Edward Boyle and Edith Durham Correspondence
MS 405/203 – Edward Boyle and Edith Durham Correspondence
MS 405/30 – Edward Boyle and Edith Durham Correspondence
MS 405/94 – Edward Boyle and Edith Durham Correspondence
MS 405/105 – Edward Boyle and Edith Durham Correspondence
MS 405/116 – Edward Boyle and Edith Durham Correspondence
MS 405/120 – Edward Boyle and Edith Durham Correspondence
MS 405/154 – Edward Boyle and Edith Durham Correspondence
University of Leeds Library, Special Collections, Durham, Vol. 1, Case M10 DUR
NA, FO, 371/1228 – General Correspondence, Turkey 1911
NA, FO, 371/1231 - General Correspondence, Turkey 1911
NA, FO, 371/1481 – General Correspondence, Turkey (War) 1912

Surrey History Centre Archives

Lord Onslow Private Papers, Vol. 1
G 173/21
G 173/22
5537/7/78

Somerset Heritage Centre Archives

DD/DRU 4/4 – Herbert Family Papers, Political and General Correspondence
DD/DRU 4/6 – Herbert Family Papers, General Correspondence
DD/DRU 4/10 – Papers relating to Albania
DD/DRU 31 – Speeches and notes for speeches given by Aubrey *Herbert*, 1911–1923
DD/DRU 35 – Miscellaneous correspondence, 1896–1903
DD/DRU 41 – Speeches and notes for speeches given by Aubrey Herbert, 1911–1923
DD/DRU 43 – Miscellaneous Papers
DD/DRU 47 – Correspondence of M. Edith Durham to Aubrey Herbert, M H, and Auberon II Herbert, 1914–1942
Arkivi i Kosovës (Kosovo Archive) Prishtina
XXIV/K. 1-1-1913 – Govor Kralja Nikole
Koleksioni i Aleksandar Bukvičit, viti 1902, Nr. 20

Hansard Online

Parga, House of Commons Debate, 29 June 1820 vol. 2 cc106-16 <https://api.parliament.uk/historic-hansard/commons/1820/jun/29/parga> [accessed 3 June 2022]

Treaty of Berlin – Protocol 13, House of Commons Debate, 17 April 1879 vol. 245 cc525-71037 <http://hansard.millbanksystems.com/commons/1879/apr/17/treaty-of-berlin-protocol-13-greece-and> [accessed 9 June 2022]

Congress of Berlin – Motion for an Address, House of Commons Debate, 22 July 1879, vol. 248 cc1027-90 <http://hansard.millbanksystems.com/commons/1879/jul/22/motion-for-an-address#S3V0248P0_18790722_HOC_126> [accessed 20 July 2022]

The Treaty of Berlin – Execution of the Articles, House of Commons Debate, 18 June 1880, vol. 253 cc297-9299, <http://hansard.millbanksystems.com/commons/1880/jun/18/the-treaty-of-berlin-execution-of-the> [accessed 10 May 2022]

Observations, House of Commons Debate, 2 September 1880, vol. 256 cc1119-56 <observations. (hansard, 2 September 1880) (parliament.uk)> [accessed 11 August 2022]

Treaty of Berlin – Eastern Affairs – The Principle of Nationalities, House of Commons Debate, 4 September 1880, vol. 256 cc1298-3281303 – 1305 <observations. (hansard, 4 September 1880) (millbanksystems.com)> [accessed 11 August 2022]

The Treaty of Berlin, House of Commons Debate, 18 June 1880, vol. 253 cc297-9 <the treaty of berlin – execution of the articles. (hansard, 18 June 1880) (millbanksystems.com)> [accessed 15 August 2022]

Treaty of Berlin – Eastern Affairs – The Principle of Nationalities, House of Commons Debate, 4 September 1880, vol. 256 cc1298-3281303 – 1305 <observations. (hansard, 4 September 1880) (parliament.uk)> [accessed 15 June 2022]

Treaty of Berlin – Protocol 13 – Greece and Turkey – Rectification of Frontier. – Resolution, House of Common Debate, 17 April 1879, vol. 245 cc525-70528 <http://hansard.millbanksystems.com/commons/1879/apr/17/treaty-of-berlin-protocol-13-greece-and> [accessed 9 June 2022]

Congress of Berlin – Motion for an Address, House of Commons Debate, 22 July 1879, vol. 248 cc1027-90 <http://hansard.millbanksystems.com/commons/1879/jul/22/motion-for-an-address#S3V0248P0_18790722_HOC_126> [accessed 20 July 2022]

Secondary sources

Books

Abdylhamiti, Sulltan. *Kujtimet e Mia nga Politika*. Shkup: LogosA, 2011.

Abdyli, Ramiz. *Kryengritja e Përgjithshme e Vitit 1912 dhe Lëvizja e Oficerëve*. Prishtinë: Arkivi kombëtar i Kosovës –Vjetar XXVIIXXVIII, 2002.

Abdyli, Ramiz. *Lëvizja Kombëtare Shqiptare, 1908–1912, Vol. 1 dhe 2*. Prishtinë: Instituti I Historisë, 2004.

Abdyli, Tahir. *Lëvizja Kombëtare Shqiptare 1900–1903*. Prishtina: Rilindja, 1982.

Ahmad, Feroz. *The Young Turks and the Ottoman Nationalities – Armenians, Greeks, Albanians, Jews, and Arabs 1908–1918*. Salt Lake City: The University of Utah Press, 2014.

Alexis, Heraclides and Dialla Ada. *Humanitarian Intervention in the Long Nineteenth Century: Setting the Precedent*. Manchester: Manchester University Press, 2015.

Allcock, John B. and Antonia Young. *Black Lambs and Grey Falcons – Women Travelling in the Balkans*. New York: Bergham Books, 2000.

Anamali, Skënder and Kristaq Prifti. *Historia e Popullit Shqiptar, Vol. II*. Tirana: Botimet Toena, 2002.

Anderson, Benedict. *Imagined Communities: Reflections on the Origin and the Spread of Nationalism*. London: Verso, 1983.

Anderson, Frank Maloy and Amos Shartle Hershey. *Handbook for the Diplomatic History of Europe, Asia, and Africa 1870–1914*. Washington: Government Printing Office, 1918.

Bajraktari, Jusuf. *Lidhja shqiptare e Prizrenit dhe Vendi i Saj në Histori*. Prishtina: University of Prishtina, 2008.

Bassett, Richard. *For God and Kaiser: The Imperial Austrian Army, 1619–1918*. New Haven: Yale University Press, 2015.

Beaconsfield, Earl of. *Home Letters*. London: John Murray, 1885.

Bebbington, David. *William Ewart Gladstone: Faith and Politics in Victorian Britain*. Michigan: William B. Publishing Company, 1993.

Bebbington, David. *The Mind of Gladstone: Religion, Homer, and Politics*. Oxford: Oxford University Press, 2004.

Biagini, Antonello, and Giovanna Motta. *Empires and Nations from the Eighteenth to the Twentieth Century, Vol. 2*. Newcastle upon Tyne: Cambridge Scholars Publishing, 2014.

Bible Society: *The Thirteenth Report of the British and Foreign Bible Society*. London: Forgotten Books, 1817.

Blaquiere, Edward. *Narrative of a Second Visit to Greece*. Cambridge: Cambridge Library Collection, 2014.

Bonaparte, Prince Louis Lucien. *Albanian Dialects*. London: The Centre for Albanian Studies, 2014.

Bourne, Kenneth, and Cameron Watt, eds., *British Documents on Foreign Affairs, Vol. 20, The Ottoman Empire under the Young Turks 1908–1914*. (Washington: University Publications of America Inc., 1985). 6–12.

Boyar, Ebru. *Ottoman Turks and the Balkans – Empire Lost, Relations Altered*. London: I.B.Tauris, 2007.

Brailsford, Henry Noel. *Macedonia, Its Races and Their Future*. London: Methuen, 1906.

Broadhead, Philip, and Damian Keown. *Can Faith Make Peace?: Holy Wars and the Resolution of Religious Conflict*. London: I. B. Tauris, 2007.

Broughton, Lord. *Travels in Albania and Other Provinces of Turkey in 1809 & 1810, Vol. I*. London: Murray, 1858.

Brundskill, Ian. *Great Military Lives – A Century in Obituaries: Atatürk*. London: Times Books, 2005.

Buchan, John. *Greenmantle*. Oxford: Oxford University Press, 1993.

Buckle, George. *The Life of Benjamin Disraeli Earl of Beaconsfield, Vol. VI*. New York: The Macmillan Company, 1920.

Buxton, Noel. *Europe and the Turks*. London: John Murray, 1907.

Byron, George Gordon. *The Life, Writings, Opinions, and Times of the Right Hon George Gordon Noel Byron, Lord Byron, Vol. 1 of 3*. London: Matthew Iley, 1825.

Byron, George Gordon. *Letters and Journals of Lord Byron: With Notices of His Life, Volume 1*. London: John Murray, 1830.

Byron, George Gordon. *The Works of Lord Byron: Including the Suppressed Poems*. Paris: A and W. Galignani, 1831.
Carlisle, Rodney P. *Eyewitness History, World War I*. New York: Facts on File, 2007.
Carmichael, Cathie. *Ethnic Cleansing in the Balkans – Nationalism and the Destruction of Tradition*. London: Routledge, 2002.
Carnegie Endowment. *Report of the International Commission to Inquiry into the Causes and Conduct of the Balkan Wars*. Washington: Carnegie Endowment, 1914.
Çeku, Ethem, and Bejtullah Destani. *Gjeneral G. F. Phillips: Komiteti 'Mbrojtja Kombëtare e Kosovës' – Dokumente Historike nga Arkivat Britanike 1913–1921*. Tiranë: Instituti i Çështjeve Kombëtare & Centre for Albanian Studies, 2015.
Clark, Christopher. *The Sleepwalkers: How Europe Went to War in 1914*. London: Allen Lane, 1012.
Clayer, Nathalie. *Në Fillimet e Nacionalizmit Shqiptar – Lindja e Një Kombi me Shumicë Myslimane në Evropë*. Tiranë: Përpjekja, 2012.
Cochran, Peter. *The Gothic Byron*. Newcastle upon Tyne: Cambridge Scholars Publishing, 2009.
Cockerell, Charles. *Travels in Southern Europe and the Levant, 1810–1817*. London: Paternoster Row, 1903.
Dauti, Daut. Çështja Shqiptare në Diplomacinë Britanike 1877–1880. Shkup: Logos A, 2012.
Демири, Мариглен, and Здравко Савески. *Национализмот во (н) контекст: соработка на Албанците и Македонците од Илинденското востание до Народноослободителната војна*. Скопје: Левичарско Движење Солидарност, 2014.
Dërmaku, Ismet. *Lidhjet Shqiptaro-Maqedone dhe Çështja e Reformave në Turqinë Evropiane në Fund të Shek. XIX dhe në Fillim të Shek. XX*. Prishtinë: Vjetari i Arkivit të Kosovës, XXI, 1979.
Destani, Bejtullah, ed., *Faik Konitza*. London: Centre for Albanian Studies, 2000.
Destani, Bejtullah, ed., *M. Edith Durham: Albania and the Albanians – Selected Articles and Letters, 1903–1944*. London: Centre for Albanian Studies, 2001.
Destani, Bejtullah, and Robert Elsie, eds., *The London Conference and the Albanian Question 1912–1914 – The Dispatches of Sir Edward Grey*. London: Centre for Albanian Studies, 2016.
Disraeli, Benjamin. *The Rise of Iskander*. London: Saunders and Otley, 1833.
Disraeli, Benjamin. *The Works of Benjamin Disraeli, Earl of Beaconsfield, Volume II*. New York and London: M. Walter Dunne, 1904.
Durham, Edith. *The Burdon of the Balkans*. London: Edward Arnold, 1905.
Durham, Edith. *High Albania*. London: Edward Arnold, 1909.
Durham, Edith. *Struggle for Scutari*. London: Edward Arnold, 1914.
Durham, Edith. *Twenty Years of Balkan Tangle*. London: Allen & Anwin, 1920.
Effendi, Wassa. *The Truth on Albania and the Albanians*. London: National Press Agency, 1879.
Elliot, Arthur. *The Life of George Joachim Goschen – First Viscount Goschen 1831–1907*. London: Longmans, 1911.
Elsie, Robert. *Albanian Literature – Short History*. London: I. B. Tauris, 2005.
Elsie, Robert. *Historical Dictionary of Albania*. Plymouth: Scarecrow Press, 2010.
Elsie, Robert. *A Biographical Dictionary of Albanian History*. London: I. B. Tauris, 2012.
Elsie, Robert. *Gathering Clouds*. London: Centre for Albanian Studies, 2015.
Elsie, Robert, and Bejtullah Destani, eds., *The Cham Albanians of Greece – A Documentary History*. London: I. B. Tauris, 2013.

Elsie, Robert, and Bejtullah Destani, eds., *The Balkan Wars – British Consular Reports from Macedonia in the Final Years of the Ottoman Empire*. London: I. B. Tauris, 2014.

Elsie, Robert, and Bejtullah Destani, eds., *The Blaze in the Balkans, M. Edith Durham, Selected Writings 1903–1914*. London: I. B. Tauris, 2014.

Elsie, Robert, and Bejtullah Destani, eds., *The Macedonian Question in the Eyes of British Journalists 1899–1919*. London: Centre for Albanian Studies, 2015.

Evans, Arthur. *Ancient Illyria – An Archaeological Exploration*. London: I. B. Tauris, 2006.

Evans, Arthur. 'Albanian Letters'. In *Arthur Evans, Albanian Letters: Nationalism, Independence and the Albanian League*, edited by Bejtullah Destani and Jason Tomes, 1–224. London: I. B. Tauris, 2017.

Evans, James. *Great Britain and the Creation of Yugoslavia: Negotiating Balkan Nationality and Identity*. London: I.B. Tauris, 2008.

Eyck, Erich, and Bernard Miall. *Gladstone*. London: Routledge, 1966.

Falaschi, Renzo. *The Memoirs of Ismail Kemal Vlora and His Work for the Independence of Albania – with Historical Notes and Supplements*. Tirana: Toena, 1997.

Faveyrial, Jean Claud. *Historia e Shqipërisë*. Tirana: Plejad, 2004.

Fawcett, Edmund. *Liberalism: The Life of an Idea*. New Jersey: Princeton University Press, 2014.

Fetiu, Muharrem. *Komiteti i Stambollit*. Prishtinë: SAS, 2017.

Finlay, George. *History of the Greek Revolution, Vol. 1*. Edinburgh and London: William Blackwood and Sons, 1861.

Fitzherbert, Margaret. *The Man Who Was Greenmantle – A Biography of Aubrey Herbert*. London: John Murray, 1983.

Foreign Office Handbook, Historical Section No. 17 *Albania*. London: Foreign Office, 1920.

Frashëri, Kristo. *The History of Albania – A Brief Survey*. Tirana: Naim Frashëri, 1964.

Frashëri, Sami. *Shqipëria – Ç'ka Qënë, çështë E ç'do Të Bëhetë*. Tiranë: Mësonjëtorja e Parë, 1999.

Frashëri, Sami. *Personalitetet Shqiptare në Kâmûs Al-a'lâm*. Shkup: Logos – A, 2002.

Gawrych, George. The Crescent and the Eagle: Ottoman Rule, Islam and the Albanians, 1874–1913. London: I.B. Tauris 2006.

Gephardt, Katarina. *The Idea of Europe in British Travel Narratives, 1789–1914*. New York: Routledge, 2016.

Gillard, David, ed., *British Documents on Foreign Affairs – Reports and Papers from the Foreign Office Confidential Print, Part 1, Series B, vol. 19, The Ottoman Empire: Nationalism and Revolution 1885–1908*. Washington: University Publications of America, 1985.

Gillard, David, ed., *British Documents in Foreign Affairs, vol. 20 – The Ottoman Empire under the Young Turks 19081914*. Washington: University Publications of America, 1985.

Gladstone, William Ewart. *Juventus Mundi: The Gods and Men of the Heroic Age*. London: Macmillan, 1869.

Gladstone, William Ewart. *Bulgarian Horrors and the Question of the East*. New York: Lovell, Adam, Wesson & Company, 1876.

Goldsworthy, Vesna. *Inventing Ruritania – the Imperialism of the Imagination*. London: Hurst, 2013.

Gooch, George Peabody. *History of Modern Europe 1878–1919*. New York: Henry Holt and Company, 1925.

Gooch, George Peabody, and Harold Temperly, eds., *British Documents on the Origins of the War 1898–1909, V. 5, The Near East: The Macedonian Problem and Annexation of Bosnia*. London: His Majesty's Stationery Office, 1928.
Grey, Edward. Twenty Five Years 1892–1916, Vol. 1 and 2. New York: Frederik A. Stokes Co., 1925.
Guibernau, Montserrat. *The Ethnicity Reader: Nationalism, Multiculturalism and Migration*. Cambridge: Polity Press, 2010.
Guy, Nicholas. *The Birth of Albania: Ethnic Nationalism, the Great Powers of World War I and the Emergence of the Albanian Independence*. London: I. B. Tauris, 2012.
Gwynn, Stephen, and Gertrude Tuckwell. *The Life of the Rt. Hon. Sir Charles W. Dilke*. London: John Murray, 1917.
Hadživasiljević, Jovan. *Arbanaska Liga Arnautska Kongra i Srpski Narod u Turskom Carstvu 1878–1882*. Beograd: Ratnik, 1909.
Hall, Catherine, Keith McClelland, Nick Draper, Kate Donnington, and Rachel Lang. *Legacies of British Slave-Ownership: Colonial Slavery and the Formation of Victorian Britain*. Cambridge: Cambridge University Press, 2014.
Hall, Derek. *Albania and the Albanians*. London: Pinter, 1994.
Hall, Derek. *The Balkan Wars 1912–1913: Prelude to the First World War*. London: Routledge, 2000.
Hall, Richard C., ed., *War in the Balkans: An Encyclopaedic History from the Fall of the Ottoman Empire to the Breakup of Yugoslavia*. Oxford: ABCCLIO, 2014.
Halleck, Friz Greene, ed., *The Works of Lord Byron in Verse and Prose*. Hartford: Silas Andrus & Son, 1840.
Hamiti, Abdullah. *Nezim Frakulla Dhe Divani i Tij Shqip*. Shkup: Logos A, 2008.
Hammond, Andrew. *The Debated Lands: British and American Representations of the Balkans*. Cardiff: University of Wales Press, 2007.
Hammond, Andrew. *British Literature and the Balkans: Themes and Contexts*. London: Rodopi, 2010.
Hanioğlu, Şükrü. *The Young Turks in Opposition*. Oxford University Press, 1995.
Hanioğlu, Şükrü. *Preparation for a Revolution: The Young Turks, 1902–1908*. Oxford: Oxford University Press, 2001.
Heaton Armstrong, Duncan. *The Six Month Kingdom*. London: I. B. Tauris & Centre for Albanian Studies, 2005.
Heller, Joseph. *British Policy towards the Ottoman Empire 1908–1914*. London: Frank Cass, 1983.
Helmreich, Ernst Christian. *The Diplomacy of the Balkan Wars 1912–1913*. New York: Russell & Russell, 1969.
Herbert, Aubrey. *Mons, Anzac and Kut – A British Intelligence Officer in Three Theatres of the First World War, 1914–18*. London: Leonaur, 2010.
Herbert, Aubrey. *Ben Kendim: A Record of Eastern Travel*. London: Hutchinson, 1924.
Herbert, Aubrey. 'Diary'. In *Albania's Greatest Friend: Aubrey Herbert and the Making of Modern Albania – Diaries and Papers 1904–1923*, edited by Bejtullah Destani and Jason Tomes, 90–5. London: I. B. Tauris, 2011.
Hinsley, Francis Harry, ed., *British Foreign Policy under Sir Edward Grey*. Cambridge: Cambridge University Press, 1977.
Hobhouse, John. *A Journey through Albania and Other Provinces of Turkey in Europe and Asia to Constantinople during the Years 1809 and 1810*. London: James Cawthorn, 1813.

Hobsbawm, Eric. *Nations and Nationalism since 1780*. Cambridge: Cambridge University Press, 1992.

Hodge, Carl Cavanagh, ed., *Encyclopaedia of the Age of Imperialism 1800–1914, Vol. 1*. London: Greenwood Press, 2008.

Holland, Henry. *Travels in the Ionian Isles, Albania, Thessaly, Macedonia, etc. during the Years 1812–1813*. London: Hurst, 1815.

Holland, Robert, and Diana Markides. *The British and the Hellenes: Struggle for Mastery in the Eastern Mediterranean 1850–1960*. Oxford: Oxford University Press, 2006.

Hosaflook, David, ed., *Albania and the Albanians in the Annual Reports of the British and Foreign Bible Society, 1805–1955*. Tirana: Institute for Albanian and Protestant Studies, 2017.

Hosaflook, David, ed., *Lëvizja Protestante te Shqiptarët 1816–1908*. Shkup: ITSHKSH, 2019.

Hroch, Miroslav. *European Nations: Explaining Their Formation*. London: Verso, 2015.

Hughes, Smart. *Travels in Sicily, Greece and Albania*. London: Mawman, 1820.

Iley, Mathew. *The Life, Writings, Opinions, and Times of the Right Hon George Gordon Noel Byron, Lord Byron, vol. 1 of 3*. London: M. Iley, 1825.

Imami, Petrit. *Srbi i Albanci Kroz Vekove*. Beograd: FreeB92, 1999.

Ismajli, Rexhep. *Tekste të vjetra*. Pejë: Dukagjini, 2000.

Jackh, Ernest. *The Rising Crescent – Turkey Yesterday Today and Tomorrow*. New York: Farrar & Reinhart, 1944.

Jelavich, Barbara. *History of the Balkans – Eighteenth and Nineteenth Centuries*. Cambridge: Cambridge University Press, 1983.

Jelavich, Barbara, and Charles Jelavich. *The Establishment of the Balkan National States: 1804–1920*. Seattle: University of Washington Press, 2000.

Johnson, Lonnie. *Central Europe: Enemies, Neighbours, Friends*. Oxford: Oxford University Press, 1996.

Jolliffe, Thomas Robert. *From Corfu to Smyrna through Albania and the North of Greece*. London: Black, Young and Young, 1827.

Jones, L. E. *An Edwardian Youth*. London: Macmillan, 1956.

Judah, Tim. *The Serbs: History, Myth, and the Destruction of Yugoslavia*. New Haven: Yale University Press, 1997.

Kemal, Ismail. *The Memoirs*. London: Constable, 1920.

Kesley, D. M. *Life and Public Services of Hon, W M. E. Gladstone*. Philadelphia: National Publishing Co., 1898.

Kieser, Hans Lukas. *Turkey beyond Nationalism: Towards Post-Nationalist Identities*. London: I.B. Tauris, 2006.

Kiossev, Alexander. 'The Dark Intimacy'. In *Balkan as Metaphor – Between Globalization and Fragmentation*, edited by Dušan Bjelić and Obrad Savić, 165–86. Massachusetts: The MIT Press, 2005.

Kirmizi, Abdulhamit. *Ferid Pashë Vlora – një jetë shtet*. Shkup: Logos A, 2018.

Knight, Fredrik Edward. *Albania: A Narrative of Recent Travel*. London: Simpson Low, Marston, Searle & Rivington, 1880.

Kondis, Basil. *Greece and Albania, 1908–1914*. Thessaloniki: Institute for Balkan Studies, 1976.

Kostovicova, Denisa. *Kosovo: The Politics of Identity and Space*. London: Routledge, 2005.

Ković, Miloš. *Disraeli and the Eastern Question*. Oxford: Oxford University Press, 2011.

Krivokapić, Marija, and Neil Diamond. *Images of Montenegro in Anglo-American Creative Writing and Film*. Newcastle upon Tyne: Cambridge Scholars Publishing, 2017.

Kuneralp, Sinan, and Gül Tokay, eds., *Ottoman Diplomatic Documents on the Origins of World War One – Macedonian Issue 1879–1912 Vol. II*. Istanbul: Isis Press, 2011.

Kyrias, Parashkevi. *The School for Girls Kortcha*. Chicago: Women's Board of Missions of the Interior, 1913.

Lake, Marilyn, and Henry Reynolds. *Critical Perspectives on Empire: Drawing the Global Colour Line*. Cambridge: Cambridge University Press, 2008.

Lear, Edward. *Journals of a Landscape Painter in Albania*. London: Richard Bentley, 1851.

Ledbetter, Kathryn. *Tennyson and Victorian Periodicals: Commodities in Context*. London: Rutledge, 2016.

Lichnowsky, Karl Marx. *My Mission to London*. London: Cassell, 1918.

Livanios, Dimitris. *The Macedonian Question – Britain and the Southern Balkans 1939–1949*. Oxford: Oxford University Press, 2008.

Lloshi, Xhevat. *Përkthimi i V. Meksit dhe Redaktimi i G. Gjirokastritit 1819–1827*. Tirana: Onufri, 2012.

Lopičić, Vesna, and Biljana Mišić – Ilić, eds., *Values across Cultures and Times*. Newcastle upon Tyne: Cambridge Scholars Publishing, 2014.

Lowe, Cedric James, and M. L. Dockrill. *The Mirage of Power – British Foreign Policy 1902–1914*. London: Routledge and Kegan Paul, 1984.

Macfie, Alexander Lyon. *The End of the Ottoman Empire, 1908–1923*. London: Routledge, 2013.

Mackenzie, Muir Georgina, and Adelina Paulina Irby. *Travels in the Slavonic Provinces of Turkey-in-Europe Vol. 1 and 2*. London: Daldy, Isbister & Co, 1866.

Mackenzie, Muir Georgina, and Adelina Paulina Irby. *Travels in the Slavonic Provinces of Turkey in Europe*. London: Daldy, Isbister & Co., 1877.

Mackridge, Peter. *Language and National Identity in Greece, 1766–1976*. Oxford: Oxford University Press, 2009.

Malcolm, Noel. *Kosovo: A Short History*. London: Macmillan, 1998.

Malcolm, Noel. *Agents of Empire – Knights, Corsairs, Jesuits and Spies in the Sixteenth-Century Mediterranean World*. London: Penguin, 2015.

Malcolm, Noel. *Useful Enemies – Islam and the Ottoman Empire in the Western Political Thought, 1450–1750*. Oxford: Oxford University Press, 2019.

Malcolm, Noel. *Rebels, Believers, Survivors – Studies in the History of the Albanians*. Oxford: Oxford University Press, 2020.

Mango, Andrew. *Atatürk – The Biography of the Founder of Modern Turkey*. New York: The Overlook Press, 2002.

Marchand, Leslie, ed., *Lord Byron: Selected Letters and Journals*. Cambridge: Harvard University Press, 1982.

Mathew, Henry Colin Grey. *Gladstone 1809–1898*. Oxford: Oxford University Press, 1997.

Mazower, Mark. *The Balkans – From the End of Byzantium to the Present Day*. London: Phoenix, 2001.

Mazower, Mark. *Salonica – City of Ghosts: Christians, Muslims and Jews 1430–1950*. London: Harper Perennial, 2005.

Mazurkiewicz, Anna, ed., *East Central Europe in Exile Volume 1*. Newcastle upon Tyne: Cambridge Scholars Publishing, 2013.

McCarthy, Justin. *Death and Exile: Ethnic Cleansing of the Ottoman Muslims 1821–1922*. Princeton: New Jersey, 1995.

McCarthy, Justin. *The Ottoman Peoples and the End of the Empire*. London: Arnold, 2001.

Medlicott, William. *The Congress of Berlin and After: A Diplomatic History of the Near East Settlement, 1878–1880*. London: Frank Cass & Co. Ltd, 1963.

Michail, Eugene. *The British and the Balkans – Forming Images of Foreign Lands 1900-1950*. London: Bloomsbury, 2011.

Mikić, Đorđe. *Izveštaji Austrougarskih Konzula iz Prizrena, Mitrovice i Skoplja o Prilikama na Kosovu u Prvim Mesecima Ustavnosti u Turskoj, Avgust-Decembar 1908*. Prishtinë: Vjetari I Arkivit të Kosovës, 1975.

Miller, William. *The Macedonian Claimants*. London: The Contemporary Review, 1903.

Miller, William. *The Ottoman Empire and Its Successors 1801-1927*. New York: Routledge, 2012.

Mishkova, Diana, ed., *We the People – Politics of National Peculiarity in Southeastern Europe*. Budapest: Central European University Press, 2009.

Moneypenny, William. *The Life of Benjamin Disraeli Earl of Beaconsfield, Vol. I*. New York: The Macmillan Company, 1910.

Moore, Thomas. *Life, Letters, and Journals of Lord Byron*. London: John Murray, 1839.

Moore, Thomas. *Life of Lord Byron, Vol. I. (of VI.) with His Letters and Journals*. London: Murray, 1854.

Morley, John. *The Life of William Ewart Gladstone 1878-1898, Vol. II, 1878-1898*. New York: Macmillan, 1907.

Morley, John. *The Life of William Ewart Gladstone, Vol. 1: 1809-1859*. Cambridge: Cambridge University Press, 2011.

Morrison, Kenneth, and Elizabeth Roberts. *The Sandžak: A History*. London: Hurst, 2013.

Morritt, John, and G. E. Marindin. *The Letters of John B. S. Morritt of Rokeby: Descriptive of Journeys in Europe and Asia Minor in the Years 1794-1796*. Cambridge: Cambridge University Press, 1914.

Motyl, Alexander J. *Encyclopaedia of Nationalism – Leaders, Movements, and Concepts, Vol. 2*. London: Academic Press, 2001.

Munro, Henry. *The Berlin Congress*. Washington: Government Print, 1918.

Myzyri, Hysni. *National Education during the Albanian Renaissance 1884-1912*. Tirana: Mileniumi i Ri, 2007.

Nash, Geoffrey. *From Empire to Orient – Travellers to the Middle East 1830-1926*. London: I.B. Tauris, 2005.

Nash, Robert. *The Great Pictorial History of World Crime, Vol. 2*. London: Rowman & Littlefield, 2014.

Osmani, Jusuf. *Vrasja e konsullit Rus Shqerbinit më 1903 në Mitrovicë sipas burimeve arkivore*. Prishtinë: Arkivi Kombëtar i Kosovës, Vjetari XXVII XXVIII: 2002.

Растовић, Александар. *Велика Британија и Србија 1903-1914*. Београд: Историјски Институт, 2005.

Pears, Edwin. *Forty Years in Constantinople*. London: Herbert Jenkins Ltd., 1916.

Pearson, Owen. *Albania and King Zog – Independence, Republic and Monarchy 1908-1939*. London: The Centre for Albanian Studies, 2004.

Penwith, Lord Courtney. *Nationalism and War in the Near East*. Oxford: Clarendon Press, 1915.

Pichler, Robert, ed., *Legacy and Change: Albanian Transformation from Multidisciplinary Perspectives*. Hamburg: LIT Verlag Münster, 2014.

Polanski, Hristo Andonov. Kontributi për Lidhjet Maqedono-Shqiptare në të Kaluarën. Shkup: Jehona, 1967.

Potts, Jim. *The Ionian Islands and Epirus: A Cultural History*. Oxford: Oxford University Press, 2010.

Prishtina, Hasan. *A Brief Memoir of the Albanian Rebellion of 1912*. Prishtinë: Rrokullia, 2010.

Рудић, Срђан. *Велика Британија и Македонско питање 1903–1908*. Београд: Историјски Институт, 2011.
Qiriazi – Dako, Sevasti. *Jeta ime*. Shkup: ITSHKSH & ISSHP, 2016.
Quanrud, John. *Gerasim Kyrias and the Albanian National Awakening 1858–1994*. Tirana: Institute for Albanian & Protestant Studies, 2016.
Rapatzikou, Tatiani. *Anglo-American Perceptions of Hellenism*. Newcastle: Cambridge Scholars Publishing, 2007.
Reed, Fred A. *Salonica Terminus*. Burnaby: Talonbooks, 1996.
Robbins, Keith. *Politicians, Diplomacy and War in Modern British History*. London: The Hambledon Press, 1994.
Rodogno, Davide. *Against Massacre: Humanitarian Interventions in the Ottoman Empire 1815–1914*. Princeton: Princeton University Press, 2012.
Rokeby, John Morrit. *A Grande Tour: Letters and Journeys 1794–96*. London: David & Charles, 1985.
Ruches, Pyrrhus J. *Albania's Captives*. Chicago: Argonaut, 1965.
Rutar, Sabine. *Beyond the Balkans: Towards an Inclusive History of Southeastern Europe*. Wien: Lit Verlag, 2014.
Sandes, Flora. *An English Women-Sergeant in the Serbian Army*. London: Hodder and Stoughton, 1916.
Sarınay, Yusuf, Yıldırım Ağanoğlu, Sebahattin Bayram, and Mümin Yıldıztaş, eds., *Osmanli Arsiv Belgelerinde Arnavutluk - Shqipëria në Dokumentet Arkivale Otomane*. Istanbul: T.C. Basbakanlik Devlet Arsivleri Genel Müdürlügü, 2008.
Schmidl, Erwin A., ed., *Peace Operations between War and Peace*. London: Frank Cass, 2000.
Schwandner, Stephanie, and Bernard Fisher, eds., *Albanian Identities: Myth and History*, London: Hurst & Company, 2002.
Seton-Watson, Robert William. *The Rise of Nationality in the Balkans*. New York: Howard Fertig, 1966.
Seton-Watson, Robert William, *Britain in Europe 1789–1914 – A Survey of Foreign Policy*. Oxford: Oxford University Press, 1945.
Seton-Watson, Robert William. *Disraeli, Gladstone and the Eastern Question*. New York: Norton Library, 1972.
Shaw, Stanford, and Ezel Kural Shaw. *History of the Ottoman Empire and Modern Turkey: Vol. 2, Reform, Revolution, and Republic: The Rise of Modern Turkey 1808–1975*. Cambridge: Cambridge University Press, 1977.
Skendi, Stavro. *The Albanian National Awakening 1878–1912*. New Jersey: Princeton University Press, 1967.
Smith, Anthony D. *Ethno-Symbolism and Nationalism: A Cultural Approach*. London: Routledge, 2009.
Stickney, Pierpont Edith. *Southern Albanian or Norhern Epirus 1912–1923*. Redwood City: Stanford University Press, 1926.
Stulli, Bernard. *Albansko Pitanje 1875–1882*. Zagreb: Jogoslovenska Akademija Znanosti i Umjetnosti, 1978.
Sultana, Donald. *Benjamin Disraeli in Spain, Malta and Albania 1830–32*. London: Tamesis Books, 1976.
Swire, Joseph. *Albania: The Rise of a Kingdom*. London: William & Notgate, 1929.
Tanner, Marcus. *Albania's Mountain Queen – Edith Durham and the Balkans*. London: I. B. Tauris, 2014.
Taylor, A. J. P. *The Trouble Makers: Dissent over Foreign Policy 1792–1939*. London: H. Hamilton, 1957.

Tierney, Stephen. *Accommodating National Identity: New Approaches in International and Domestic Law*. The Hague: Kluwer Law International, 2000.
Todorova, Maria. Imagining the Balkan. Oxford: Oxford University Press, 1997.
Toynbee, Arnold. *The Western Question in Greece and Turkey*. London: Constable, 1922.
Urquhart, David. *The Spirit of the East, Vol. 1*. London: Henry Colburn, 1830.
Verli, Marenglen. *Shqiptarët në Optikën e Diplomacisë Austro-Hungareze 1877-1918*. Tiranë: KLEAN, 2014.
Wace, Alan, and Maurice Thompson. *Nomads of the Balkans*. London: Methuen, 1914.
Wallace, Lillian Parker, and William Askew, eds., *Power, Public Opinion, and Diplomacy*. Cambridge: Duke University Press, 1959.
Walsh, Robert. *Narrative of a Journey from Constantinople to England*. Philadelphia: Carey, Lea & Carey, 1828.
Wheeler, Mark. 'Not So Black As It's Painted - The Balkan Political Heritage'. In *The Changing Shape of the Balkans*, edited by Francis Carter and Harry Norris, 3-13. London: UCL Press, 1996.
Woods, Charles. *The Danger Zone of Europe*. Boston: Little, Brown and Co., 1911.
Woodhouse, C. Montague. *The Philhellenes*. London: Hodder and Stoughton, 1969.
Youngs, Tim, ed., *Travel Writing in the Nineteenth Century: Filling the Blank Spaces*. London: Anthem Press, 2006.
Zacharia, Katerina, ed., *Hellenisms: Culture, Identity, and Ethnicity from Antiquity to Modernity*. Aldershot: Ashgate Publishing, 2008.
Zefi, Frok. *Mikel Summa - Arqipeshkëvi i Shkupit 1695-1777*. Zagreb: Unija Zajednica Albanaca u Republici Hrvatskoj, 2003.
Zekolli, Shefqet. *Veprimtaria e Hasan Prishtinës - Dokumente*. Shkup: ITSHSH, 2012.
Zürcher, Erik J. *The Young Turk Legacy and Nation Building: From the Ottoman Empire to Atatürk's Turkey*. London: I. B. Tauris, 2012.

Printed Journal Articles

Buxton, Noel. 'Balkan Geography and Balkan Railways'. *The Geographical Journal* 32, no. 3 (September 1908): 217-34.
Çelik, Bilgin. 'Romanya'da Bir Jön Türk: Ibrahim (Ethem) Temo ve Romanya'daki Faaliyetleri'. *International Journal of History Studies* 2, no. 2 (September 2010): 363-75.
Dedijer, Vladimir. 'Sarajevo Fifty Years After'. *Foreign Affairs* 42, no. 4 (July 1964): 569-84.
Draper, Stark. 'The Conceptualization of an Albanian Nation'. *Ethnic and Racial Studies* 20, no. 1 (September 1997): 123-44.
Durham, Edith. 'My Golden Sisters: A Macedonian Picture'. *The Monthly Review* 15, no. 5 (1904): 54:65.
Feroz, Ahmad. 'Great Britain's Relations with the Young Turks, 1908-14'. *Middle Eastern Studies* 2, no. 4 (December 1966): 302-29.
Inglis, Sarah. 'Origins of the Albanian National Awakening'. *Haemus Journal* 2, no. 2 (2013): 77-87.
Kolonja, Shahin. 'Një Puhi e Re në Maqedoni'. *Gazeta Drita*, no. 2 (1904): 38-9.
Martel, Gordon. 'Liberalism and Nationalism in the Middle East: Britain and the Balkan Crisis of 1886'. *Middle Eastern Studies* 21, no. 2 (April 1985): 172-91.
Perkins, James. 'The Congo of Europe: The Balkans and Empire in Early Twentieth Century British Political Culture'. *The Historical Journal* 58, no. 2 (May 2015): 565-87.
Perkins, James. 'Peasants and Politics: Rethinking the British Imaginative Geography of the Balkans at the Time of the First World War'. *European History Quarterly* 47, no. 1 (December 2016): 55-77.

Psilos, Christophoros. 'Albanian Nationalism and Unionist Ottomanization, 1908 to 1912'. *Mediterranean Quarterly* 17, no. 3 (Summer 2006): 26–42.

Radovich, Frances. 'The British Court and Relations with Serbia, 1903–1906'. *East European Quarterly* 14, no. 4 (Winter 1980): 461–72.

Sencer, Emre. 'Balkan Nationalisms in the Ottoman Parliament 1909'. *East European Quarterly* 38, no. 1 (March 2004): 34–45.

Shanfelt, Gary. 'An English Lady in High Albania: Edith Durham and the Balkans'. *East European Quarterly* 30, no. 3 (September 1999): 283–300.

Skendi, Stavro. 'Beginnings of Albanian Nationalist and Autonomous Trends: The Albanian League, 1878–1881'. *The American Slavic and East European Review* 12, no. 2 (April 1953): 219–32.

Tennyson, Alfred. 'Montenegro'. *The Nineteenth Century: A Monthly Review*, no. 3 (May 1877): 358.

Ünal, Hasan. 'Ottoman Policy during the Bulgarian Independence Crisis, 19089: Ottoman Empire and Bulgaria at the Outset of the Young Turk Revolution'. *Middle Eastern Studies* 34 (October 1998): 135–76.

Ünal, Hasan. 'Britain and Ottoman Domestic Politics: From the Young Turk Revolution to the Counter Revolution, 1908–9'. *Middle Eastern Studies* 37, no. 2 (April 2001): 1–22.

Woodville, Richard Caton. 'Sketches in Albania, A Meeting of the Albanian League'. *The Illustrated London News* 4 (1880): 10–12.

Woods, Charles. 'Albania and the Albanians'. *The Geographical Review* 5, no. 4 (April 1918): 258–73.

Wolff, Larry. 'The Western Representation of Eastern Europe on the Eve of World War I: Mediated Encounters and Intellectual Expertise in Dalmatia, Albania, and Macedonia'. *The Journal of Modern History* 86, no. 2 (June 2014): 381–407.

PhD Thesis

Perkins, James Andrew. 'British Liberalism and the Balkans 1875–1925'. PhD diss., Birkbeck University. 2014.

Psilos, Christopher. 'The Young Turk Revolution and the Macedonian Question 1908–1912'. PhD diss., University of Leeds. 2000.

Tallon, James. 'The Failure of Ottomanism: The Albanian Rebellions of 1909–1912'. PhD diss., University of Chicago. 2012.

Tokay, Ahsene Gül. 'The Macedonian Question and the Origins of the Young Turk Revolution 1903–1908'. PhD diss., SOAS University of London. 1994.

Online Journal Articles

Abbott, George Frederick. 'Young Turks in Albania'. *The Saturday Review of Politics, Art and Science*, no. 3 (January 1910): 659–63. http://0-search.proquest.com.wam.leeds.ac.uk/docview/876924107?pq-origsite=summon.

Ashworth, Lucian M. 'David Mitrany and South-East Europe: The Balkan Key to World Peace'. *The Historical Review/La Revue Historique* 3, no. 2 (January 2006): 203–24. https://doi.org/10.12681/hr.190.

Clark, Bruce. 'Shifting Western Views on Turkey'. *Asian Affairs* 43, no. 2 (May 2012): 193–203. http://dx.doi.org/10.1080/03068374.2012.682365.

Licursi, Emiddio Pietro. 'Empire of Nations: The Consolidation of Albanian and Turkish National Identities in the Late Ottoman Empire, 1878–1913'. *Columbia University*

(May 2011): 35–41. http://academiccommons.columbia.edu/download/fedora_content/download/ac:131865/CONTENT/.

Skendi, Stavro. 'Language as a Factor of National Identity in the Balkans of the Nineteenth Century'. *Proceedings of the American Philosophical Society*, 119, no. 2 (April 1975): 186–9. http://www.jstor.org/stable/986634.

Sohrabi, Nadir. 'Reluctant Nationalists, Imperial Nation-State, and Neo-Ottomanism: Turks, Albanians, and the Antinomies of the End of Empire'. *Social Science History* 42, no. 4 (March 2018): 835–70. https://doi.org/10.1017/ssh.2018.4; https://www.cambridge.org/core.

Tokay, Ahsene Gül. 'Macedonian Reforms and Muslim Opposition during the Hamidian Era: 1878–1908'. *Islam and Christian–Muslim Relations* 14, no. 1 (July 2003): 51–65. http://dx.doi.org/10.1080/09596410305258.

Website or Webpage Articles

Balliol College Archives & Manuscripts. 'His Majesty's Appointment of J. P. Morrier: Papers of the Morier Family'. Accessed 28 March 2022. http://archives.balliol.ox.ac.uk/Modern%20Papers/Morier%20family/morierfam-biog.asp.

BBC. 'Letters and Journals of Lord Byron'. Accessed 30 April 2022. http://www.bbc.co.uk/programmes/b00xmx42.

Berkowitz, Michael. 'Moses Gaster'. Accessed 23 August 2022. https://www.ucl.ac.uk/library/specialcollections/mosesgaster.

Cambridge Library Collection. 'The London Greek Committee'. Accessed 11 December 2021. https://cambridgelibrarycollection.wordpress.com/2014/08/21/thelondongreekcommittee/.

Crampton, Richard. 'Balkans'Britannica'. Accessed 15 March 2022. http://www.britannica.com/EBchecked/topic/50325/Balkans.

Frashëri, Sami Bey. 'What Will Become of Albania'. Accessed 9 August 2022. http://www.albanianhistory.net/texts19_2/AH1899_1.html.

Freundlich, Leo. 'Albania's Golgotha: Indictment of the Exterminators of the Albanian People'. Accessed 10 May 2022. http://www.albanianhistory.net/texts20_1/AH1913_1.html.

Kings Collections. '43. Letter to Byron from the London Greek Committee'. Accessed 10 December 2021. http://www.kingscollections.org/exhibitions/specialcollections/byron/greece/letterfromlondongreekcommittee.

Lucio. 'Miscellany: Disraeli Goes Albanian'. Accessed 16 February 2017. https://0searchproquestcom.wam.leeds.ac.uk/docview/484613998?pqorigsite=summon.

'The Albanian Question'. Accessed 15 April 2018. http://0search.proquest.com.wam.leeds.ac.uk/docview/478840433/pageview/FA92C44923D64587PQ/1?accountid=14664.

The Balkan Committee. 'Mr. A. Herbert's Retirement'. Accessed 22 August 2022. https://paperspast.natlib.govt.nz/newspapers/CHP19130113.2.82.2.

'The Declaration of Albanian Independence'. Accessed 15 April 2018. http://0-search.proquest.com.wam.leeds.ac.uk/docview/478835786?pq-origsite=summon.

The Spectator. 'The Albanian League'. Accessed 13 June 2022. http://archive.spectator.co.uk/article/5th-october-1878/2/the-albanian-league-has-completely-thrown-off-the-.

The Spectator. 'The News of the Week'. Accessed 6 July 2022. http://archive.spectator.co.uk/article/14th-september-1878/1/news-of-the-week.

Žižek, Slavoj. 'You May!' Accessed 25 March 2022. http://www.lrb.co.uk/v21/n06/slavojzizek/Youmay.

Index

Abbott, George Frederick 81–82, 176, 179, 203
Abdul Hamid II, Sultan 38, 97–98, 114, 152
Abdullah Pasha Dreni 39
Adriatic 7, 11, 34, 40, 55, 101, 109, 117–118, 131, 133, 145–146, 154, 157, 159
Akçura, Jusuf 93
Albanian Committee 5, 29, 47, 137, 140–144, 147–149, 151, 156, 160–161, 184, 186–187
Albanian Independence 23, 49, 53, 65, 117–118, 131
Albanian language 2, 9, 15, 34, 65, 76, 82, 84–85, 87–92, 129
Albanian League (League of Prizren) 2, 4, 24, 29–30, 33–34, 37–43, 45, 48, 89, 158
Albanian nationalism 2–3, 14, 16, 45, 57, 61, 64–66, 73, 81, 85–86, 90, 92–94, 99, 103, 112, 115, 146, 147, 157–159
Albanian Nationality 2, 4–5, 32–37, 55, 65, 93, 112–113, 123, 128, 131, 134, 139, 141–143, 147, 156, 158–160
Albanian National Renaissance 33
Albanian Question 3, 4, 20–21, 24–25, 27, 29–31, 37–39, 42–44, 47–51, 54, 57, 61, 63, 68–69, 77, 81–82, 96, 101–103, 105, 108–120, 125–126, 141–144, 153, 157–159, 168, 170, 187, 195
Ali, Amir 151
Ali, Mohamed 151
Ali Pasha Gucia 38, 39
Ali Pasha (Tepelena) 11–20, 22–23, 25, 30, 33, 38–39, 86
All India Muslim League 151
American Protestant Mission 91
Anatolia 39
Antivari 27, 31, 37
Apis, Colonel 102
Argyll, Duke 24

Asquith, Herbert 59, 82, 119–120, 145, 150
Athens 2, 9, 58, 137, 155
Attica, 9, 12
Austria-Hungary 11, 24, 30–31, 33, 41–42, 44, 51–56, 61, 63–64, 75, 78–79, 85, 101–102, 105–106, 108–109, 111, 115, 122, 125–127, 130–132, 146, 155, 159
Autonomy 4, 29, 31–32, 36, 45, 50, 51–52, 54, 57–58, 63, 65, 68, 71, 82, 92, 94–95, 98, 101–104, 106, 110–119, 124, 126, 128–142, 156–158
Aziz Pasha Vrioni 110

Balfour 63
Balkan (Balkans) 1–5, 7–13, 18–19, 21–25, 31–34, 36–38, 42, 44–45, 47–48, 59, 63–68, 77, 79, 82, 85–87, 98–99, 102, 105, 107–108, 111–112, 114–125, 130–132, 139, 141–149, 154–160
Balkan Committee 48–49, 51–58, 61–63, 104, 123–124, 131, 134, 138, 140, 142, 156, 158, 160
Balkan League 103, 109, 120, 127, 130, 135
Balkan Wars 4–5, 10, 57–59, 116–120, 127–134, 138, 140, 145–147, 157, 159
Balkanism 9–10, 23
Bardhi, Frang 91
Bashkimi Club 97
Bathurst, Earl 23
Bax-Ironside 111
Belgrade 2, 49, 58, 62, 79, 102, 108, 116–117, 122, 127, 145, 148
Berchtold, Leopold 113, 118
Berlin Congress 122
Bible 87, 88, 124
Bismarck, Otto von (Prince) 7, 30–31, 33, 35–36, 41–42
Black Hand 102, 116
Boçari, Marko (Marco Botzaris) 16

Bogdani, Pjetër 83–84, 92
Boletini, Isa 69, 70, 75, 94, 99, 102, 112–114, 140
Bonaparte, Lucien 87
Bosnia and Herzegovina 7, 23, 31, 58, 79, 149
Boyle, Edward 126, 130, 184
Brailsford, Henry 51–53, 57–58, 123, 131, 133
Bright, John 24
Britain 1, 3, 4, 7, 10–12, 14–17, 21, 23–24, 30, 32–34, 38, 40, 43–44, 48–53, 55, 58, 61–64, 67–68, 77–81, 87, 104, 106, 108, 110, 113, 119, 122–126, 128, 132, 137, 139, 141–144, 150, 152–153, 155–157
British and Foreign Bible Society (BFBC) 87, 124
Brochart 83
Bucharest 7, 55, 117–118
Budakova, Hasan 94
Budapest Convention 30
Bulgaria (Bulgarians) 7, 18, 23–25, 28, 30–31, 37, 44, 47–48, 52–54, 56–58, 62, 67, 78, 80, 82, 85, 92, 94–95, 103, 107, 111, 114–117, 123, 140, 142
Burney, Vice Admiral 132–133, 153
Bustani, Suleiman 104
Buzuku, Gjon 83
Buxton, Charles 52
Buxton, Noel 51–53, 57, 63
Byron, Lord 7, 10, 12–20, 22, 24–25, 32, 52–53, 133, 149, 156
Byzantine 8

Callamas 40
Calvert, Edmund, 28
Çamëria 154
Canterbury, Archbishop 51
Carnarvon 137, 150
Carnegie Report 132
Cartwright, Fairfax 98, 107–108
Catholics 23, 27, 31, 33, 41, 45, 84–85, 109, 118, 130
Cemal, Ahmet 94
Cetinje 109, 121, 124, 129, 132
Childe Harrold 15
Churchill, Winston 120, 145

Clark, Christopher 145, 148
Cockerell, Charles 17
Connaught, Prince Arthur 150
Conference of Ambassadors 4, 42, 128, 133, 141, 145, 149, 155, 157
Congress of Manastir 92–93, 95, 100
Conservative Party 3, 34
Constantinople 7–8, 17, 19, 27–30, 34–38, 41–45, 48, 61–65, 67–70, 74–78, 80–82, 89–90, 96–98, 102–103, 105–106, 108, 110–114, 119, 138–140, 144, 152
Cooper, Harry 27
Corfu 10–11, 19, 21, 33, 47, 87
Corti, Count 31, 41
Cowen, Joseph 35–37
Crackenthorpe, Dayrell 137
Crete 24, 55, 78, 138
Crispi, Francesco 31
Croatia 7, 11, 24, 27, 137
Cullen 28
Cunningham 133
CUP, also Committee for Union and Progress 72, 80, 92, 94–97, 99, 103
Curri, Bajram 70, 75, 112–113, 117

Dahmad Mahmud Pasha 71
Dakin, Douglas 16
Dalmatia 137
Danilo, Prince 129
Dardania 8, 24, 66
Darwin, Charles 24, 93
De Bunsen 127–128
De Giorgis, General 54
Demir Hisar 54
De Rada, Jeronim 55
Dervish Pasha 43, 89, 90
Dibra 28, 81, 147
Dilke, Charles 34–36, 38, 41
Dino, Rashid Bey 143
Diocletian 8
Disraeli, Benjamin 3–4, 18–23, 25, 27, 30–31, 33–34, 37–38, 40–42, 44, 53, 59, 141, 158, 160
Draga, Nexhip 75, 93, 117
Drummond, Henry 35
Drury, Henry 12

Dubrovnik 24
Durham, Edith 1, 5, 44, 51–54, 56, 62, 64, 80, 82, 88, 94, 105, 107, 109, 121–135, 138, 141, 150, 160
Durrës 83, 118, 126, 131, 133, 147

Eastern Question 4, 21, 32, 35, 37–38, 40, 42, 101, 107, 122
Edinburgh 38
Ellis, William 121
Engjëlli, Pal 83
England 21, 36, 40–41, 62, 78, 80, 111, 121–122, 128, 130, 144–145, 147, 149, 153
Enver Bey 72–73, 76, 81, 95
Emin Bey 48
Epirus 13, 22, 31, 33, 40, 42–44, 87, 138, 154–155
Esat Pasha Toptani 94, 110
Ethem Pasha 67
European Powers 11, 34–35, 37–38, 48, 52, 61, 64, 66, 101–102, 108, 110, 118, 124, 158
Evans, Arthur 24, 51
Exarchate 48

Fairholme, Colonel 54
Fehmi, Hasan 96
Ferdinand, Franz 130, 133–134, 155
Ferid Pasha 69, 76
Ferizaj 72, 75–76, 98–99
Feroz, Ahmad 80
Fishta, Gjergj 91
Fitzmaurice, Lord 35, 38, 42, 44–45, 77, 79–82, 119
Foreign Office 35, 39, 45, 52, 58–59, 62, 72, 74, 78–82, 105–109, 111, 124–128, 133, 140, 143, 145, 151, 154–155
Frakulla, Nezim 84
France 11, 36, 40–42, 79, 83, 88, 106, 114, 122
Frashëri, Abdyl 29, 34, 36, 39, 43
Frashëri, Naim 90
Frashëri, Sami 65–66, 68, 88–93
Fremantle, Admiral 104–105
Fuad, Prince 151

Galip Bey 74–75
Garibaldi, Giuseppe 101, 121, 128, 149
Garibaldi, Ricciotti 101–102
Gaster, Moses 141–143
Gawrych, George 2, 65
Gegë 88, 91
Gennadius 36
Germany 30–31, 41–42, 61, 72, 77, 79, 106, 119, 127, 146, 155
Gjakova 39
Gjakova, Riza Bey 112–114
Gjilani 116
Gjirokastra 154
Gjoka, Prenk 48
Gladstone, Herbert 51
Gladstone, William 3–4, 21–25, 27, 35, 37–38, 41–44, 48–49, 51, 53, 56, 58, 62, 68, 77, 120, 128, 130, 137, 145, 156, 158
Gocevac, Milorad 62
Goetze, Sigmund 59
Goschen, Lord 35–36, 38, 41–42, 44–45, 108, 146
Gothic 17–21
Graves, Richard 73
Granville, Earl 35–36, 41
Greece 4, 7–9, 11–16, 20–21, 31, 33–36, 38, 40, 42–44, 48, 52, 56–58, 62, 64, 67, 73, 78, 86, 88, 97–98, 102–103, 107, 114–115, 130, 138–139, 146, 148–149, 154, 158
Greek Committee 16, 53
Greene, Kirby 28, 30, 39, 44–45
Grey, Edward 55, 58–59, 61, 63–64, 78–82, 98, 104–106, 109, 111–114, 120, 126–128, 143, 145–150, 152–156, 160
Grujić 112–113
Gruda 41–42
Gucia 39–41
Guildford, Earl 17
Gurakuqi, Luigj 104

Hairi Pasha 73
Halil Bey 73
Hamilton, William 11
Hammond, Andrew 10
Harcourt, William 24
Hawkins, John 11
Hayredin Bey, 69

Heaton-Armstrong, Duncan 152
Herbert, Aubrey 5, 24, 51–53, 56, 59, 62, 81, 119, 133, 137–156, 160
Herbert, Henry 137
Hima, Dervish 71, 94
Hobhouse, John 12, 14–15, 17–18, 32
Hobsbawm, Eric 86
Holland, Henry 13, 15, 17, 36
Hoti 41–42
Hughes, Thomas 9, 22–23

Ilaz Pasha Dibra 29
Ilinden Uprising 49–50, 55, 63
Illyria 11, 13, 24, 66, 83, 86, 88, 91
Illyricum 12–13, 87
India 4, 37, 67, 78, 108, 127, 145, 151, 154, 157, 159
Ippen, Theodor Anton 90
Irby, Adelina Paulina 23
Ireland 37, 50, 137
Ishtip 54
Islam (Islamic) 3, 8–10, 14, 23, 25, 56–57, 82, 84, 93
Istanbul Society 89
Italy 11, 16, 31, 33, 36, 41, 55, 57, 83, 85, 87, 98, 101, 105–106, 108–109, 115, 117–118, 121–122, 125, 146, 155
Ivanaj, Nikollë 101–102
Izvolski, Count 81

Janina 4, 11, 13–17, 19–20, 25, 29, 33–35, 38–41, 43–44, 51, 92, 110, 160
Jews 62–63, 141–142, 144, 154, 160
Judge, Mark H. 141–142

Kabashi, Rrustem 94
Karatheodory Pasha 30–31
Kastrati, Jup 71
Kazazi, Gjon Nikollë 83
Kemal, Ismail, also Ismail Qemali or Ismail Bey 63, 67–69, 71–72, 76, 80–81, 92, 96–97, 102, 104–105, 110–112, 117–118, 133, 143, 148, 150
Kemal, Mustafa 73
Kërçova (Kičevo) 54
King Alexandar 122
King Edward 61, 64

Kolonja, Shahin 92
Komiteti Qendror i Shqipërisë (Central Committee of Albania) 102
Konitza, Faik 49, 143
Kopitar, Bartolomeo 87
Korais, Adamantios 86
Korça 54, 83, 90
Kosovo 2, 4, 7, 10, 14, 23–24, 28–29, 32–33, 35, 38, 43, 45, 50–51, 54, 56, 58–59, 63–64, 67, 69–76, 79, 81, 84, 89, 94, 97–99, 102–13, 109–113, 116–118, 120, 126–127, 130, 132, 138–139, 147, 160
Kristoforidhi, Konstantin 88
Kruševo 50, 54
Kukeli, Kyazim 137
Kumanovo 54, 117
Kyoprolu 110

Labour Party 51
Lamb, Harry 95–97, 126–128, 133, 152, 154–155
Lamington, Lord 141
Lansdowne 55, 64
Latin Alphabet 81, 84–85, 92, 98, 103
Layard, Henry 27–28, 30, 34, 38, 41, 44
Leake, William Martin 11–12, 17, 88
Lear, Edward 13, 18
Leybourne, G. W. 47–48
Liberal (Liberalism) 3–5, 17, 21–22–25, 28, 32, 34–35, 37–38, 40–42, 44, 47, 49–57, 59, 62, 67–68, 70, 77, 79, 83–84, 96–97, 120–125, 128–130, 134–135, 137–143, 145–146, 148–149, 151, 153, 155–156, 158–160
Libohova, Mufid 93, 95, 110
Libya 68, 101, 108, 115
Lichnovsky, Prince 146
Lipich 45
Lloyd George, David 148, 153
London 4, 15–16, 28, 30, 33–36, 39, 44–45, 47, 49, 58, 63, 65, 70, 77–78, 80–81, 104–105, 110–112, 119–121, 124–125, 127–128, 132–134, 137, 141, 143–149, 151–154, 157, 159–160
London Greek Committee 16
Lowther, Gerald 61, 78, 80–82, 106–108, 111–113, 119
Lyons, Lord 40

Macedonia (Macedonian) 1, 3, 5, 7, 12–14, 24, 35, 43, 47–52, 54–59, 61–82, 84, 92, 94–95, 98–99, 102–104, 107, 109, 111–118, 120, 122–124, 126–127, 133, 138, 140–142, 158–159
Macedonian Relief Committee 123
Mahmud V 97
Mahmud Shevket Pasha 97
Maitland, Thomas 23
Malcolm, Noel 2, 8, 10
Manastir 4, 14, 19, 28, 50–51, 54–56, 64, 67–68, 70, 72–76, 82, 88, 91–95, 97, 112, 114, 117, 124, 126–127
Manchester Guardian 24–25, 43, 126, 128
Mansuell 82
Mazower, Mark 115
Mehmet Ali Pasha (Ali Pashë Maxharri) 30, 38–39
Mehmet Pasha Bushati 19
Meshari 83
Milovanović 107–108
Mirdita 31
Mitrovica 32, 56, 69–70, 75, 138
Mohamed, Ali Dusé 151
Montenegro 7, 13–14, 18, 23, 25, 27–28, 31, 33–45, 59, 67, 79, 83, 101–105, 111, 114, 116, 121–122, 126–130, 132, 144, 146–148, 158
Morica 55
Morley, John 21, 82
Morrier, Phillip 11
Morrit, John 7, 9
Mufid Bey Libohova 95
Muslims 14, 22–25, 27–28, 32, 41, 45, 52, 54, 56, 66, 72, 78, 84–85, 88, 94, 118, 127, 130, 140–145, 154, 160
Mürzsteg Agreement 54, 56, 61
Musurush Pasha 47

Naço, Nikolla 71
Napoleonic Wars 11, 17
Nazim Pasha 115
Neratow 106
Nevinson, Henry 51, 57, 107, 109
Nicholson, Harold 51
Nightingale, Florence 23
Nijazi Bey 73–74, 76, 95, 97–98

Nikola, King 126, 131–132
Noga, Filip 143, 148
Novi Pazar 14, 32, 56, 70, 79, 139

Onslow, Lord 113, 127
Orthodox 8, 9, 14, 52, 55, 62, 66, 84–85, 87–89, 91, 96, 103, 118, 127, 130, 151
Ottoman Parliament 34, 76, 80, 92–93, 95–96, 104–105, 110, 138, 159
Ottoman Union Society 70

Paget, Arthur 17, 141
Parga 11, 22–23
Paris Peace Conference 14
Pašić, Nikola 102, 127
Patriarchate 48, 98
Peja (Ipek) 69, 147
Pelasgians 22, 66
Phillips, Thomas 15
Phillips, General 133, 150, 152–153, 155
Piccolomini, Enea 84
Plava 39–41
Podgorica (Podgoritza) 101
Prespa 54
Preveza 15, 40
Princip, Gavrilo 116
Prishtina 27–28, 113
Prishtina, Hasan 93, 106, 110–112, 114, 117, 152
Prizren 29, 33, 39, 43–45, 89–90, 98, 110, 147
Protestant 91, 151
Psykharis, Ioannis 86

Qiriazi, Gjergj 82
Qiriazi, Sevasti 90
Queen Draga Obrenović 49, 122
Queen Victoria 150

Radenković, Bogdan 98
Resna 54, 73
Reval Agreement 159, 161, 74
Rifat Pasha 27
Rilindja 33, 83, 85, 87–88, 90–91
Riza, Ahmed 92, 95–96
Riza Tewfik Bey 138
Rome 31, 34, 55, 83, 106, 109

Rostkovski, Arkadievich 70
Rumania 7, 18, 67, 71, 151
Rumelia 7–8, 56
Russia (Russians) 11, 16–17, 20, 27–28, 30–31, 36–37, 40, 42–45, 48, 51, 54–56, 61–62, 64, 67, 69–70, 74, 78–81, 103, 106, 111, 114, 119, 122, 132, 141, 144, 146–147, 151, 156–157, 159–160
Russell, Lord 23–24
Russo-Japanese War 62
Russo-Turkish War 25, 157
Ryder, C. F. 141, 143–144

Sabahudin, Prince 71–72
Sabri, Ejup 73
Sadik Pasha 30, 74
Sadullah Bey 30
Said, Edward 8
Salis, John de 127–128
Salisbury, Marquees 28, 30–31, 34–35, 41, 47–48
Sandes, Flora 10
Sanjak 14, 32, 70, 79, 107, 139, 147
San Stefano 27–30
Sarajevo 128, 133, 155
Scutari, see also Shkodra 13, 61, 121, 129, 132
Ščerbin, Grigorije Stepanovič 70
Seferi, Idriz 99
Serbia (Serbian, Serbs) 7, 10, 14, 18, 23–24, 27–28, 37–38, 43–45, 49, 51–54, 56, 58–59, 62, 64, 67, 69, 73, 75, 79–80, 83, 98, 102–103, 107–118, 122–123, 127–128, 130–132, 134, 140, 145–149, 154
Seton-Watson, R. W. 50, 52, 57–59, 123, 127, 131, 134, 137, 149
Shaw, George Bernard 50
Shemsi Pasha 69, 70, 74
Shën Gjin 131, 147
Shkolla e Vashave (School for Girls) 90
Shllaku, Hasan 94
Shoqëria e Zezë për Shpëtim (Black Society for Salvation) 117
Shtime 51
Skouloudis 36
Skanderbeg 19, 47, 86–87, 91, 93, 152
Skendi, Stavro 2
Skene, Henry 14

Shkodra 4, 13–14, 31, 33, 39, 43–44, 47–48, 51, 61–62, 65, 68, 82, 89–90, 94, 99, 109–110, 112, 116, 121, 124, 126–127, 129, 132–133, 141, 146–147, 149–153, 155
Skopje 43, 54, 62, 74–75, 83, 98, 103, 106, 110, 113–114, 116–117, 119
Slavs 2, 23–24, 30, 36, 43, 53, 62–63, 66, 85, 87, 114, 131, 137, 140
Smyrna 42
Sofia 89, 102, 111, 114, 115
Spencer, Herbert 24
Steed, Henry Wickham 134
St. John 44–45
Stranieri 95
Symonds, Arthur 140
Syreja Bey Vlora 67, 110

Taksim 110, 114, 117, 119
Tanzimat 65, 93
Taylor, A. J. P. 52–53, 124
Tefik Pasha 69
Temo, Ibrahim 49, 70–71, 94
Tennyson, Alfred 24–25
Thallóczy, Lajos 90
Thessaly 13, 31, 40, 42
The Times 7, 24, 52, 81, 104, 111, 126, 134, 140, 142
Thompson, Lady 52
Todorova, Maria 8–10
Topulli, Bajo 73
Topulli, Çerçiz 76
Toskë 88, 91
Toynbee, Arnold 51, 58
Treaty of Berlin 30, 37–38, 41–42, 51, 55, 79, 116, 122–123, 158
Treaty of Paris 23
Troubridge, Admiral 133
Turhan Pasha 69
Turkey 7–8, 11, 23, 28, 32, 35, 42, 57, 62, 77–78, 107–108, 115–116, 119–120, 138–139
Turkism 3, 66, 92–93, 95, 99, 159
Tuzi 129–130
Tyrell, William 77

Ulqin 35, 41–43, 45, 79
Urquhart, David 20–21

Vaso, Pasha 65, 88, 90
Vienna 12, 31, 36, 49, 55, 63, 79, 87, 90, 98, 106–109, 113, 115, 117–118, 125, 127, 130–131, 134, 146, 151
Vlora 40, 68, 71, 110, 118, 126, 133, 137
Vrioni, Mehmet 34

Walsh, Robert 7
Waring, L. F. 58
Weardale, Lord 104–105
West, Rebecca 134
Wied (Prince Wied) 151–153, 155

Woodhouse 14, 17
Woodville, Richard 43, 73

Yastrebov 45
Young Turks 3, 49, 61, 70–78, 80–82, 85, 90, 92–99, 102–105, 114, 119, 125, 128, 138, 159
Yugoslavia 4, 7, 127, 134

Zavalani, Fehim 73, 82
Zichy, Count Ferenc 27
Žižek, Slavoj 9, 10
Zographos, Christakis 154

www.ingramcontent.com/pod-product-compliance
Lightning Source LLC
Chambersburg PA
CBHW052111300426
44116CB00010B/1630